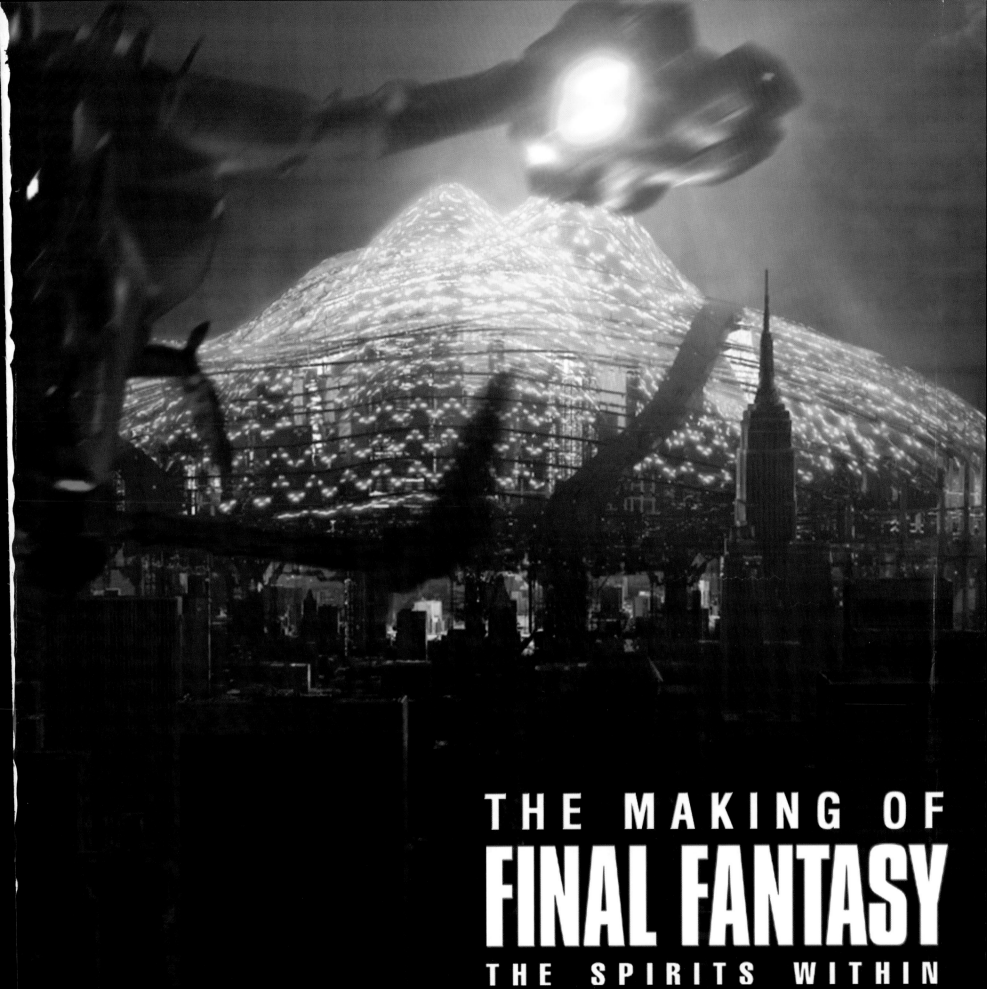

THE MAKING OF
FINAL FANTASY
THE SPIRITS WITHIN

2

5

FINAL FANTASY
THE SPIRITS WITHIN

FOREWORD

12

CONCEPT ART

58

STORYBOARDS

142

ANIMATION

188

LIGHTING

196

VFX

Contents

92 SETS & PROPS

AIR

122 LAYOUT

130 MOTION CAPTURE

204 COMPOSITING

210 BRINGING IT ALL TOGETHER

216 SCRIPT

237 EXTRAS

If you ask me what I think "spirits" are, I would say that they are matters of energy. The fact that the numerous challenges we've had to overcome in the making of this movie have all come together in the end, I believe is the result of the combined efforts of a lot of energy that have so diligently worked together to support this project.

Spiritual energy is comprised of waveforms. These waveforms vary according to one's temperament and each waveform has its own unique characteristics. If two opposing waveforms overlap, the two forces cancel each other out and become a neutralized waveform. On the other hand, should two forces happen to be complementary to each other, their forces will continue to develop and create limitless potentials.

Jun, Chris Lee, Moto-san, Andy, Tani, Chris Capp, Al Reinert, Jeff, Elliot, Randy, Hayashida-san, Seshita, Fujii, Okusawa-san, Naoko-san, Meghan, Ken—just to name a few. (All of your names come to mind, but I am running out of space to list them all!) I am convinced that all of these countless people have brilliantly succeeded in working together as complementing forces that have brought to life something that has never before been seen. Although I cannot list all of your names here, the point that remains is that our accomplishment is the result of the combined efforts of everyone's waveform and its energy.

There are so many different facets to the making of this movie. The development of hyperReal CG characters has been technically more challenging than initially anticipated, and has lead us through a series of hurdles to overcome. Of course, there was the challenge of operating a large-scale project to think about. Confusions and communication difficulties deriving from staff members from over 20 different countries of the world had to be meted out as well. Overcoming all of these obstacles has in fact funneled strength into (the making of) this movie.

There was also the business side of the movie to consider. The essence of a true business rests in the ability to take someone's vision and to somehow turn out statistically sound operations even while deliberately shutting ones eyes to the vision itself. Yet in the end, we've managed to ride it out gracefully, much like a surfer catching a huge wave.

I lost my mother 13 years ago, and when I think of her soul I imagine a single bubble surfacing out of a sorrow-filled abyss. The theme for this movie was inspired by this (newfound) theory. In other words, if spirits are matters of energy, this would mean that just as any other energy we create that transforms itself from the form of light to heat and then to physical energy, the energy itself will never truly disappear. If all souls continue to exist in some shape or form after death, I would say that this understanding alone will help ease one's pain by at least half, if not close to zero. It also has made me realize that I should live my life to its fullest by cherishing each moment that has been given to me. It has helped me realize the importance of building off of day-to-day experiences. The making of this movie has taken me through a succession of experiences that I had never known of before. The painful moments included, all of these experiences have been most meaningful and enjoyable. Through this book, I hope to share a little bit of what I have experienced on this fantastic journey. I also wish that this will yet inspire the birth of a new ring of waveforms.

Finally, to all those who have shared this journey with me, I thank you for being there.

Hironobu Sakaguchi

F O R E W O R D

今回の映画製作においての、私自身の目標は、生命の最も基本的なレベル、つまりサバイバル（生存していく）という問題に直面した際の、心の感情、また心そのものの存在を、ビジュアル化することのできるストーリーを作り上げることでした。神話や魔法の世界ではなく、生命のスピリチュアル（精神的）側面に焦点をおきたかったのです。

インタラクティブビデオゲームの技術的側面と今日の映画製作における驚くべきビジュアルエフェクトを併せ持つ、新しいエンターテインメントの形を作り上げたいと思っていました。そして、その目標を達成できたと感じています。多くの人にとってまったく新しい形のアニメーションを提示する映画が出来上がりました。また、映画業界において、新しいジャンルを構築する、新たなスタンダードを設定したいとも考えていました。

今回の映画は、基本的には SF ストーリー、魅力的なキャラクター、充実したアクション、および興味を掻き立てる設定に基づいています。 しかし、われわれのアーティスト達が映画上でここまで詳細なリアリズムを作り上げることが出来たのも、ひとえにコンピューターグラフィックス技術の驚異的な発展によるものです。

もちろん、アーティストやアニメーター達の多大な努力を忘れては、この映画は語れません。彼ら、そして製作に関係した全ての人たちが、この映画を創るために限りなく時間を費やしてきました。この映画の製作には 4 年の年月がかかっています。通常の映画制作期間としては、かなり長いものですが、この作品のスケールを考えると、必ずしも長すぎるわけではありません。

ひとたび映画をご覧いただければ、登場人物に親近感がわき、また映画全編に通じるテーマをよりよく理解してもらえることを、願っています。また、見終わって、あれは実写だったのか、CG だったのか・・という疑問を持たれるほどの出来になっていれば、とも願っています。

本書によって、読者の皆様が、この映画の製作にかかわる全工程を、よりよく理解できるようになることを願っています。この映画を製作するということ自体が、すでに素晴らしい経験であったと確信しています。

坂口博信

INTRODUCTION

It has taken several years and the combined efforts of over 300 visionaries, artists, animators and technicians, along with the latest software and computers, to simulate a full range of human emotions and movements with hyperReal human characters and backgrounds all in CGI for *Final Fantasy: The Spirits Within*. However, this reality began as a fantasy for one man, Hironobu Sakaguchi, a legendary game designer with a love of movies.

In 1997, Square opened a new U.S. digital studio in Honolulu, Hawaii. Long known for pushing the envelope of technology, Square had amassed an enormous worldwide following for its Final Fantasy role-playing games. Heading the new Honolulu studio, Sakaguchi pushed hard to create an ultra-sophisticated digital studio that could take CGI production to new visual levels with cinematic animations.

"The whole thing started four years ago, when we decided to build a top-notch production studio like Industrial Light and Magic or Pixar," says Sakaguchi. "Making a feature film was the best testing ground. We needed to see if we could create realistic computer graphics that could withstand scrutiny on a big screen. So I decided to make a full-length feature film."

For Sakaguchi's dream to succeed, it also needed someone whose experience spanned both the video game and movie industries. That rare combination came in the form of Jun Aida, a former employee of Osaka-based video game giant Capcom. While at Capcom, Aida produced the Jean-Claude Van Damme movie *Street Fighter*, which was based on one of Capcom's biggest game properties.

As president of Square USA, he brought an understanding of how to get things accomplished in Hollywood. He also brought some much-needed connections. "By 1998 we had the screenplay done, and I was running around like crazy trying to make a deal with the actors," says Aida. "It was very difficult. Back then, even now, we are still a nobody. They would ask, 'What have you guys done? Video games? The director, Sakaguchi, what has he done?'"

These two men teamed up with Chris Lee, a high-powered studio executive with a yen for games.

"I was president of Tri-Star pictures at the time and I had been wanting to do more feature films based on PlayStation games," says Lee. "Then Jun (Jun Aida, President of Square USA) approached me with a 12-page treatment from Sakaguchi and said, 'I want to make Final Fantasy into a picture, and I want to do it all CGI (computer graphics).'"

Lee liked Sakaguchi's story treatment, but converting that treatment into a movie would become a four-year battle requiring huge investments of time, talent, and technology.

"I truly believe that only a gamer like Sakaguchi would have felt this was possible. For him to move to the motion picture screen with human emulation like this was an evolutionary process. Hollywood has reached the visual age of *Pearl Harbor*, *Shrek*, *The Mummy*... I mean, nobody thinks of movies as having digital effects anymore; but more than half of the movies have effects that are done on computers as well."

Besides recruiting top talents from all over the world to assemble a brilliant production team, Sakaguchi turned to screen writer Al Reinert, the Academy Award-nominated screenwriter of *Apollo 13*, to help flesh out the script. Translating Sakaguchi's concepts into a script became a daunting task with constant re-writes and a lot of additional work from screenwriter Jeff Vintar, whose credits include *Hardwired* and *The Last Hacker*.

7

When it came to recruiting voice talent, Aida had prior experience. He struck up a friendship with actress Ming-Na (*Joy Luck Club, Mulan*) during the making of *Street Fighter*, then turned to her as his first choice when casting *Final Fantasy: The Spirits Within*. The next step would be finding more marquee actors. Jack Fletcher (*Princess Mononoke, Black Mask*), an experienced voice recording and casting director, also provided assistance through his personal relationships in the film industry.

"Having Ming-Na say yes, that helped us," says Aida. "The agents would ask, 'Who is your writer,'" and we would tell them Al Reinert, and they would say, 'Oh, *Apollo 13*. Who do you have [acting] so far? Ming-Na? Oh, from *Mulan*? Maybe I should pass this on to my client.'"

And success begat more success. Aida and Fletcher were able to create a voice talent cast that included such veteran actors as Alec Baldwin (*Ghosts of Mississippi*), James Woods (*Contact*), Ving Rhames (*Pulp Fiction*), Donald Sutherland (*Space Cowboys*), Steve Buscemi (*Armageddon*), and Peri Gilpin (*Frasier*).

But even with a strong cast and studio backing, the battle to make *Final Fantasy: The Spirits Within* was just beginning. The movie would not work as a live-action movie, and no one had all of the technology needed to bring the film to life.

"The best analogy that I can think of is when Walt Disney did *Snow White*," says Lee. "*Snow White* was the first all-color, full-length cartoon, and everybody thought he was crazy. He could have gone out and hired a real actress and got some little people to play the dwarfs; but he felt very strongly that there was a better way to tell that particular story."

"When people come up to me and say, 'Final Fantasy looks so real. Why didn't you do it with real people?', I tell them, 'Because this is a better way of doing it.' The future belongs to those who dare, and I think that's what happened here."

"The theme that I want to convey is more of a complex idea of life and death and spirit, and I felt that in

HIRONOBU SAKAGUCHI, DIRECTOR

Hironobu Sakaguchi was born in November 1962. He was appointed Director of Planning and Development with the establishment of Square Co., Ltd. in 1986 and subsequently promoted to Executive Vice President in 1991. Since joining Square Co., Ltd., he has headed the Development Division. He was appointed President of Square LA, Inc. (now Square USA, Inc.) in 1995 with the establishment of a research and development base for U.S. operations. The total number of Square brand interactive game software sold surpasses 60 million units worldwide. Sakaguchi is the Executive Producer of the world-famous interactive game software *Final Fantasy* series, which has sold more than 33 million units.

He has long spoken of his desire to create "a brand-new form of entertainment uniting interactive games and motion pictures," something demanding the wide-ranging, flexible, and imaginative creativity going beyond the bounds of both conventional interactive games and motion pictures. *Final Fantasy: The Spirits Within* is a major step toward that dream.

In May 2000, Sakaguchi was honored at the Third Annual Interactive Achievement Awards Ceremony in Los Angeles during the Electronic Entertainment Expo (E3). Hosted by the Academy of Interactive Arts and Sciences, he received the prestigious Hall of Fame Award given to those who have made the most enduring, groundbreaking, and seminal contributions to the world of interactive entertainment and information.

order to best portray this idea, the story should really be set on earth with actual humans that live on earth."

— HIRONOBU SAKAGUCHI
INTRODUCTION

MOTONORI SAKAKIBARA, CO-DIRECTOR

At the age of 14, Motonori Sakakibara started making animation using his father's 8mm camera. While attending Musashino Art University, he had a "fateful" encounter with Yusei Uesugi. Together, they immersed themselves in producing films of special effects experiments. It was during the study of motion control cameras that Sakakibara learned about the existence of computer graphics.

Upon his graduation, he joined JCGL, the first CG production company in Japan, embarking into the newly born world of computer graphics. In 1992, he joined NAMCO and subsequently moved to New York where he participated in a project to create dinosaurs with hi-vision CG at HDCG in Queens.

During those years, he continued to work as an individual artist as well. He exhibited his works at the Art Show and SIGGRAPH's Electronic Theater in 1989 and 1990.

He also received gold awards from two major graphic art competitions in Japan, participated in two different exhibitions of his work, and established his position as one of the pathfinders of CG art in Japan.

In 1995, he joined Square and worked as the FMV director of *Final Fantasy VII* and *Final Fantasy VIII*. He started his full participation in the movie project during the spring of 1999, and worked on the project until its completion.

JUN AIDA, PRODUCER

Jun Aida serves as President of Square's Honolulu Studio. Originally from Japan, he has produced *Street Fighter*, the live-action box office hit film in 1994, which grossed over $100 million worldwide. In addition, Aida was responsible for the film's local distribution, marketing and promotion for North America, Latin America, Europe, and Australia. Aida has also produced successful animated TV series such as *Street Fighter*, *MegaMan*, and *DarkStalkers* for the United States market.

CHRIS LEE, PRODUCER

Chris Lee is the founder of Chris Lee Productions Inc., a multimedia entertainment and management company. His company is involved in a wide range of content creation, the production of motion pictures, television, Internet programming, music videos, commercials, and computer video games. Lee is he former President of Motion Picture Production for Columbia/TriStar Pictures where he was responsible for Academy Award®-winning films *As Good As It Gets*, *Jerry Maguire*, and *Philadelphia* among others. Originally from Hawaii, he graduated from Yale University.

12

CONCEPT ART

CONCEPT ART

In the 1870s, Jules Verne envisioned explorers searching out many of the world's great secrets in self-propelled submarines. Impressive as the prediction sounds, considering the fact that Cornelis Drebbel built a working submarine in 1620, Verne's predictions may not have been all that visionary.

In his work as Square USA's conceptual artist, Kazunori Nakazawa did not get to deal with a distant future or frontiers. Instead, Nakazawa confined his work to the grim near future of 2065, a setting that audiences may find easier to scrutinize than more distant time periods. Just because the buildings, weapons, and vehicles in *Final Fantasy: The Spirits Within* do not currently exist does not mean that audiences will forgive them for being any less realistic. They all had to be carefully constructed to create the illusion of reality. So before Aki fired her first flare or wrapped her fingers around the controls of the Black Boa, Nakazawa planned out these objects with meticulous details.

An early design of the Black Boa's controls.

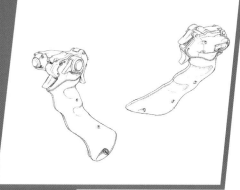

To the audience, the vehicle on the screen was 'just a jeep.' To Nakazawa, it was the futuristic cousin of the U.S. Marine Corps: Light Armor Vehicle—a 4-wheeled, all-terrain vehicle that is 6.72 meters in length, 3.30 meters wide, and 1.92 meters tall. Nakazawa specified the diameter of the vehicle's front and rear wheels, that it had a 263-horse-power engine, and that its maximum speed was 144 kilometers per hour. Audiences might see these details as super-fluous, but they would notice inconsistencies if Nakazawa's jeep moved faster in some scenes than in others.

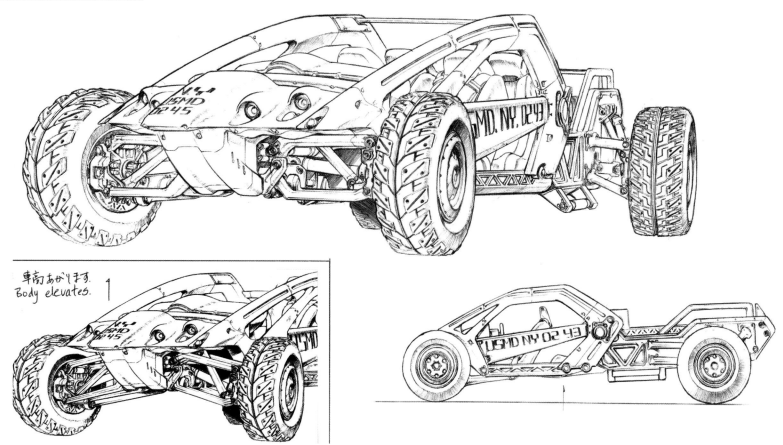

"I was told that Final Fantasy would be a realistic movie, so all the machinery and models had to be realistic," says Nakazawa. "But we're not making a documentary. So all of the vehicles look like you might expect in real life, but they cannot be boring. I wanted to create vehicles and machines that have never been shown in movies, yet maintain enough realism that they could actually work."

Not all of Nakazawa's concepts focused on working machines. He created a design for a destroyed aircraft carrier. The concept was used in an unlikely way—as a ruin in the Battlefield Wasteland scene, the scene in which Aki and company search the landscape in the desert outside Tucson, Arizona. When Neil hastily pilots the Copperhead through old wreckage to evade attacking phantoms, he flies through Nakazawa's aircraft carrier.

These images provide a perfect example of the detail involved in creating the concept art used for the movie. In the movie, it's difficult to tell what exactly the Copperhead is flying through. A couple of these images show the wrecked ship from a top-down perspective, a view that isn't witnessed in the movie.

16

17

If one theme permeated Nakazawa's concepts, it was the use of holographs. Throughout the movie, most of the futuristic equipment used by the characters had both holographic readouts and interfaces. "I do not believe that any film before Final Fantasy has had so many detailed holographs," says Nakazawa. "From the very beginning, we thought that all of the machines and the creatures' devices that appear in the movies be holographs. That was the original idea. That's why we formed a special team to work on holographs only, called the Holo Team."

This image appears during the scene in which Dr. Sid explains how Gaia can counteract the phantom presence.

The holographic image served as a key visual reference in the film.

Aki's wrist holo.

fingers go into slits

Aki rotates

rotates horizontally & vertically.

Doctor

green sphere moves like airplane control stick

cylinder-shaped holo rotates in random movement.

frame is fixed

gauge moves along with every movement.

N.Y. Treatment Room console. Holographic Normal version its operational

Nakazawa.

center ball channel

spins... slowly

turn the ball with hand.

stop the channel with fingers.

push channel switch.

data & grip appear

cylinder holo is constantly moving.

GRIP

Nakazawa   NY spiritual treatment room control holo (Aki's version)

ball moves like airplane control grip

Aki manipulating the holographic controls in an attempt to rid Gray's body of an invading phantom.

19

Hence, when Aki saves Gray's life by eradicating the phantom particle that has invaded his body, she uses a holographic sphere to control her equipment. When General Hein commandeers the Barrier City New York Control Room, the controls that his men use are also holographic. "At the very beginning, Mr. Sakaguchi said, 'I would like to have a holograph that we can touch and move to control systems,'" says Nakazawa. "We wanted the holographs and the other equipment in the Barrier City New York Control Room to be totally new, stuff with shapes and silhouettes that nobody has ever seen before."

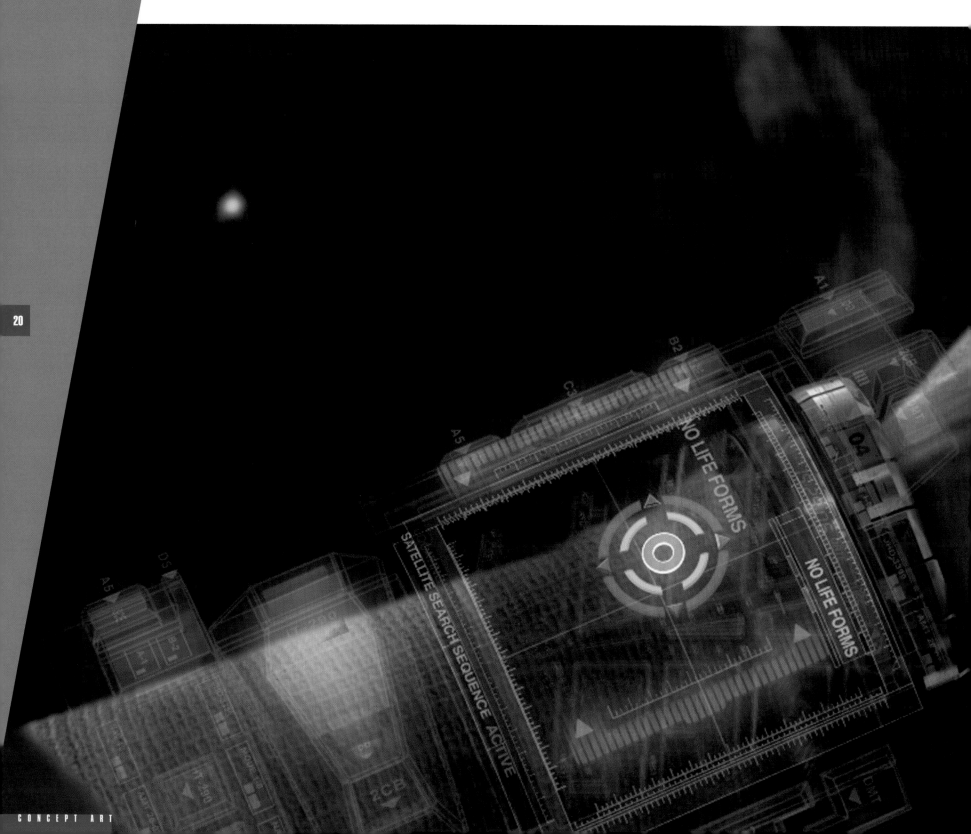

In all, Nakazawa reckons that he submitted some 3,000 conceptual designs for *Final Fantasy: The Spirits Within*. His office became a library of concept drawings bearing sketches of imaginative items that look vaguely familiar, yet mostly new. In his own way, Nakazawa must be credited for being a visionary; the mechanical furnishings of Final Fantasy are his dark vision.

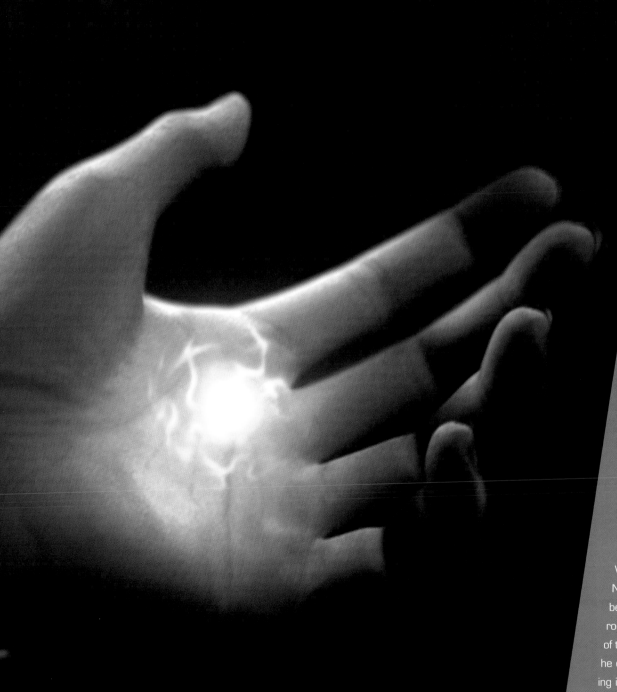

KAZUNORI NAKAZAWA, CONCEPTUAL ARTIST

Kazunori Nakazawa, the conceptual designer who devised most of the vehicles, buildings, and gadgets in *Final Fantasy: The Spirits Within*, is a true product of the age of video games. As a high school student, he and some friends created two games—*Zarth* and *Wingman*—which were published in Japan by ENIX Corporation. After graduation, Nakazawa spent over 10 years working at Toei Animation Studios and Sunrise in Japan.

In 1998, Nakazawa joined Square, where he quickly established himself as one of Hironobu Sakaguchi's most-trusted conceptual art designers. His concept work on this film has extended into almost all facets of the movie.

"I was the Art Director as far as designing everything other than characters and backgrounds," says Nakazawa. "All the vehicles, the buildings, the city details and whatnot were my designs. The only things I did not work on were the uniforms and the armor. That was designed before I arrived, and the guy who did the uniforms also did the overall cityscape for Barrier City New York."

While audiences are likely to appreciate the breadth of Nakazawa's work as it appears in the movie, they would probably be amazed to see how much of his work ended up on the cutting room floor. "The script went through a lot of revisions. Initially, a lot of the things I designed had to be scratched." Of the 3,000 designs he created for the movie, he estimates only 500 ended up appearing in the film.

AKI

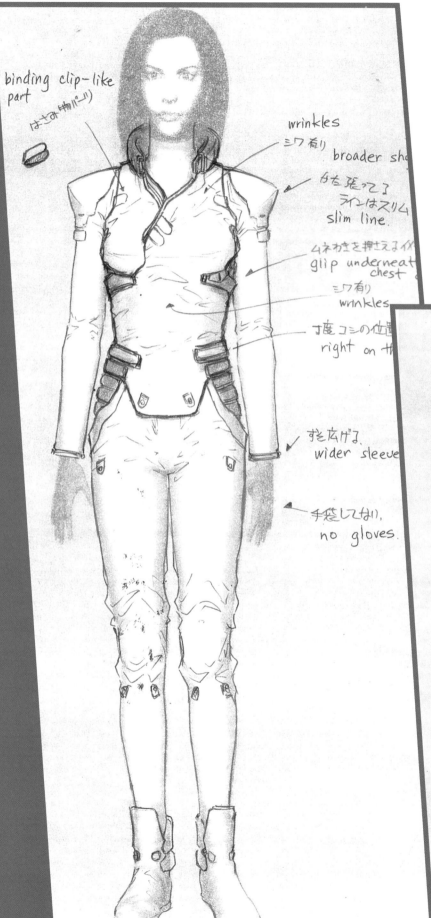

binding clip-like part
はさみ物パーツ

wrinkles
シワ有り
broader sho

白を残ってる
ラインはスリム
slim line.

ムネわきを押えるイ
glip underneat
chest

ミワ有り
wrinkles

丁度コシの位置
right on th

すそ広げる。
wider sleeve

手袋してなし、
no gloves.

Aki's form-fitting uniform.

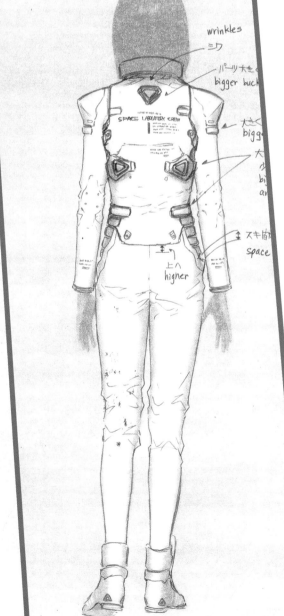

wrinkles
シワ

パーツ大き
bigger buck

大く
bigg

大
少
bi
a

±スキ間
space

上へ
higher

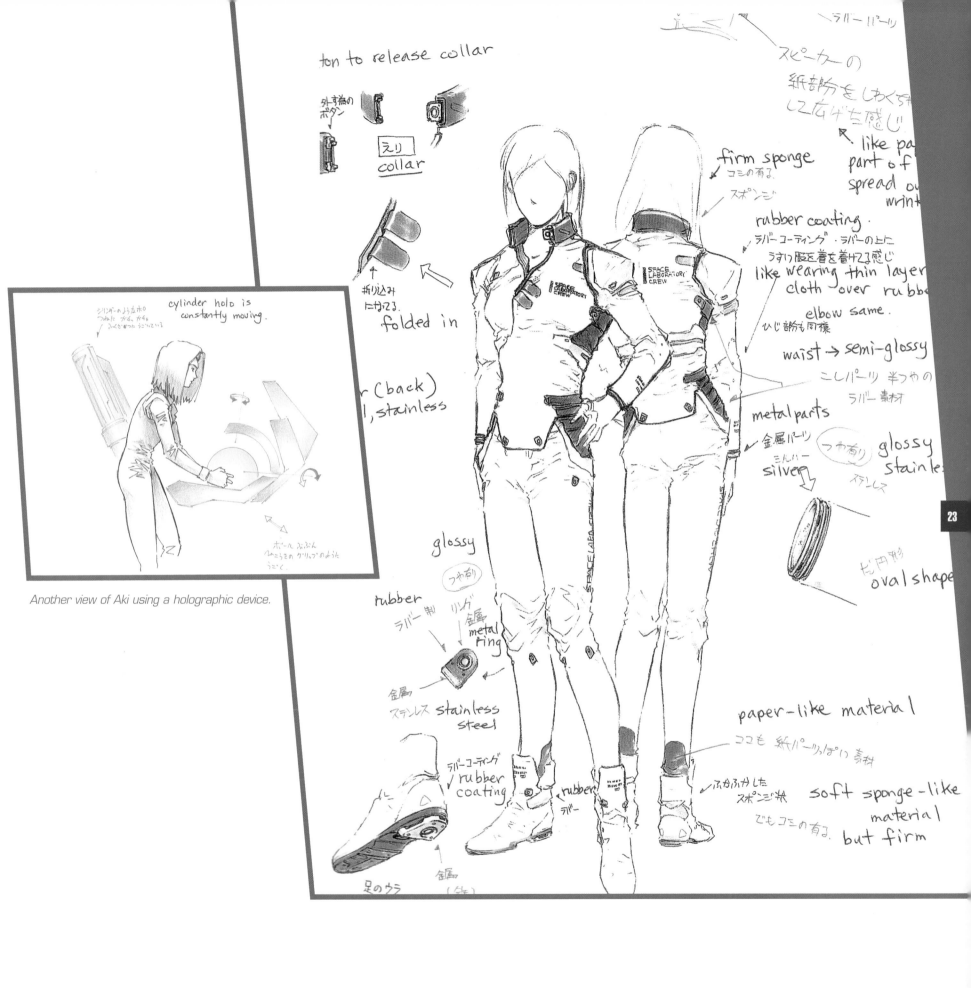

ton to release collar

外す為の
ボタン

えり
collar

ラバー パーツ
スピーカーの
紙部分をしわくちゃ
に広げた感じ

like pa
part of
spread o
wrint

firm sponge
コシの有る
スポンジ

rubber coating.
ラバーコーティング・ラバーの上た
うすい服を着を着ける感じ
like wearing thin layer
cloth over rubb

elbow same.
ひじ部分も同様

waist → semi-glossy
こしパーツ 半つやの
ラバー 素材

metal parts
金属パーツ   つや有り glossy
シルバー   stainle
silver   ステンレス

oval shape
ビジ円形

cylinder holo is
constantly moving.

Another view of Aki using a holographic device.

folded in

(back)
, stainless

glossy
つやあり

rubber
ラバー製   リング
           金属
           metal
           ring

金属
ステンレス stainless
steel

paper-like material
ココも 紙パーツっぽい 素材

ふかふかした
スポンジ状
soft sponge-like
material
でもコシの有る。 but firm

rubber
coating
ラバーコーティング

rubber
ラバー

足のウラ   金属
          (タ キ)

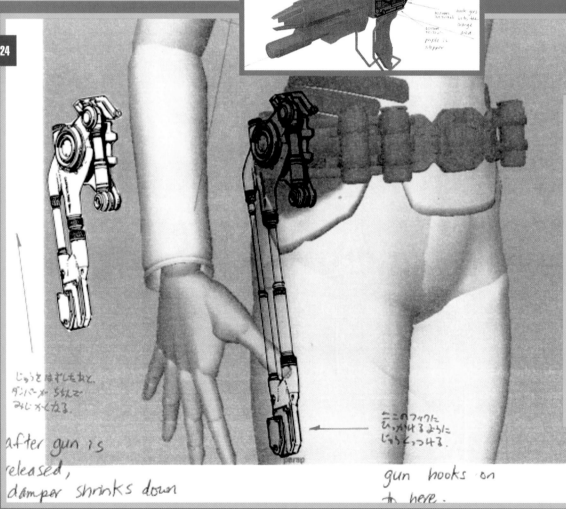

Aki's eye scope.

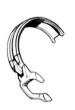

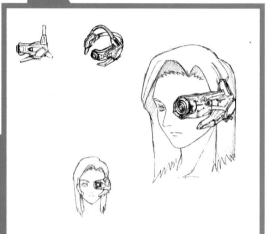

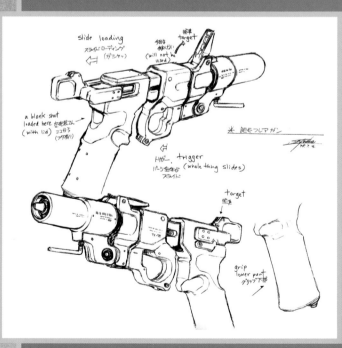

slide loading
スライドローディング
（ガシャッ）

固定 target
今回 刻印なし
（will not be used）

a blank shot
loaded here 空砲装填
（with lid）ここから
（フタ付り）

トリガー trigger
バレル全体が
（whole thing slides）
スライド

※ BEE フレアガン

target
密着

grip
lower part
グリップ下部

じゅうをはずしたあと、
ダンパーが ちぢんで
みじかくなる。

after gun is
released,
damper shrinks down

ここのフックに
ひっかけるように
じゅうをつける。

gun hooks on
to here.

Although it was cut, these concept pieces show Aki's home.

25

DEEP EYES

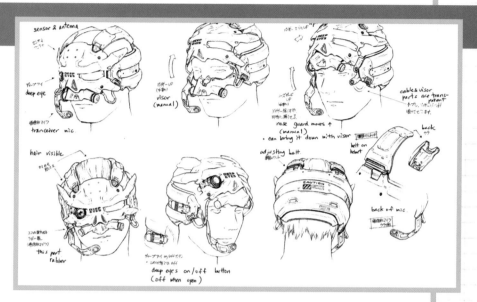

It's obvious that a great deal of care was taken in the creation of the Deep Eyes headgear.

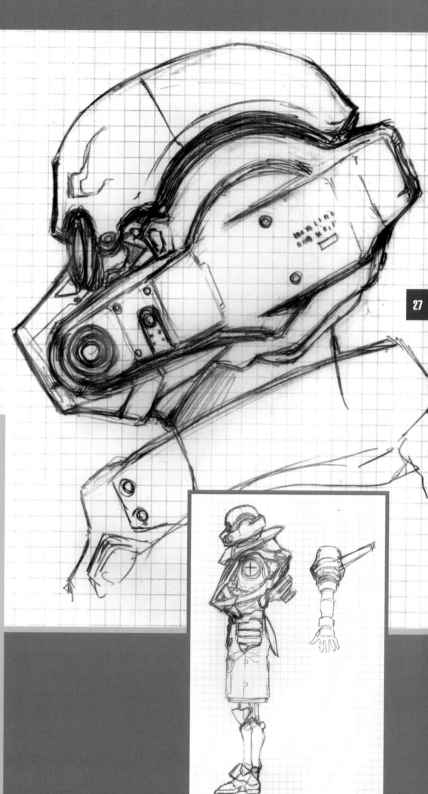

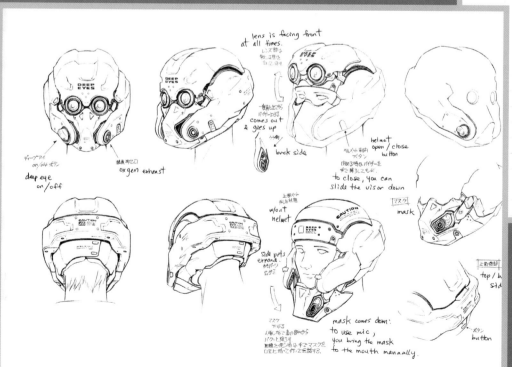

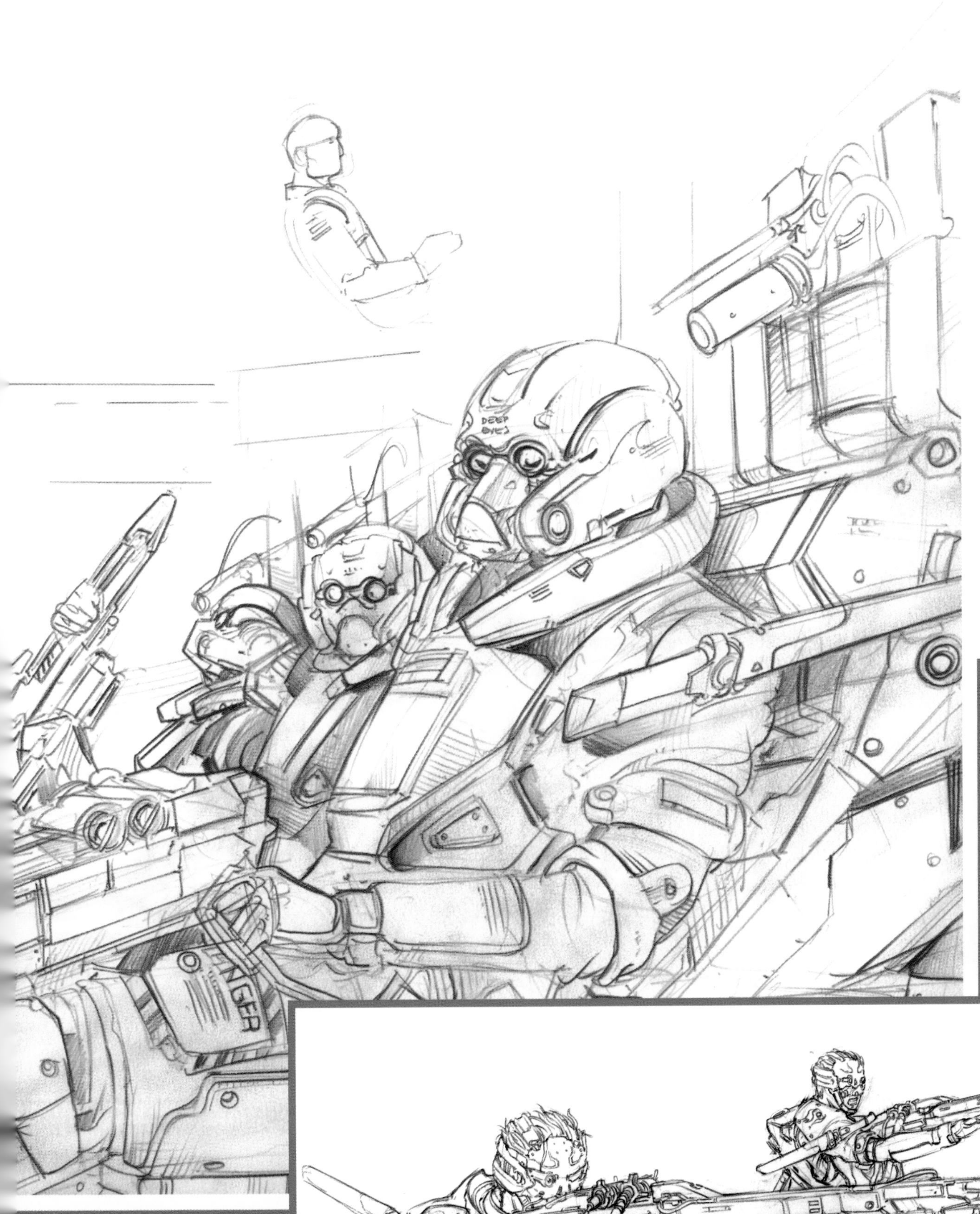

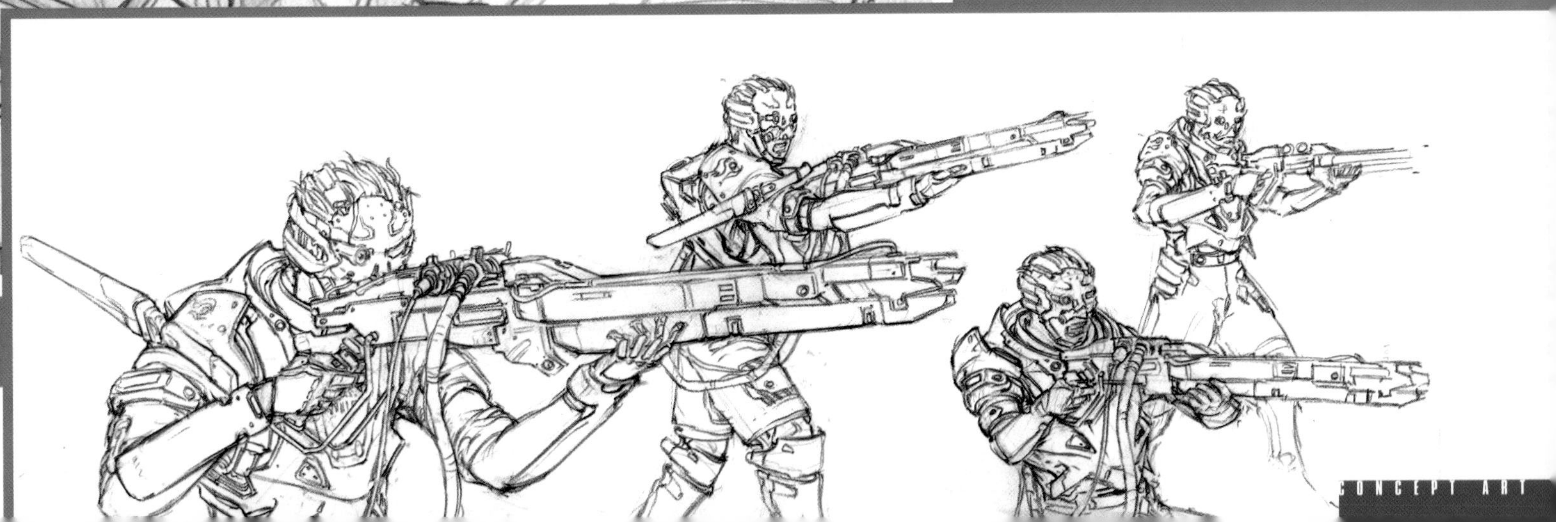

parts behind armpit area
ワキ後ろのパーツ

・復帰するゲールライト
・rear signal light

レバーをはさむと
ケーブルがはずれる
by gripping the
levers, cable is released.

パワーケーブル
コネクタ
power cable
connector

ヘリウムケーブル
コネクタ
helium cable
connector

重装兵 《パーツ》

・ヘリウムガス
タンク
・helium gas
tank

コネクタ connector

背中パーツ back parts.

ジョイント
joint

こちら上面 This side up

中心穴 center hole

・バッテリーパック
・battery pack

コネクタ
connector

ベルトジョイント部
belt joint

foot
・shin armor is
attached to shoe

ankle armor is
attached to shoe

mesh w/ calender

gloves

leather strap

APPROVE

Deep Eyes gear.

ammunition pouch

Deep Eye knife

cartridge

emergency lever (for rescue)

most soldiers wear about 4~6 of them.

重装兵《装備》 EQUIPMENTS

This part is fixed on shoulder pad.

clip

behind neck rubber material

not sharp

less sharp then top

name plate

Back joint

neck area

Behind shoulder pads inside is made of hard rubber material

cushion

inside left shoulder pad.

This material is used for flexibility.

screw for knife.

metal fittings for belt

air bag starts

after landing, release air from here

air bag prevents head from floating up during descent.

immediately after a deep they bulge up.

knee protector is worn on top of uniform

soft rubber

GENERAL HEIN

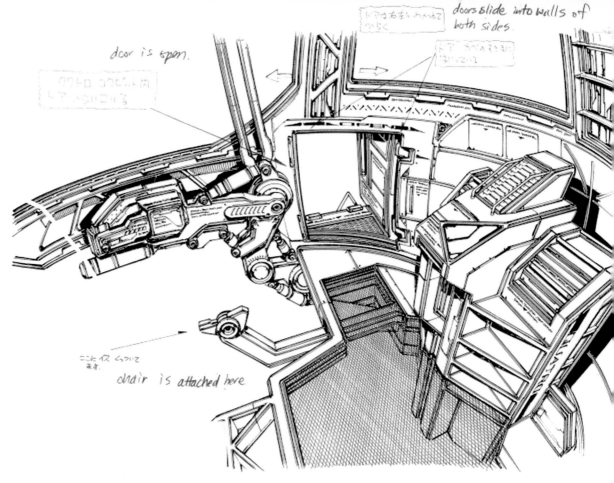

door is open.

doors slide into walls of both sides.

chair is attached here

The design of the Quatro is extremely intriguing. Although it looks quite durable, it seems somewhat susceptible to attack due to its large glass outer casing.

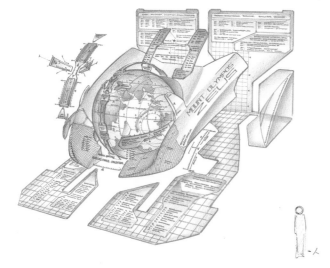

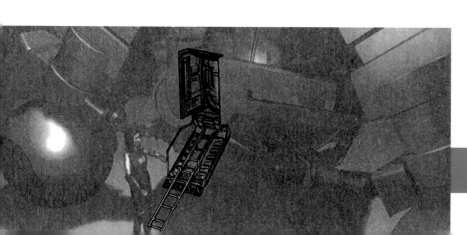

QUATRO

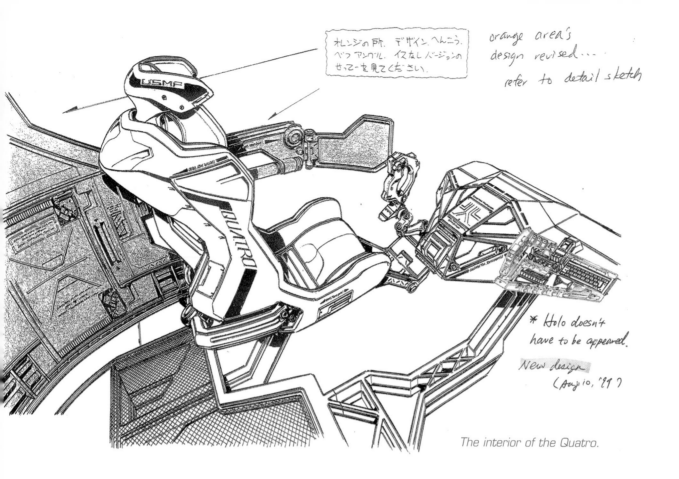

オレンジの所、デザイン、へんこう。
べつアングル、イスなしバージョンの
せってーを見てください。

orange area's
design revised...
refer to detail sketch

* Holo doesn't
have to be appeared.

New design
(Aug 10, '99)

The interior of the Quatro.

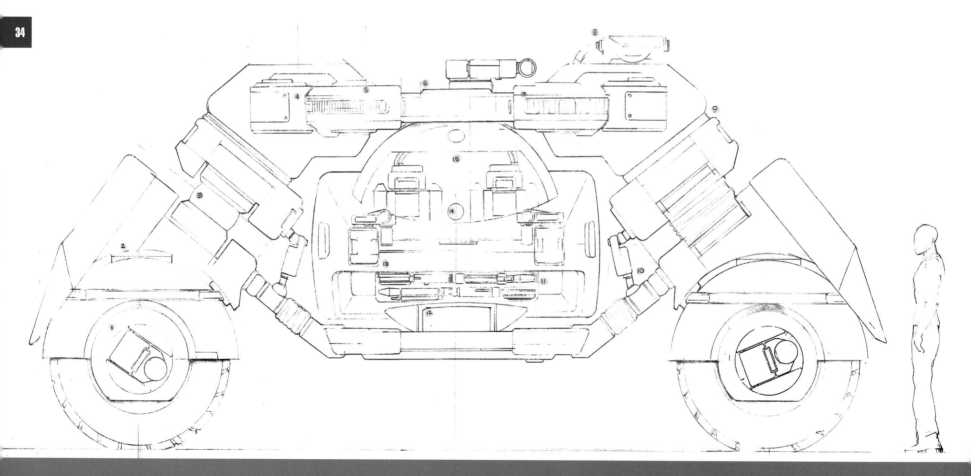

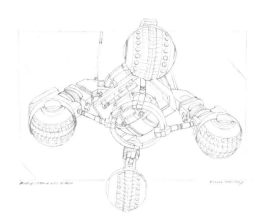

Buggy / Crane lift to Boat

Final Fantasy

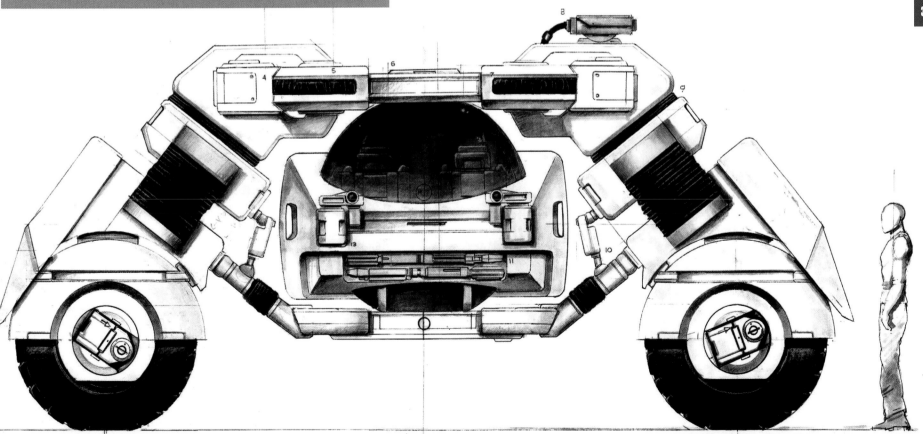

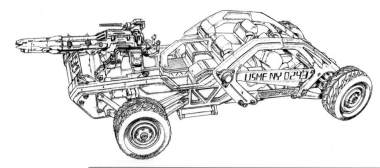

JEEP

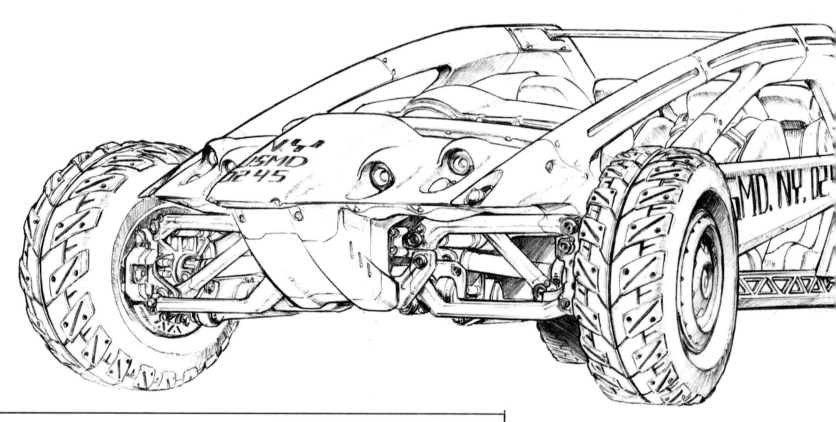

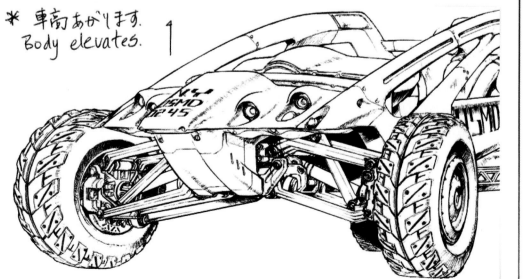

※ 車高あがります.
Body elevates.

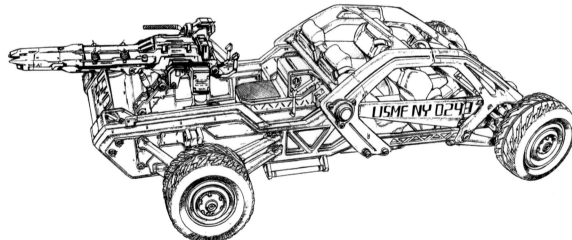

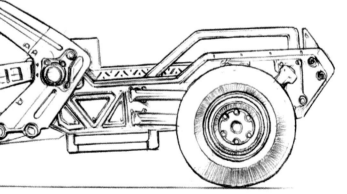

ZEUS CANNON

The Zeus Cannon was a complicated piece to construct, although it really looks majestic when in the sky.

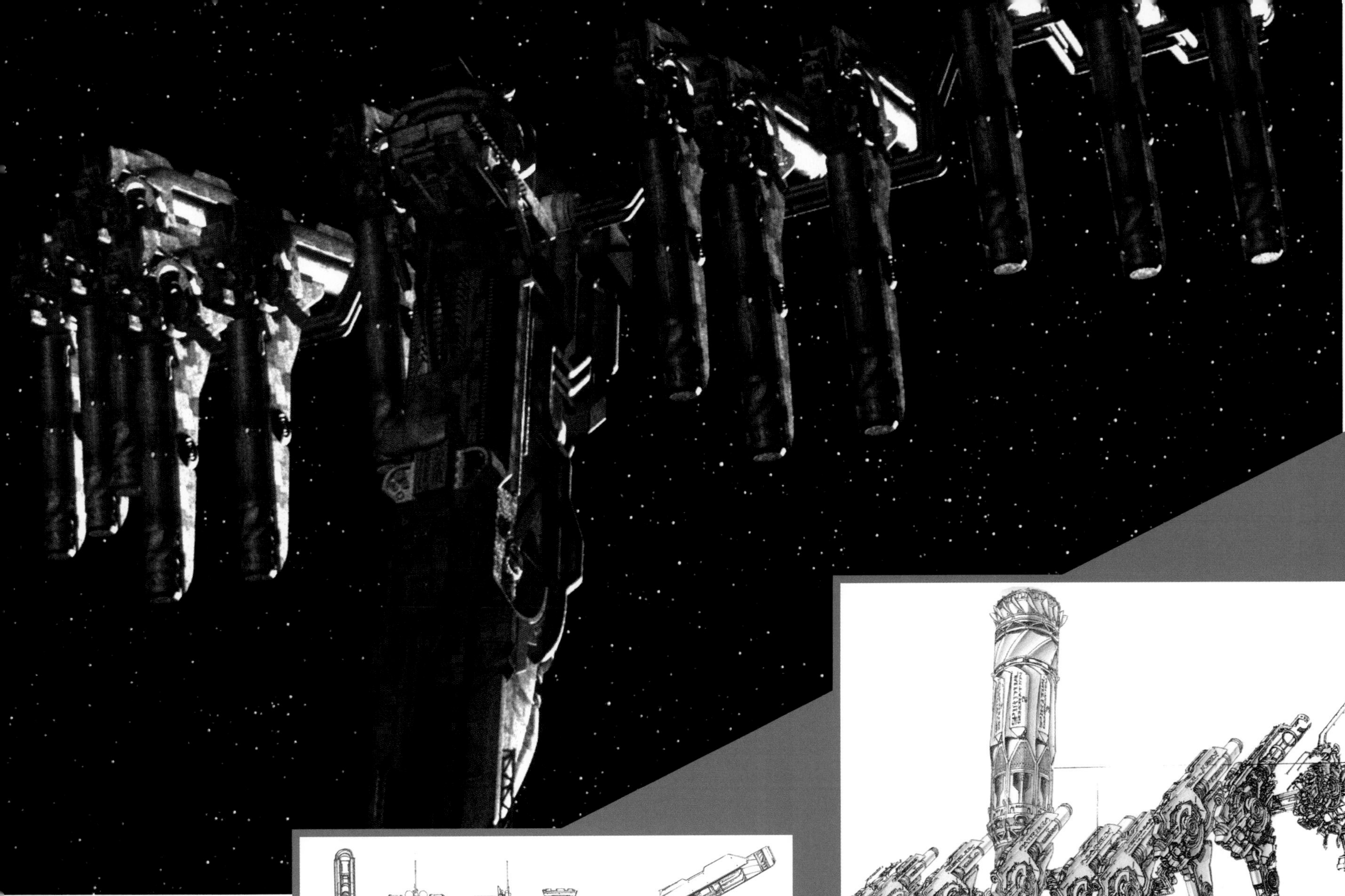

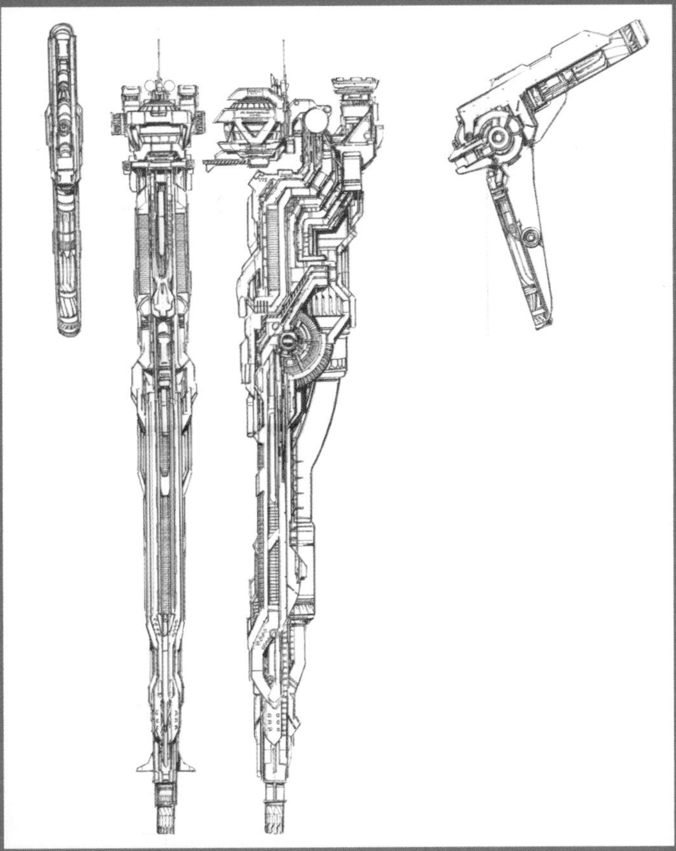

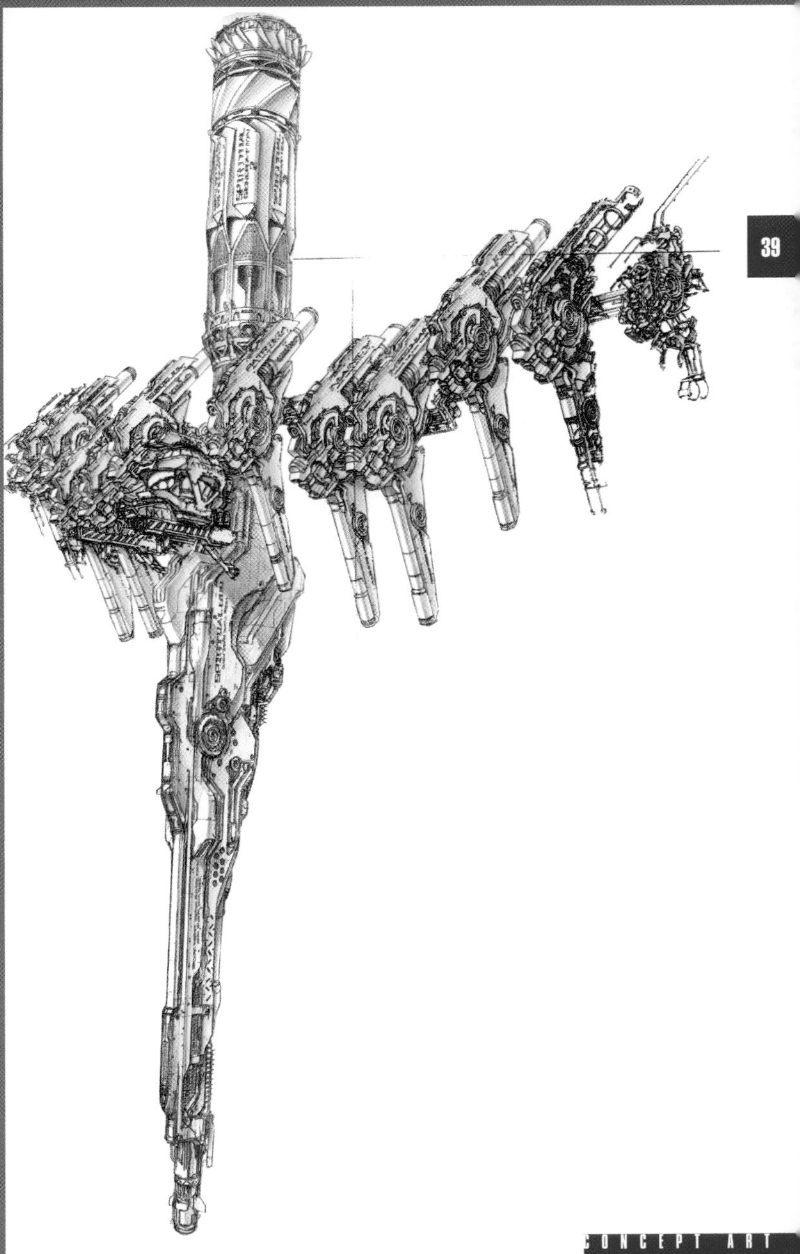

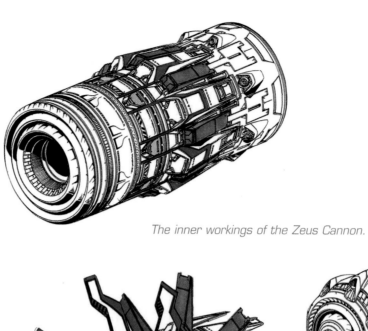

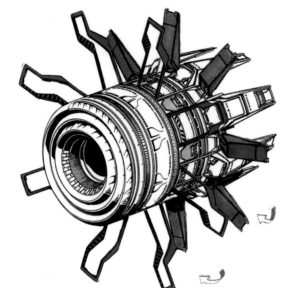

The inner workings of the Zeus Cannon.

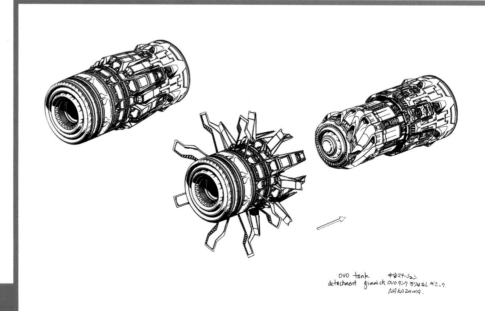

ovo tank
detachment gimmick OVOタンク 切り出しギミック
NAKAZAWA.

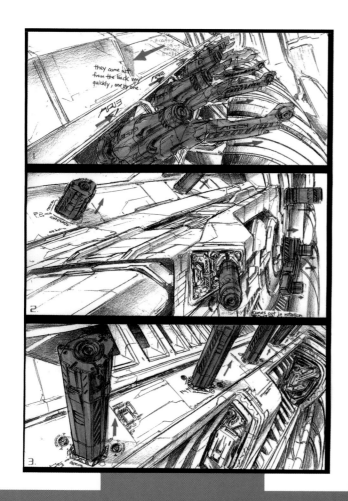

they came in
from the back way
quickly, one by one.

comes out in rotation

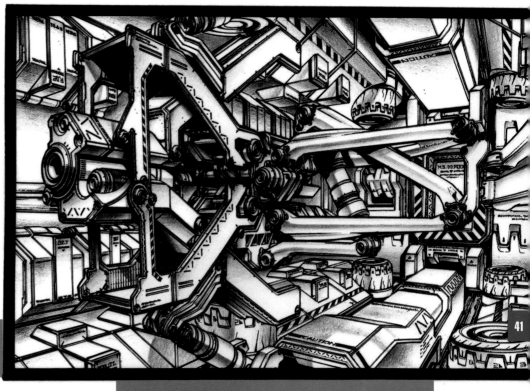

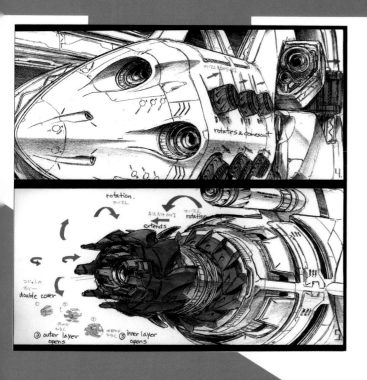

rotates & comes out

rotation.

rotation
extends

double cover
outer layer opens   inner layer opens

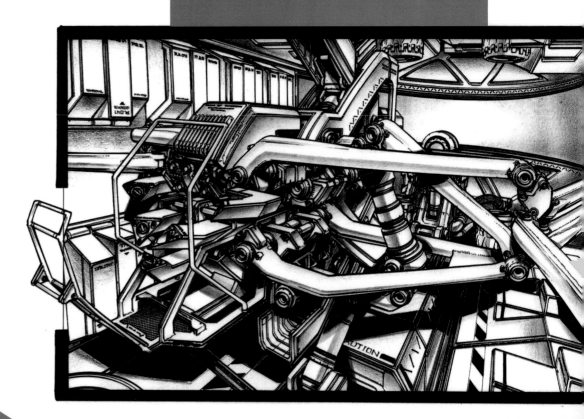

GONDOLA

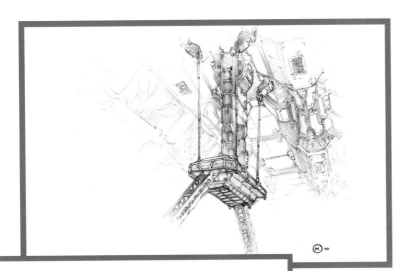

window (green)

The interior of the Gondola.

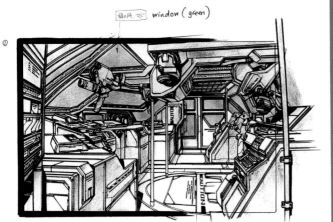

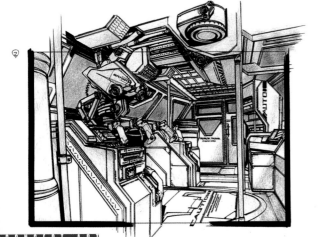

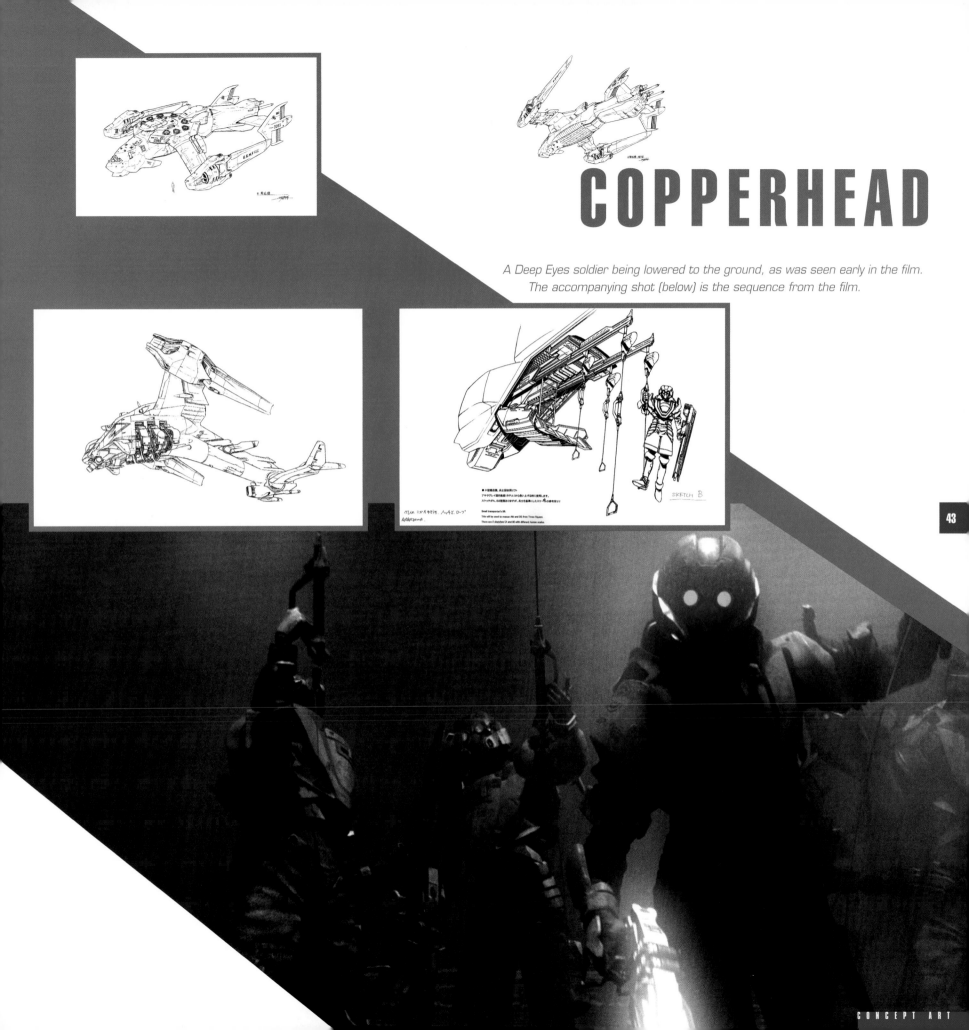

COPPERHEAD

A Deep Eyes soldier being lowered to the ground, as was seen early in the film. The accompanying shot (below) is the sequence from the film.

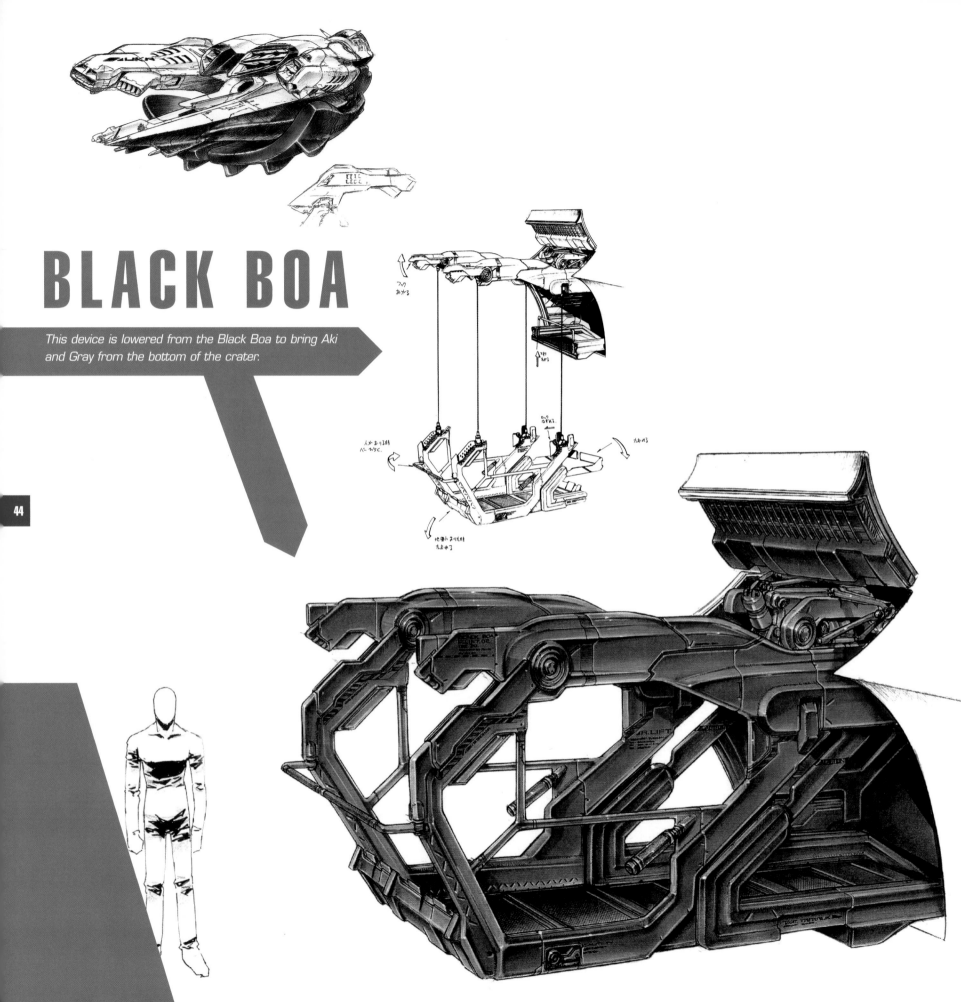

BLACK BOA

This device is lowered from the Black Boa to bring Aki and Gray from the bottom of the crater.

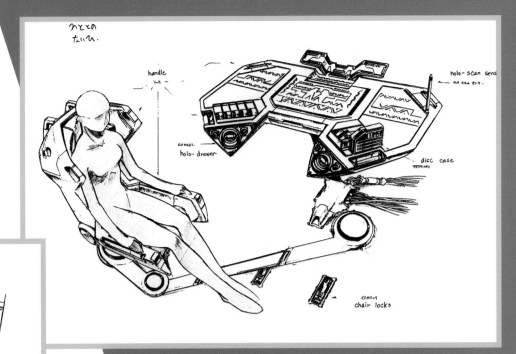

handle

holo-scan sens

holo-drawer

disc case

chair locks

The interior of the Black Boa.

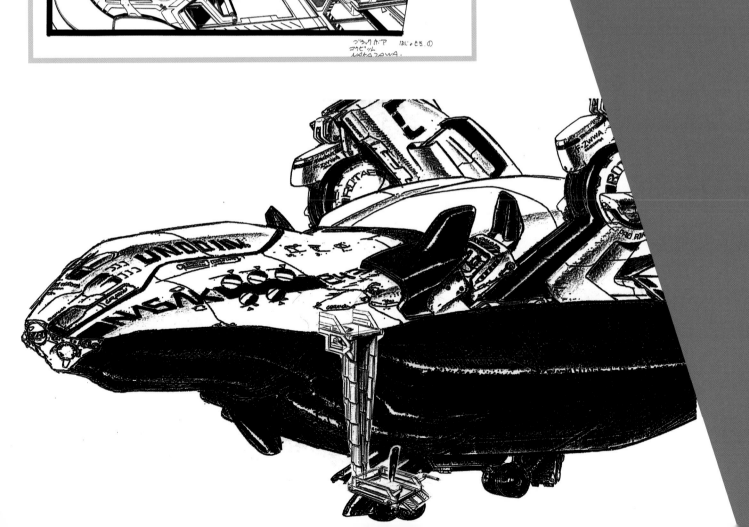

emergency sea
(normal style)

NAKAZAWA.

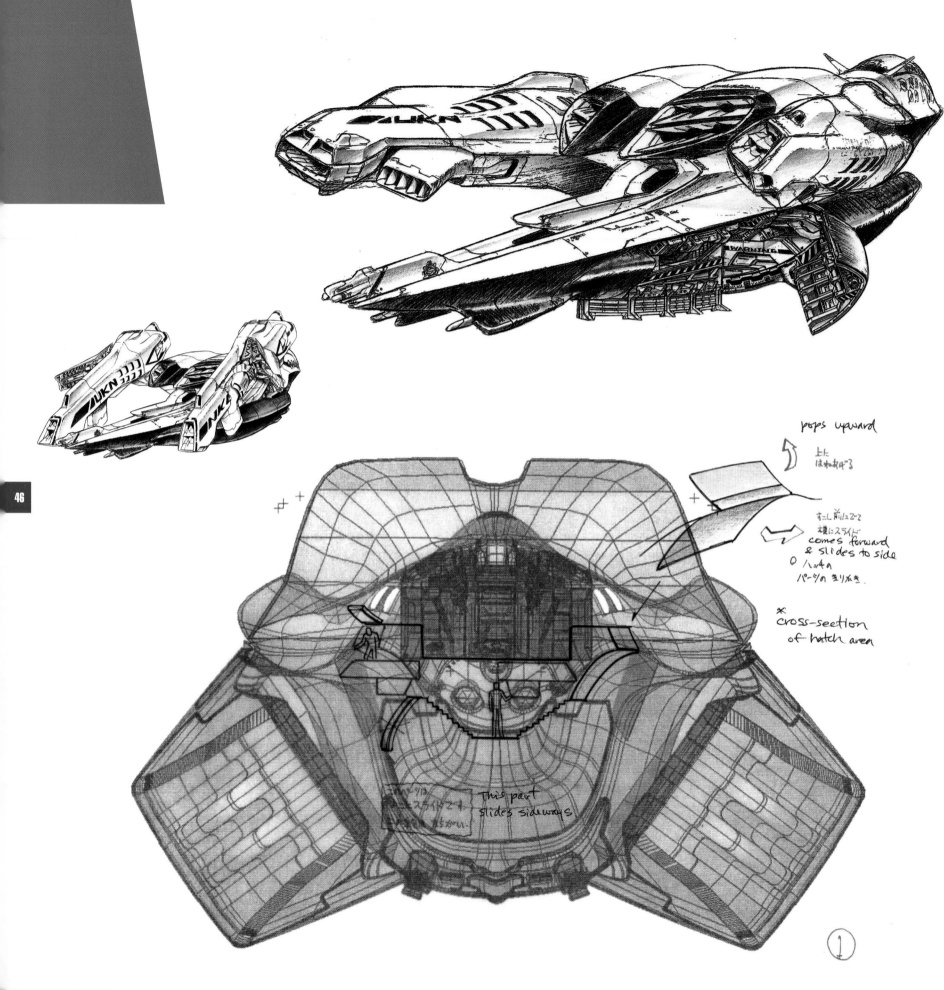

pops upward

上に
はね上げる

すこし前にズーて
横にスライド
comes forward
& slides to side
○ ハッチん
パーツのヒリ水キ

✱ cross-section
of hatch area

This part
slides sideways

①

46

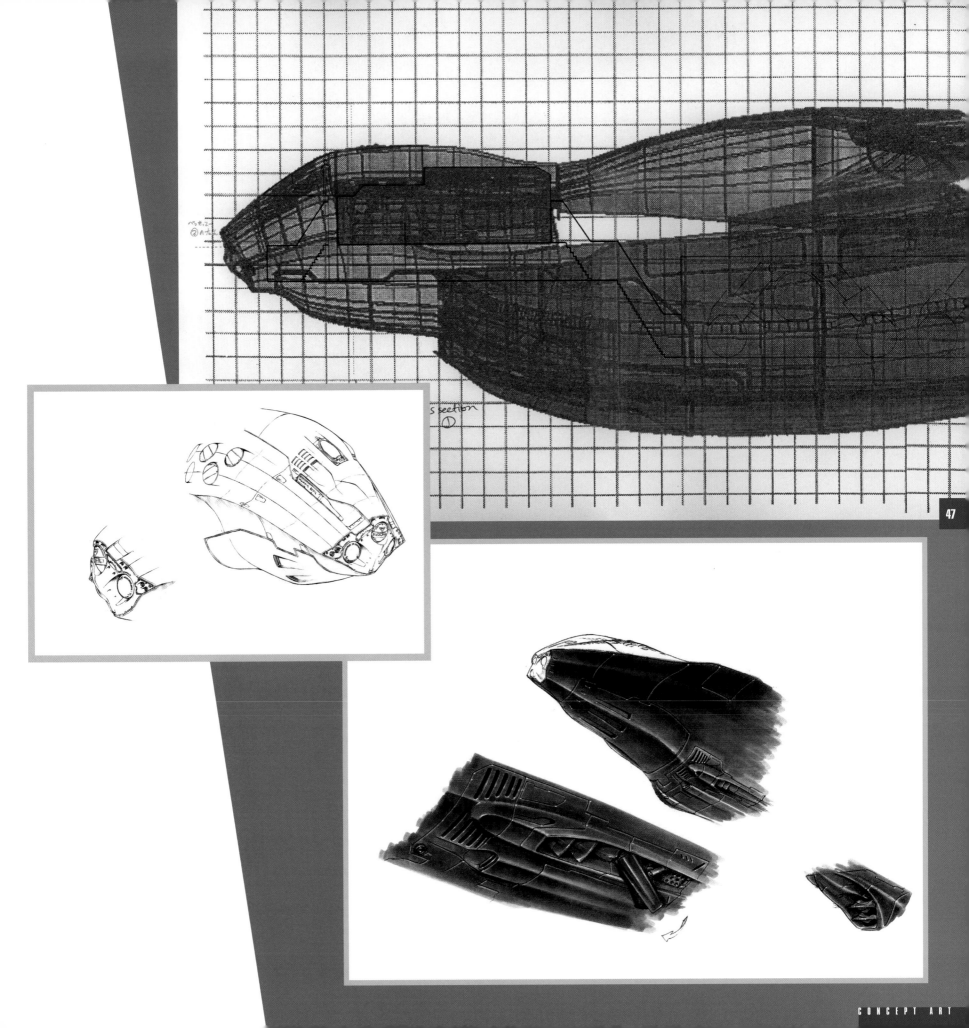

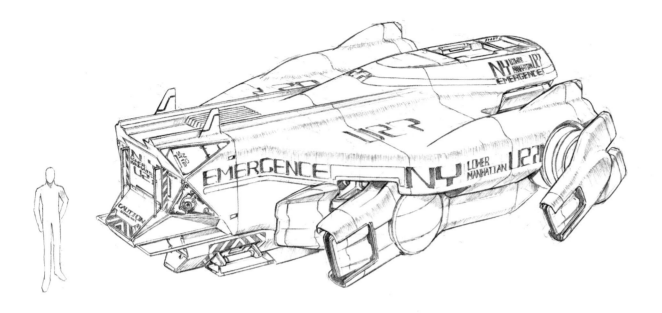

ESCAPE POD

Airport ⑤

Airport ③

ENVIRONMENTS

by Aramaki
Aug. 31, 1998

Airport ①

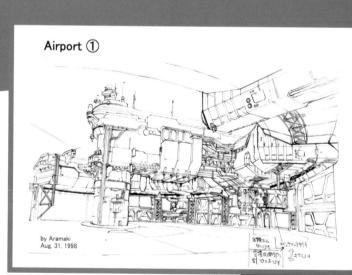

by Aramaki
Aug. 31, 1998

This beautiful scene of the airport provides stunning insight into how concept art transforms during the process.

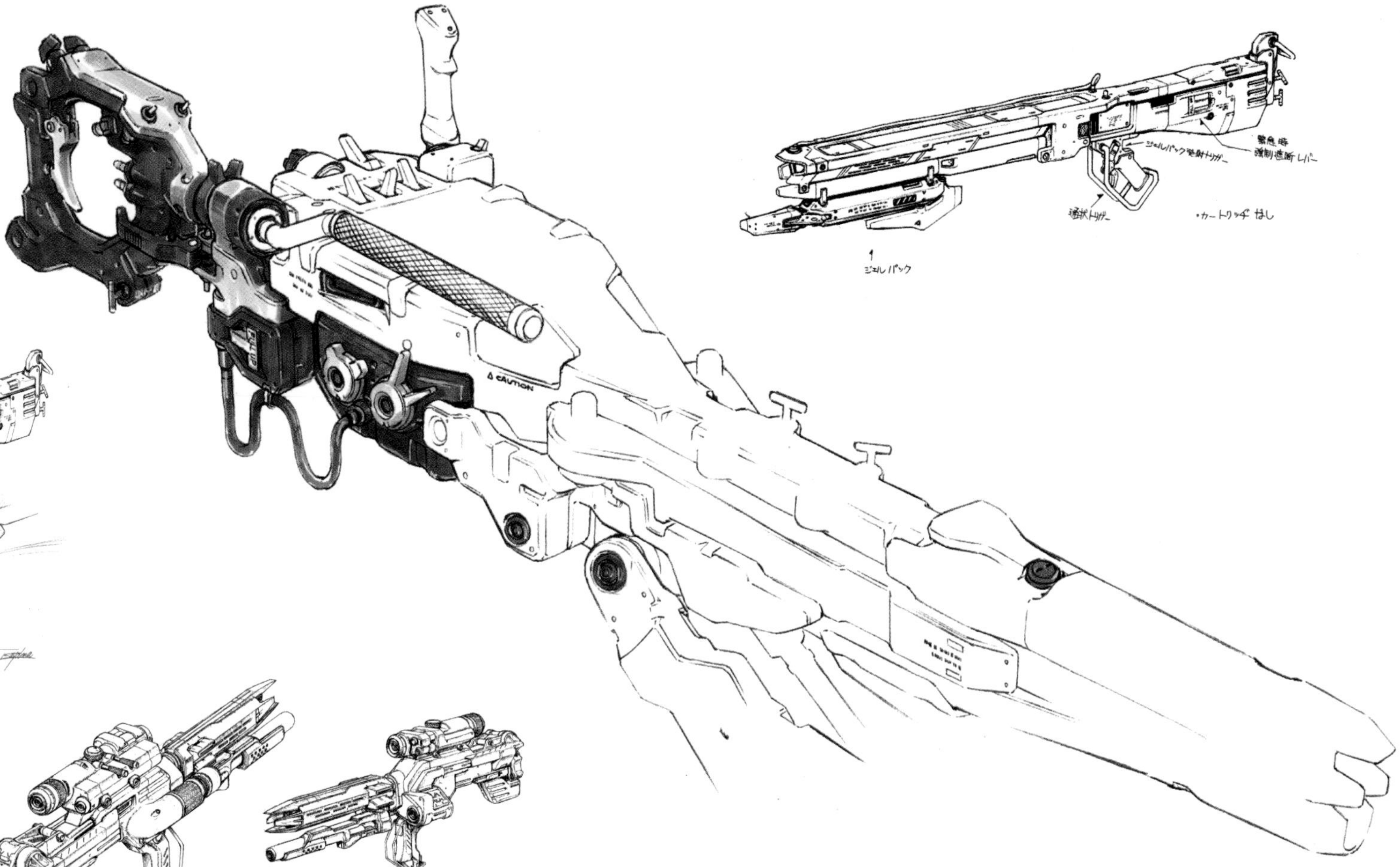
CAUTION
ジェルパック
カートリッジなし

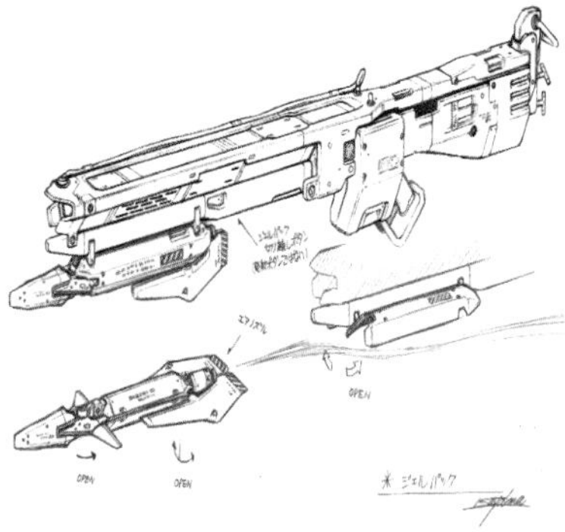

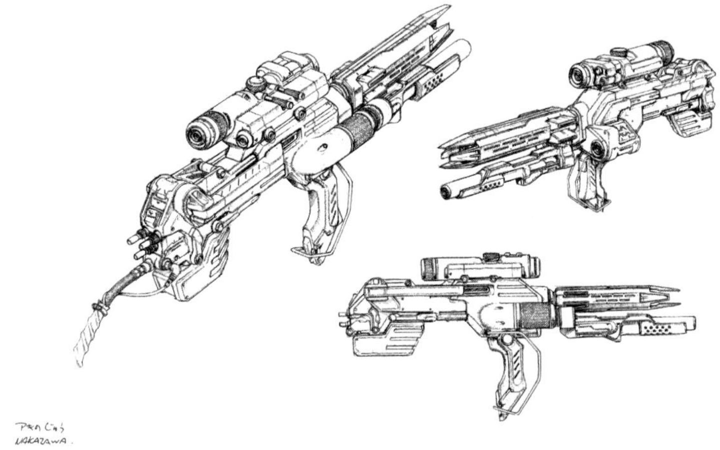

WEAPONS

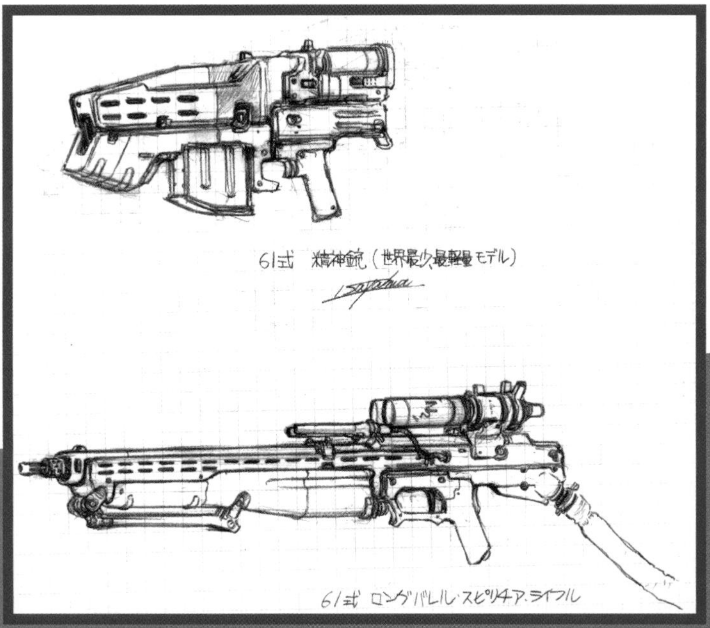
61式 精神銃（世界最少最軽量モデル）
61式 ロングバレル・スピリチュア.ライフル

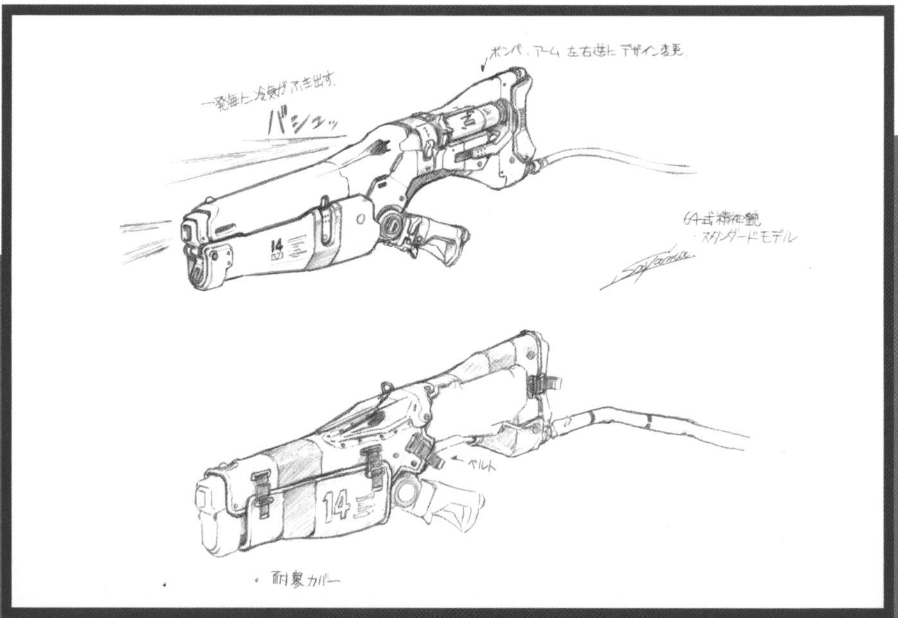
ポンパ、アーム 左右逆にデザイン変更
一発毎に冷気がふき出す
バシュッ
64式精神銃 スタンダードモデル
ベルト
耐爆カバー

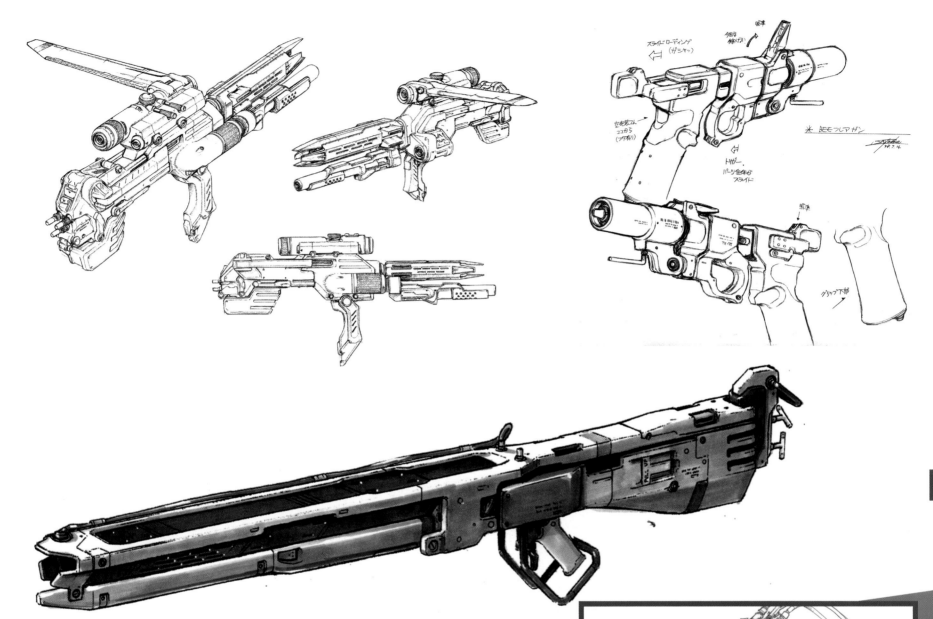

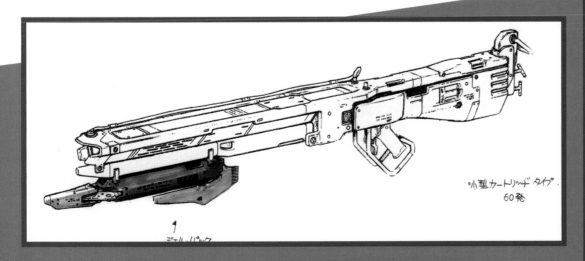

小型カートリッジ タイプ
60発

1

ジェル パック

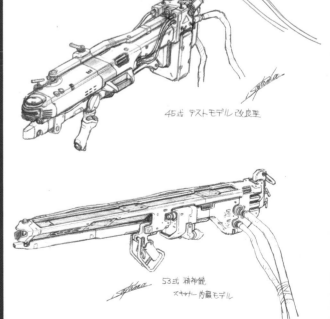

45式 テストモデル 改良型

53式 精神鋭
スキャナー 内蔵モデル

AKI'S SLEEP CHAMBER

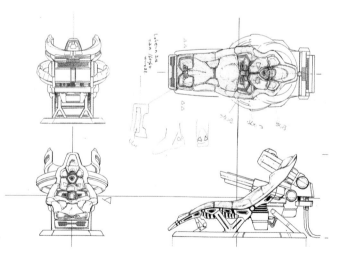

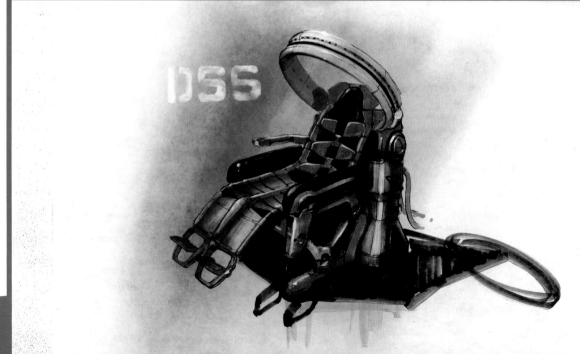

DSS

CRATER

Some early concept pieces of the meteor crater.

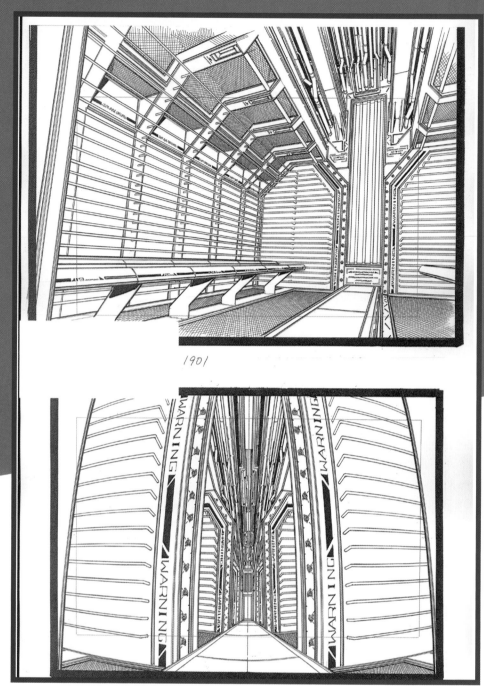

1901

CELL

BARRIER CITY
NEW YORK CITYSCAPE

EXAM ROOM

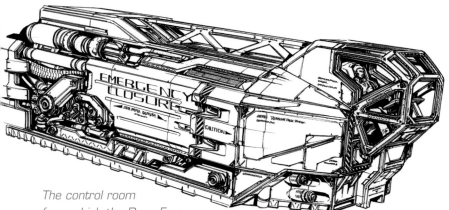

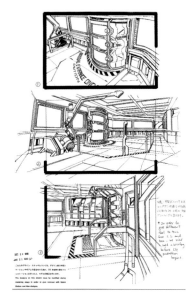

The control room
from which the Deep Eyes
receive their scans to detect a phantom
presence. In the movie, only the very
front portion of the vehicle is visible
on-screen.

The area outside of the chamber and
the chamber in which the
scans take place.

The device in which Gray under-
goes his treatment to rid
the phantom from
his body.

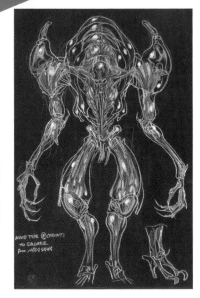

56

CONCEPT ART

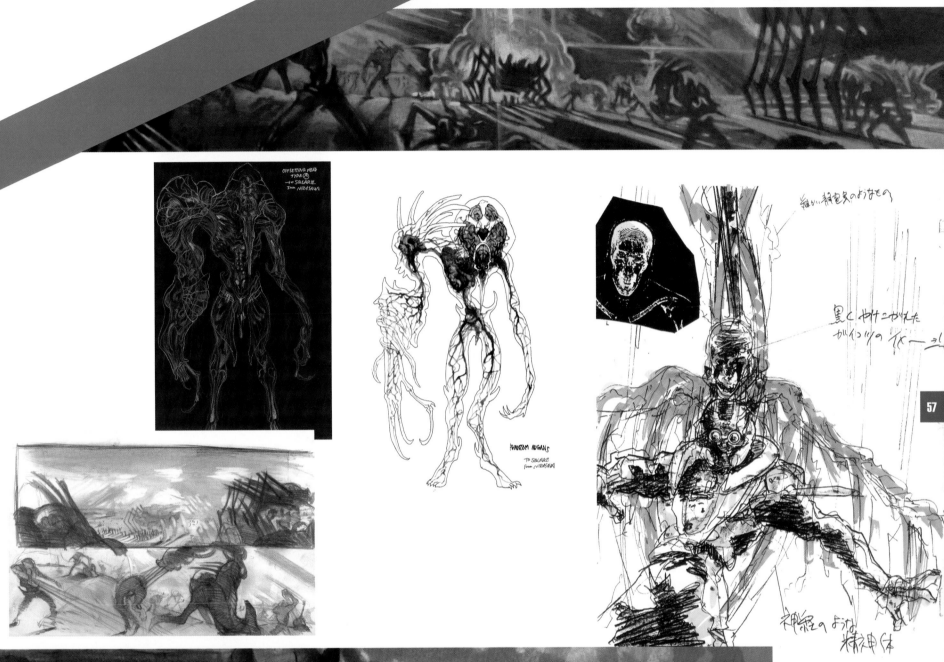

OFFSETTING HEAD
TYPE Ⓐ
→ SQUARE
From NIRASAWA

細かい静電気のようなもの

黒くやけこがれた
がいじんの スートコイ

PHANTOM AUGANS
TO SQUARE
From NIRASAWA

未開霊のような
精霊甲体

S T O R Y B O A R D S

THE STORYBOARD PROCESS

Walking the halls of Square USA's Honolulu offices used to feel like reading the Sunday morning comics. Huge rows of black-and-white sketches striped the outside walls of many cubicles in which the graphic artists and software engineers worked. Mural-like collections of these unframed scenes lined the walls, accented by an occasional color drawing. As if the walls and cubicles could not provide enough space, white boards were brought in and tattooed with even more of these illustrations.

The smaller pictures, which were generally 2.6 inches tall and 5 inches wide, had a crude quality about them—the rough, unfinished look of hastily hand-drawn pencil sketches. These drawings often showed groups of scantly detailed people in conversations, running, carrying guns, or in other poses. Though crudely drawn, these sketches conveyed movement and emotion with dead-on accuracy.

A sample set of storyboards.

The larger pictures, on the other hand, were more refined. Generally drawn on 11-inch by 17-inch sheets, these drawings were composed of carefully ruled lines meeting in perfectly squared corners, all drawn with fine-tipped pens. Unlike the smaller sketches, this art was mostly about objects and places. It was highly detailed and nearly lifeless—a space ship, a building, a gun, a room. And even when there were people in these renderings, their bodies seemed frozen.

The smaller works were created by Staging Director Tani Kunitake and his team of storyboard artists. The larger pieces were created by Square's conceptual artists, led by Kazunori Nakazawa. These were the teams that took the script and ideas and turned them into visual images; the place where Hironobu Sakaguchi's vision of *Final Fantasy: The Spirits Within* took its first steps toward becoming a reality.

STORYBOARDS

Audiences may not know Staging Director Tani Kunitake by name, but they certainly know his work. Kunitake worked on *The Matrix*, *Armageddon*, *Blade*, and *Fight Club*. At age 34, Kunitake has participated on an enviably long list of blockbuster hits.

The work he and his team did on *Final Fantasy: The Spirits Within* was deceptively vital. In a very real sense, Kunitake choreographed the movie, converting the script into visual pictures like frames in a comic book to illustrate the look, mood, and even the camera angles for each scene.

"Basically, I was part Art Director, part Storyboard Supervisor,"

says Kunitake. "My job was supervising a crew of storyboard artists and dealing with the continuity of the movie. I worked very closely with Sakaguchi-san. We talked about the script and worked out his ideas visually, and that continued all the way through the editing process."

In live-action films, movie directors have the luxury of seeing actors and sets. Because *Final Fantasy: The Spirits Within* had no on-screen actors and no real sets, storyboarding took on extra significance and required additional steps.

Tani in his creative working environment.

The office where the storyboards come to life.

Kunitake, who only spent seven months working on *The Matrix*, spent three full years tinkering with this film. "On a project like this, we had to illustrate everything. We had to illustrate all our coverage shots and close-ups. You really wouldn't board some of these things on a regular production. But we couldn't go out to a location and start blocking out camera coverage on this project, so we had to make everything up. We had to plan it out early on and it took a lot more time for pre-production development."

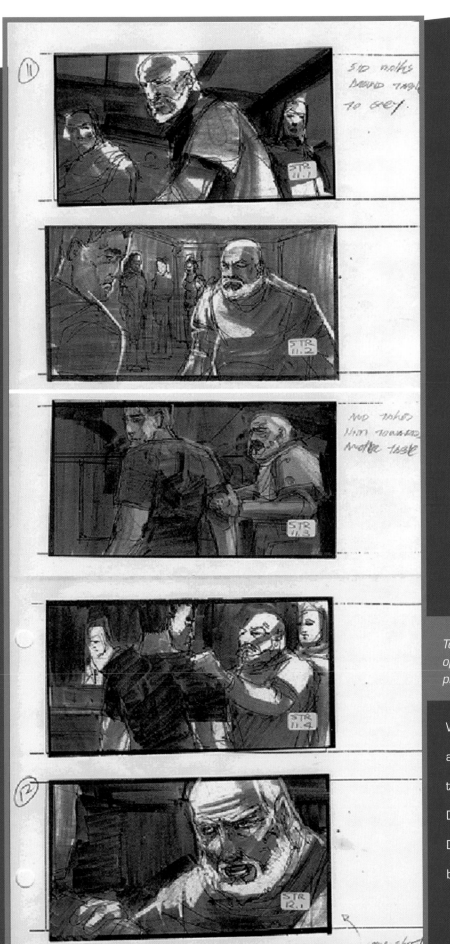

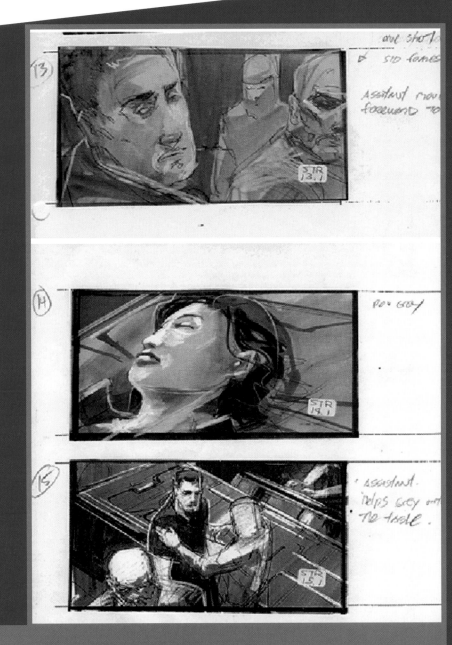

To the novice, this storyboard sequence may seem quite unimportant. However, the opposite is true. A sea of emotions is emphasized in these eight shots, as Dr. Sid pleads with Gray to help the injured Aki.

When the production team looked at the storyboard illustrations, they learned to look at more than the picture itself. The man on the street might look at one of these pictures and think it was just about a couple of people talking. To Andy Jones, Animation Director, it might hold information about how a scene should be motion captured. To David Seager, the Lighting Supervisor, it might hold clues about how the scene should be lit.

"I guess that's why I was called Staging Director instead of the Storyboard Supervisor," says Kunitake. "My role included initial camera direction. If there was a vehicle, we might suggest opening the walls so the camera could see in from outside. The world that Sakaguchi-san had in mind was very rich, so we had to make sure that a sense of continuity ran throughout the whole film."

To achieve that continuity, Kunitake had to break every scene from the movie into standard-sized illustrations—the index card-sized pictures lining the walls of Square USA. According to Kunitake, each of his artists could produce anywhere from 12 to 24 pictures per day. Sound like a lot? He estimates that the final storyboard contained 1,500 illustrations!

Check out this dramatic transformation, as Tani sketches Gray's dream sequence. The process is simply amazing.

"The storyboard was kind of like a comic book," says Kunitake. "We put the illustrations into a story reel. We organized the pictures into scenes and looked at them on the wall, and as soon as the scenes got approved by Sakaguchi-san, we would put them into a story reel for him."

Sakaguchi's story reel was a slideshow presentation, a primitive representation of the entire movie with hand-drawn illustrations instead of movie frames and an audio track with Square USA's employees performing scenes that would later be dubbed using professional actors. "We created a pre-edited film as a slide show and added in scratch (meaning "temporary") recorded voices so that we could see if the scenes played out well early on. If they weren't working at this stage, they definitely would not work once we started animating and doing the motion capture."

Although he was born and raised in Detroit, Tani Kunitake has a Hawaiian connection—his father is from the Big Island of Hawaii.

Kunitake started his career in Detroit designing cars for Honda and Ford, but he soon switched from cars to movies, working for such places as Digital Domain and Industrial Light and Magic as a storyboard artist. His list of credits includes *Fight Club*, *Blade*, and *The Matrix*.

"I mainly worked as a concept artist," says Kunitake. "On *The Matrix*, I got a little bit more involved with the storyboards, so I had more to do with the narrative. I was mostly involved with illustrations [made] directly from the script."

But the public will be less familiar with one of Kunitake's favorite projects: *I Am Legend*, a Ridley Scott film based on a classic Richard Matheson horror novel. The movie was cancelled, but Kunitake still speaks wistfully of the project. "I had a pretty good run for a while. Then there was a big project that never got made: *I Am Legend* with Ridley Scott. That one wasn't so lucky. It got shut down. *I Am Legend* was always one of my favorite books, and I was a big fan of *Night of the Living Dead* and *The Omega Man*."

HEIN'S SUICIDE ATTEMPT

If *Final Fantasy: The Spirits Within* has one scene that reflects the importance of storyboards, it is the scene in which a very distraught General Hein prepares to commit suicide as he flees the ruins of Barrier City New York in a transport.

It must be remembered that by this scene, Hein had betrayed the Council, cleared the way for phantoms to invade Barrier City New York and kill its civilian population, and abandoned his soldiers while they were under attack. In other words, he begins this scene as a less than sympathetic character.

The scene opens with the sight of bullets floating weightlessly inside the dim cabin of Hein's ship. "We follow that downward spiral of the camera down, following the path of the bullets as Hein unloads his gun," explains Staging Director Tani Kunitake. "He's thinking and methodically pulling back the ejection (on his pistol), letting the shells fly."

Note how initially in the storyboards the bullet is facing a different direction than in the finished piece.

"The camera goes down to an extreme close up, then Hein gets interrupted. He's thinking about erasing himself, but gets interrupted by the computer. And this is where he looks up and sees destination, and then he has the idea to follow through with his original plan to go to the Zeus Cannon."

As far as the data was concerned, it did not matter if this scene was done from a blatant barrel's-eye view or seen from a totally obscure angle. Storyboarding decided to handle the scene in an artistic and somewhat mysterious fashion, concentrating on the mood of the scene and never fully spelling out the details of Hein's self-destructive plan.

"This shot came very quickly and very easily," says Kunitake. "We were able to storyboard it within a day. What we wanted to do was get caught up in the emotion of Hein's downward spiral. This is where he was heading, out of control, and it kind of worked nicely with the zero gravity aspect of being in orbit. We followed this spiral trail down to the temple of his head, and in doing this we were also able to hide the blatant suicide attempt. We don't show the full frame, the suicide is very much subtly indicated, and then you see Hein unloading the bullets. He's never pulled the trigger, and then he lets the gun drop."

But the success of this scene depended on invisible wizardry as well as storytelling magic. Although it looks as if the camera is getting closer and closer to Hein as it spirals down toward him in the beginning of the scene, the virtual camera is actually moving away while the lens zooms in for a tighter shot. By the time the picture is focused on Hein's face, the camera is physically outside of his transport.

"We did the scene in a virtual camera environment, so we were able to use a wider lens on the way down, and then go into as extreme 200 (magnification) zoom onto Hein's face," says Kunitake. "If you had an actual physical camera, that camera would have been 100 feet away at the end of the spiraling, but it looks like it's six inches from the actor's face."

"This shot would have been impossible with real cameras, and because we tried to do it conventionally, even though it was in computer graphics, it just wouldn't work. Then Andy (Andy Jones, Animation Director) played with the virtual space, so we were able to take the camera hundreds of feet out of the room."

Storyboarding and animation worked together to create an effect that could not have been accomplished in a live action film. And the end result is what Kunitake describes as "very tasteful for a suicide attempt." What more can you say?

Hein before aborting his suicide attempt.

STORYBOARD GALLERY

It would be impossible to include all of the storyboards for the entire movie; there are just too many.

Therefore, we have selected the most important ones for most sequences in the movie.

AKI'S FIRST DREAM (DRA)

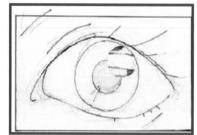

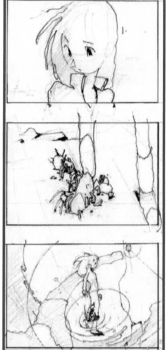

BLACK BOA LANDING (BBL)

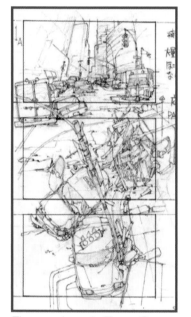

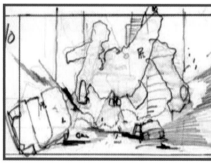

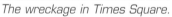

The wreckage in Times Square.

AKI'S ADVENTURE, PART A (AAA)

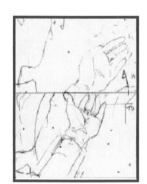

AKI'S ADVENTURE, PART B (AAB)

Gray: "This is a restricted area."

Gray: "HALT! I said HALT!" Gray then stands up and runs after Aki.

The phantom moves through the drum. The other members of the Deep Eyes follow Aki as if they were taking command of the situation.

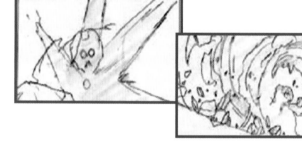

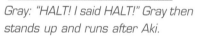

Ryan fires some bullets that pierce through the phantom and the drum, causing an explosion.

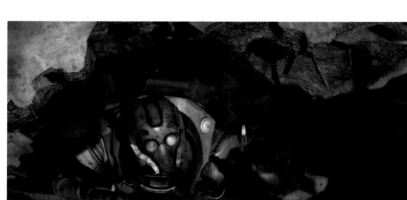

DEEP EYES UNVEILED (UNV)

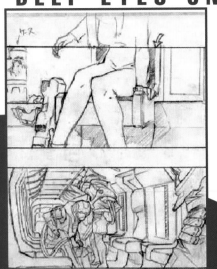

Gray takes off his helmet.

Aki: "Who are you?"

SCANNING CHAMBER (SCN)

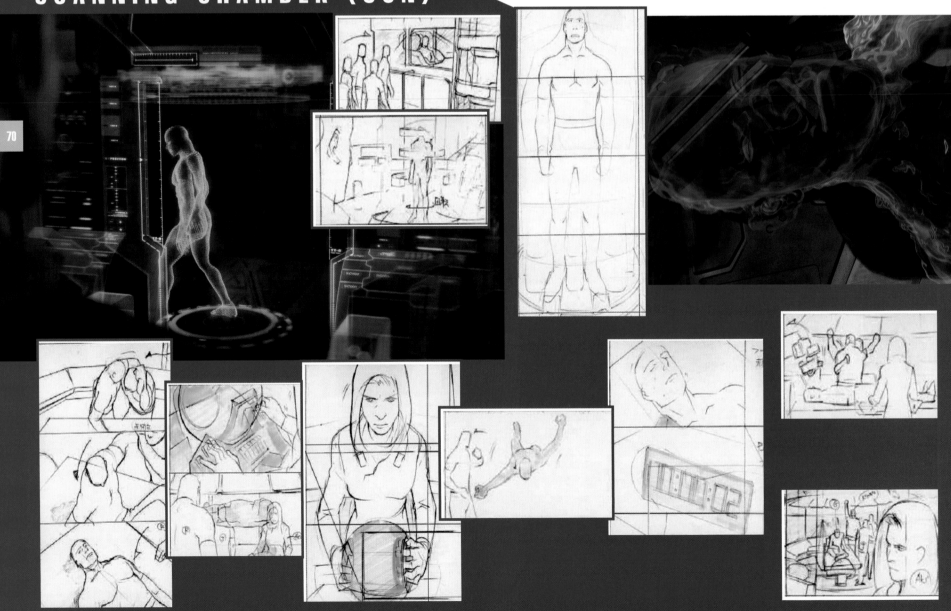

SID'S LAB A (SLA)

CONFERENCE ROOM AND HALL (CFR)

General Hein glares down toward Dr. Sid.

GONDOLA (GON)

Gray: "The council decided to postpone firing the Zeus Cannon."

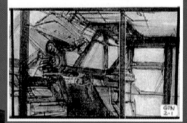

Aki: "I'm scanning the city for the seventh spirit."

Aki: "Don't please."

MILITARY COMMAND ROOM (MOA)

Hein: "My wife and daughter were killed by phantoms when the San Francisco..."

AKI'S DREAM SEQUENCE, PART B (DRB)

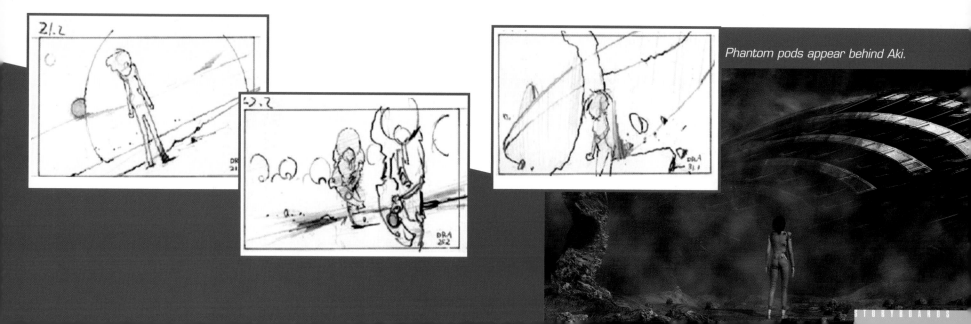

Phantom pods appear behind Aki.

AKI'S DREAM SEQUENCE, PART C (DRC)

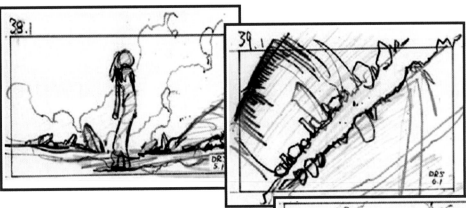

AKI'S DREAM SEQUENCE, PART D (DRD)

AKI'S DREAM SEQUENCE, PART E (DRE)

Aki appears next to Gray.

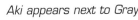

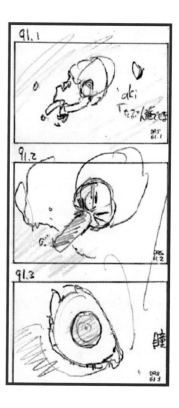

AKI'S DREAM SEQUENCE, PART F (DRF)

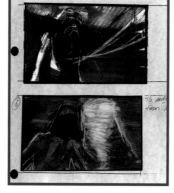

Aki drops to the ground. A glow emits from her chest.

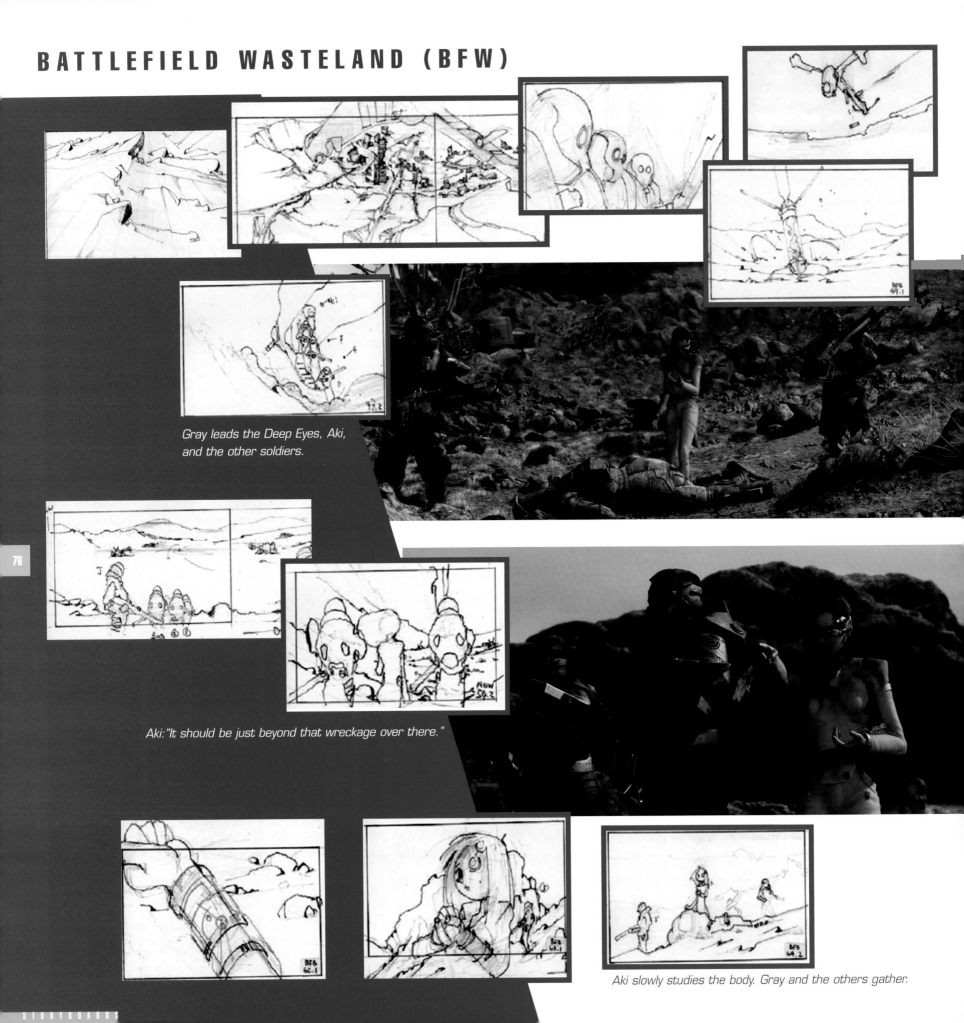

Gray leads the Deep Eyes, Aki, and the other soldiers.

Aki:"It should be just beyond that wreckage over there."

Aki slowly studies the body. Gray and the others gather.

Neil: "We have incoming."

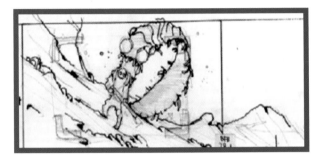

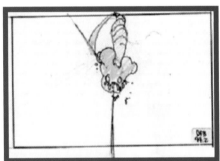

Gray: "Let's get the hell outta here."

Jane: "Get Down!" Jane yells to Gray
and the others.

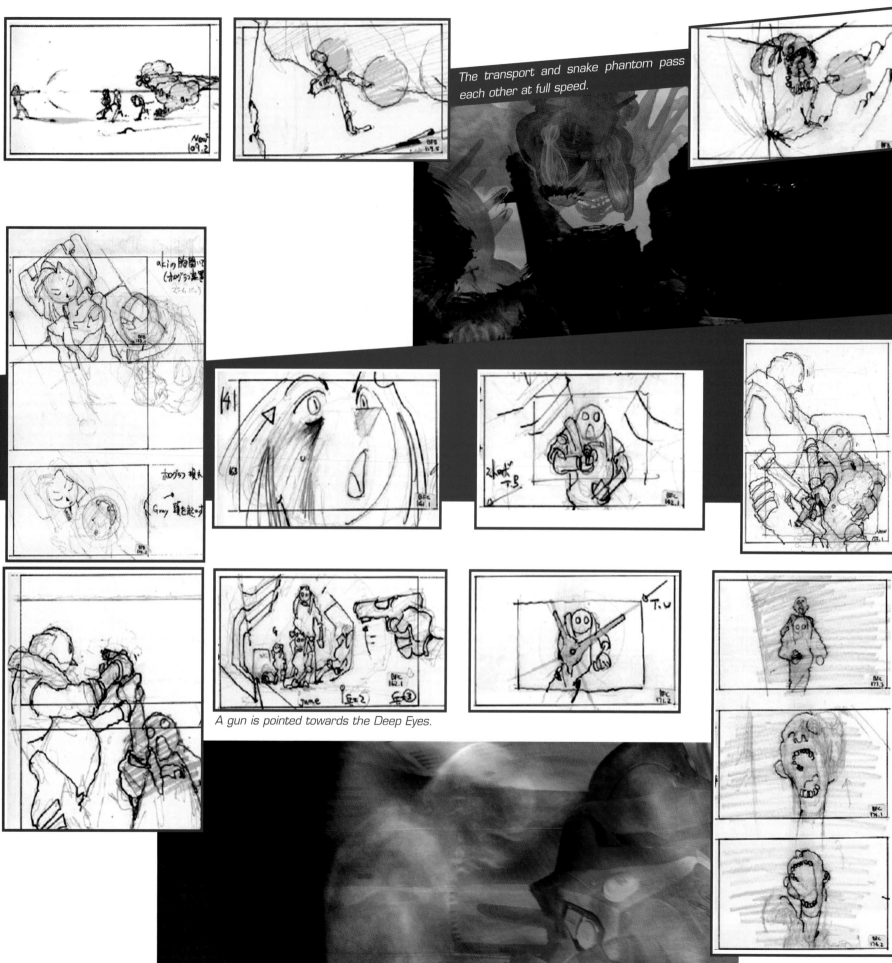

The transport and snake phantom pass each other at full speed.

A gun is pointed towards the Deep Eyes.

SPIRITUAL TREATMENT ROOM (STR)

SID'S LAB, PART B (SLB)

Hein walks toward the spiritual containment tanks.

BARRIER CONTROL ROOM (BCR)

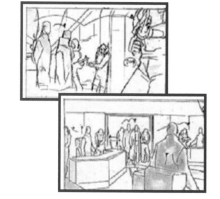
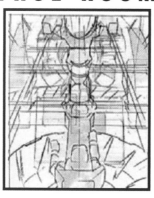

Hein approaches Soldier and says: "How many Phantoms?"

The snake phantom enters the inside of the control center.

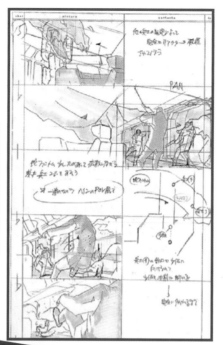
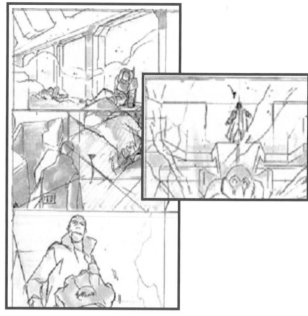

Dying Major Elliot extends his hand towards Hein.

MILITARY CELL BLOCK

The Military Cell Blocks.

MILITARY CELL BLOCK ESCAPE

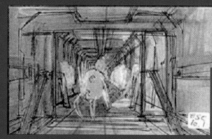

Deep Eyes and Dr. Sid are separated by phantoms from Aki and Gray by Phantoms.

BARRIER CITY NEW YORK (BNA)

PANIC (PNC)

Escape pod disengaged.

Transport explodes in the background; a meta Phantom rises up.

Jeep turns 180 degrees to a halt.

AIRPORT, PART B (AIB)

Gray: "Is anybody hurt?" Ryan is revealed
pinned in the jeep.

Ryan: "No, Doc.
No drugs."

AIRPORT (AIR)

Gray: "Neil, do you read me?"

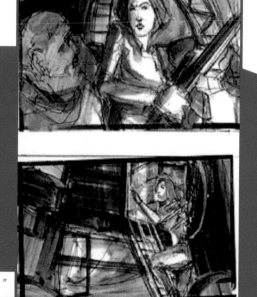

Aki: "We can't just leave everybody."

Airtray is grinding to a halt.
Meta phantom legs rising from
the airtray.

Gray: "Aki, get outta here now!"

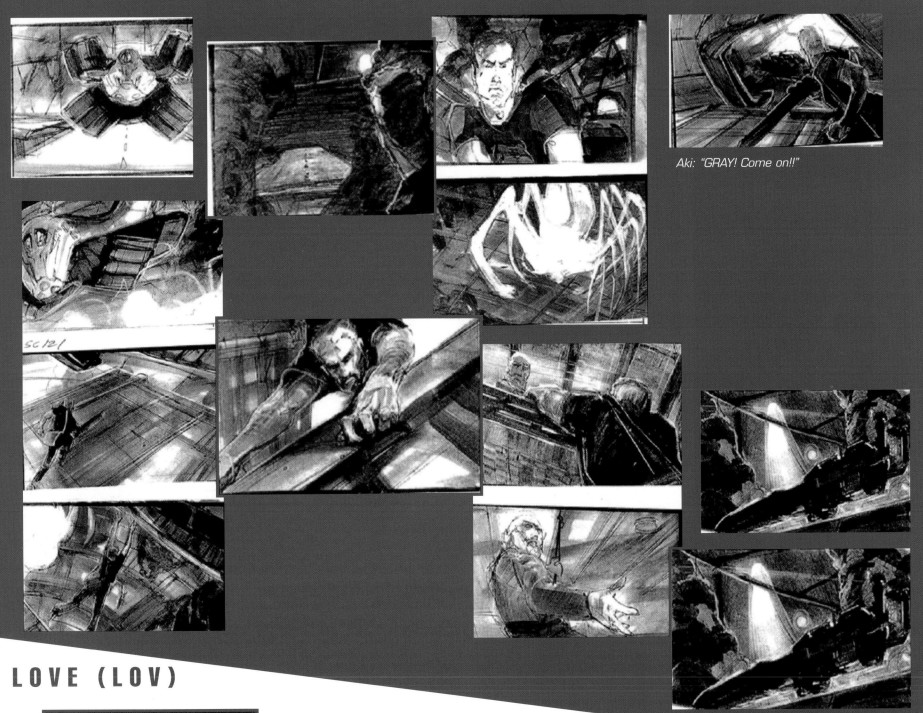

Aki: "GRAY! Come on!!"

LOVE (LOV)

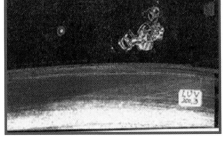

HEIN'S SUICIDE ATTEMPT (HSA)

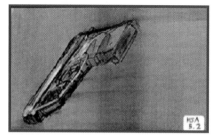

BOA/ZEUS STATION (BZS)

Aki: "I say we go."

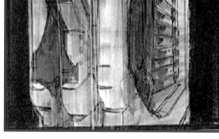

Hein: "Prepare to fire the cannon."

ENDING SPACE STATION (ESS)

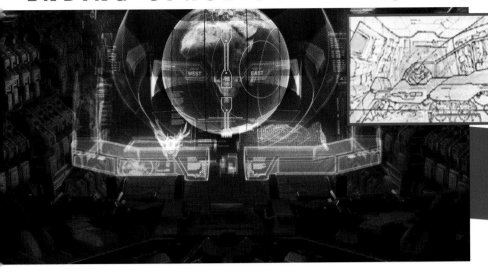

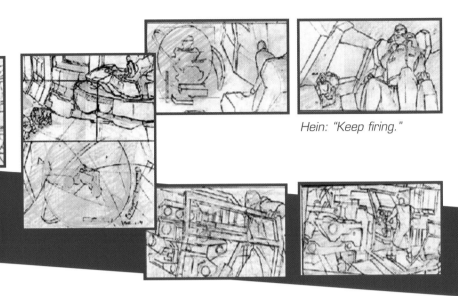

Hein: "Keep firing."

SPACE STATION FIRE (SSF)

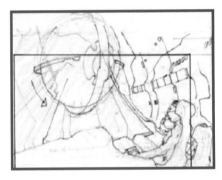

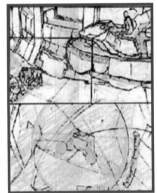

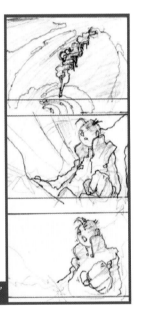

Hein: "Fire."

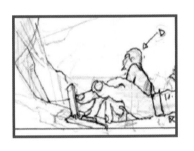

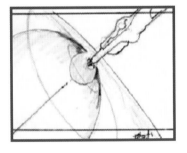

SPACE STATION EXPLOSION (SSE)

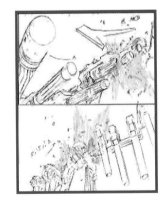

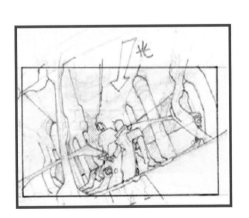

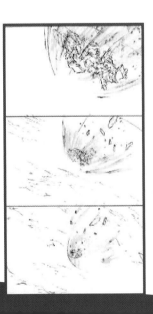

CRATER, FIRST HALF (CRA)

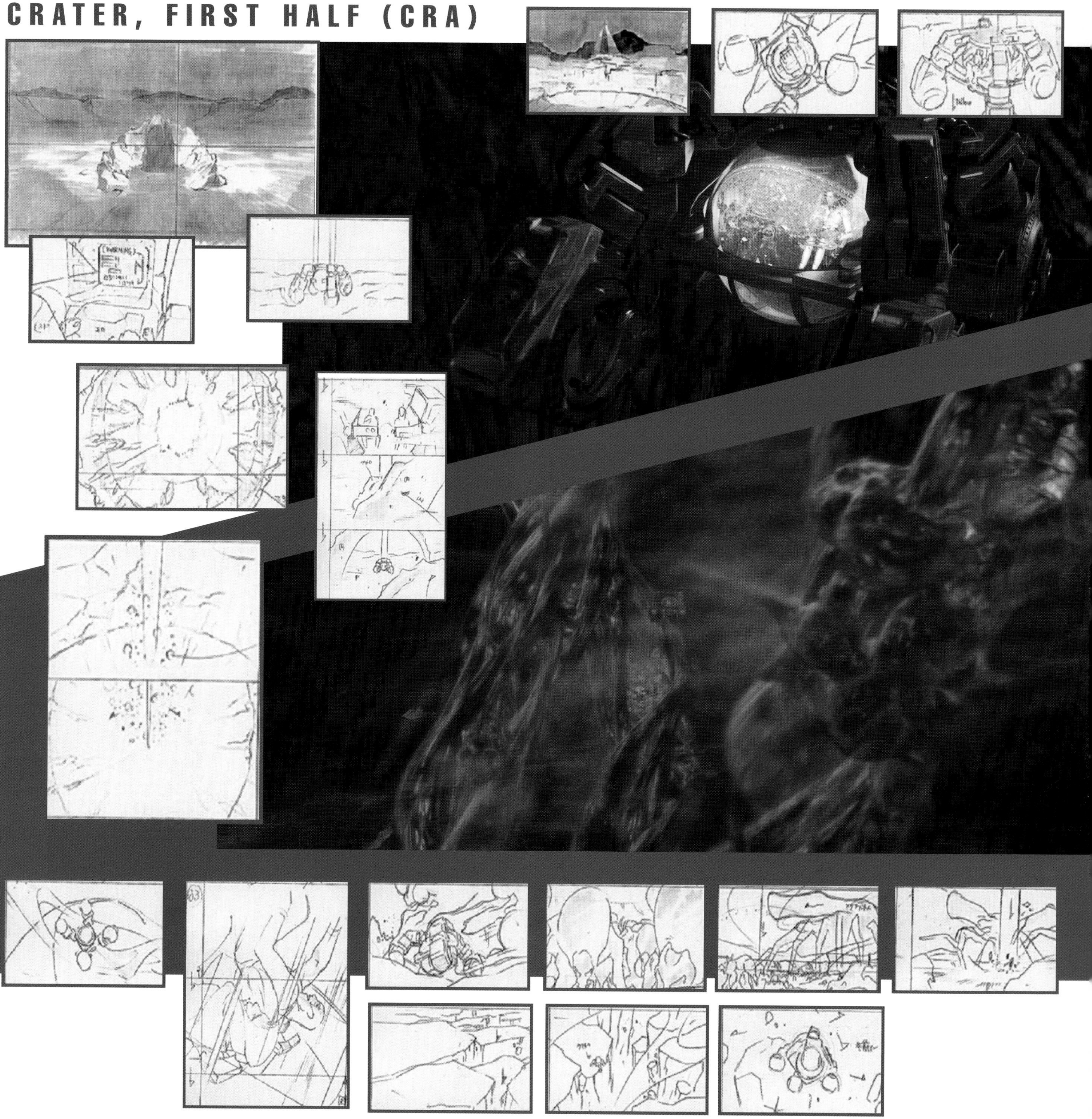

Aki looks to Gray, anticipating him to follow.

SETS AND PROPS

THE MAKING OF A VIRTUAL REALITY

Painted skies and sets are nothing new. Fifty years ago, singing cowboys sometimes rode off into painted sunsets at the end of Westerns. Mark Hamill and David Prowse didn't really enter the cavernous core of an orbiting cloud city when they had their classic light saber battle. That location was a matte painting, like so many of the settings in which science fiction cinema unfolds.

Unlike the galaxy of *Star Wars*, the world of Final Fantasy was neither long ago nor far away. It should be noted that Dr. Sid was born in 1995, the Leonid meteorite crashed into the Middle East in 2031, construction of Barrier City New York began in 2048, and the movie opens in 2065. *Final Fantasy: The Spirits Within* opens to a bleak world in which the invading phantoms have taken a grim toll. The global population totals 170 million people living in 92 cities and 481 military facilities. The task for Square USA's set designers was to bring it all to life.

SETS

Concept Artist Kazunori Nakazawa created the basic look for the movie's buildings, objects, and landscapes, however, the job of rendering his concepts into usable models fell on the teams of graphic artists in Square's Sets and Props Section.

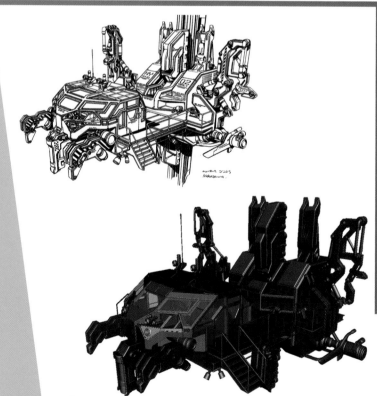

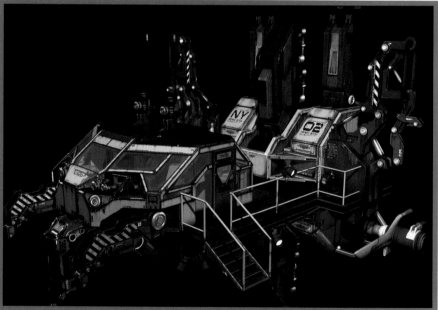

The set of the Gondola transforms from concept art to the final render.

TADAO ODAKA, SETS AND PROPS SUPERVISOR

The Sets and Props Section was responsible for creating all models except for characters and creatures that appear in the film," says Sets and Props Supervisor Tadao Odaka. "We start with the concept design, from which everything is modeled (a virtual process meaning creating a 3D image) and textured (a colored and textured skin is added to the model that forms the virtual model). I oversaw the entire (sets and props) pipeline."

According to Odaka, the Sets and Props Section turned to real-life references for help while converting Nakazawa's landscape ideas into their final movie form. "For landscapes, sometimes we would just go out and photograph or look at other landscapes. We also went on location to New York to shoot the Times Square cityscape. I would have liked to have done more of that, maybe see the Rockies for a mountain reference."

"The bulk of our sets and models were pretty much created directly on computers,"

says Sets and Props Supervisor Tadao Odaka. But there were early exceptions, such as Aki's Black Boa transport ship; this was also modeled in clay. The process of making convincing props is demanding, but Odaka says making sets is even more challenging. "Landscapes are a lot more difficult to create. The sheer amount of data involved in creating a landscape gets heavy, and the more data we put into it, the heavier it gets."

THE TRICKS OF TERA-FORMING

To accomplish these lush visual miracles, the Sets and Props Section had to build each of its virtual landscapes with an invisible layer of precision. Because the movie's character animation sometimes used motion-captured movements of real humans, the basic angles and contours of each virtual landscape had to be recreated in the motion capture studios. After all, it would not look good if Gray's posture suggested he was climbing a hill with a 10 percent slope while standing on a mountainous landscape with very steep 40 percent slopes. Careful attention had to be paid to coordinate the way the characters moved to the land beneath them. By doing so, there was always something there when they lowered their feet. Everything did not always go as planned, and sometimes Sets and Props had to touch up scenes to put them on better footing.

The Copperhead ventures toward a Barrier City.

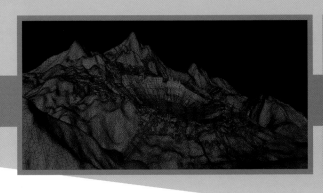

The Phantom Crater.

But the final vistas that audiences see on-screen are really a distant cousin of the landscapes that the Sets and Props Section gave to the Animation Section. "The Animation Section doesn't use the same models that sometimes get used in final rendering," says a Technical Director of Sets and Props, Steve Preeg. "Animation uses a lower resolution version of the model. When you're trying to make terrain that people walk on, you must have enough detail so that their foot has a spot to land on. The final models weren't ready yet, so we built a rough model and delivered that to animation, then they got the motion capture data in. When they applied the motion capture data, all of a sudden we had to build the terrain around each step that each person took to make sure that they're stepping on something."

A clay model of the Phantom Crater.

The final models seen in the movie are composed of hundreds of thousands of polygons meshed together to create plains, ridges, craters, and other landscape. Features such as rolls, bumps, and holes can add hundreds or even thousands of polygons to a landscape. With bigger sets such as Tucson and the Caspian stretching for miles, it would have taken several minutes for artists' computers to open these files. By simplifying the models to have fewer polygons and replacing data-heavy textures with simple shading, Sets and Props can convert an overwhelming file into something a bit more manageable.

The transformation of the Crater appears in this dramatic three-piece sequence.

"The animation model has fewer polygons than the model that we use in the render," says Preeg. "And what Remington (Remington Scott, one of the Motion Capture Directors) and the motion capture team would usually get was a rough model (of landscapes or props) of what the characters would interact with from which he could get dimensions and then build a mock-up to scale for them to use."

Of course, the mock-ups used in motion capture were even rougher than the models used in the animation studio. Since the various bumps and ramps the motion capture team created to simulate terrain were entirely invisible to the infrared cameras that captured the motion, the only thing they had to worry about was putting the bumps and dips in the proper place.

In the meantime, while the Animation Section used its rough-but-accurate models to bring scenes to life, Sets and Props fleshed out the models, adding carefully crafted textures and greater detail to make the movie's picture-perfect scenery.

During this process, different artists took on amazing new areas of specialization. "There were certain people in Sets and Props who began to consider themselves experts in dirt," remembers Preeg. "They made dirt for months and months... Between the Crater, Battlefield Wasteland, and some of the other shots, they were doing rocks and dirt for a year."

The phantoms kick up some dirt.

Fortunately, there were also highly technical ways of cheating that helped speed up the work. "We used displacement mapping for little bumps and ridges," says Preeg. "That's a process which allows you to get more detail in a single polygon rather than having to model several polygons. If we had to model everything and not have any displacement mapping, it would have been 100 times larger."

Displacement mapping was also used to cut down the work involved in creating some of the movie's man-made sets as well. When Aki goes searching for life in Old New York, much of the ruined city was a flat scene made to look more three-dimensional through the use of displacement mapping. "It's a pretty common use of displacement mapping," says Preeg. "In AAB (Aki's Adventure Part B, see sidebar on Acronyms), when she's running through destroyed New York, a lot of the buildings were a single flat polygon with displacement mapping such as 3D window sills or columns to give it depth."

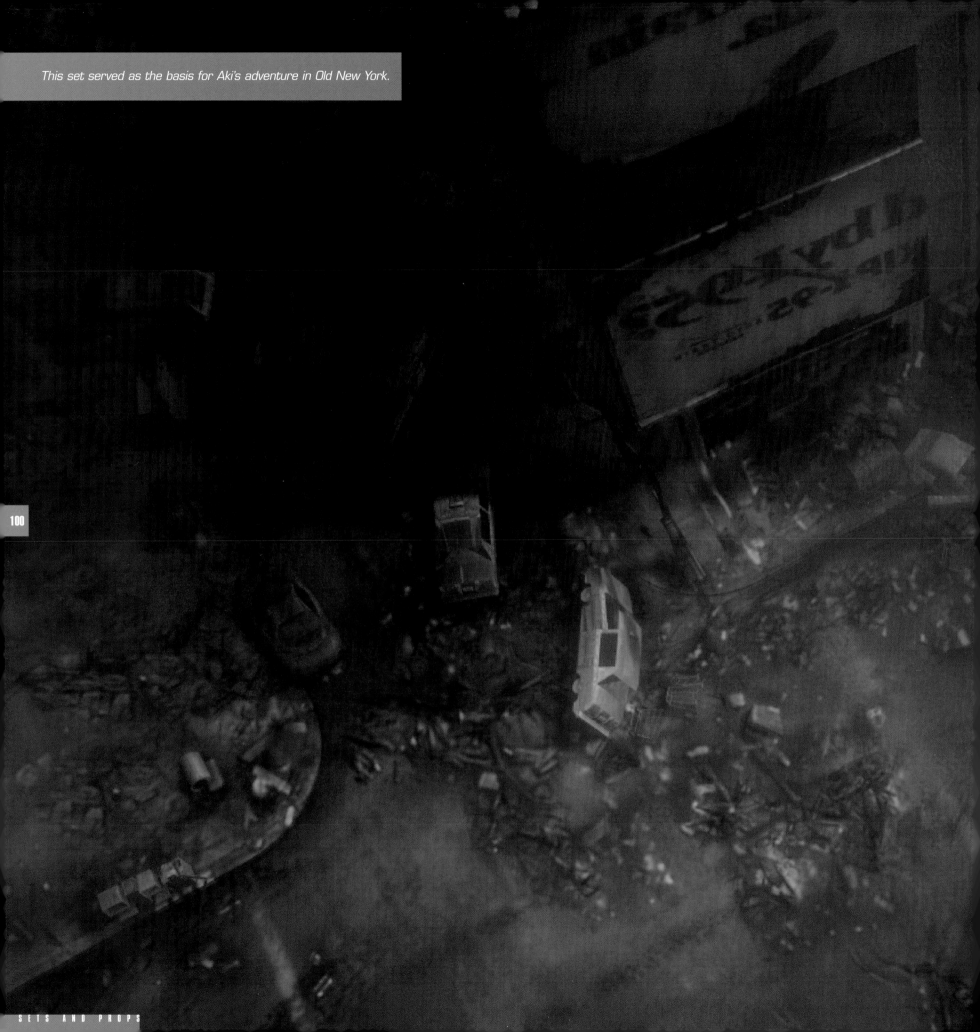

This set served as the basis for Aki's adventure in Old New York.

Unlike the sets themselves, many of the backgrounds were actually two-dimensional matte paintings. Matte painting has a longer history in movies than the relatively new technique of modeling landscapes. It is a technique in which painted backgrounds are composited onto live-action scenes to create an illusion. The combination of movement in the foreground and highly detailed backgrounds strengthens the illusion that viewers are seeing a real image. In this case, mattes were used to create backgrounds that were too vast, too expensive, or simply too inaccessible to create. The enormous government repository at the end of *Raiders of the Lost Ark* was a matte, and the workers moving through the foreground helped cause audiences to suspend their disbelief of such a massive warehouse. Although *Final Fantasy: The Spirits Within* was not a live-action film, matte painting was used to build some of its virtual sets as well.

"Even if you have models, a lot of what happens behind the models is painted," says Christian Scheurer, the illustrator who

worked both as a concept artist and matte painter on the film. "Let's say you look out of a window. They

would model the window and some of the objects in the foreground, but everything

behind that would be painted. Everything that doesn't need to be

a parallax and anything that doesn't move

can be painted."

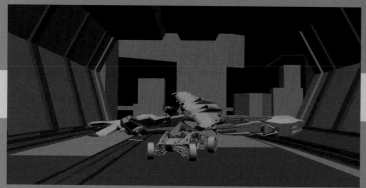

Historically, mattes were hand painted on glass, but in today's thoroughly high-tech movie industry, mattes are digitally created on high-end graphic workstations. According to Scheurer, computers have improved the process. "Now that I'm a matte painter, I actually do all my concept art digitally."

Just as two-dimensional mattes are composited behind sets in live-action motion pictures, mattes such as the more than 40 skies Scheurer created for the film were composited behind 3D-rendered landscapes and sets created by Sets and Props. "Let me give you an example," says Scheurer. "In the final scene, part of the big crater that you see in the background is painted. The sky is painted, but the rest (of the set) is 3D. In the next shots, when everything caves in, that's all 3D."

"I painted all of the skies in all the dream sequences. When the camera pans and all the phantoms are standing by the smoking pods, I painted that. The cloud effect in the nuclear explosion is actually painted. The alien planet that breaks apart is painted, too."

This image contained a matte painting.

But the matte paintings in Final Fantasy were not restricted to skies and planets. Many of the city shots include mattes

as well. "We flew in Craig Mullins, one of the best matte painters in the world. He did several city paintings. When you see

the city break into pieces and Aki's Boa as a little dot flying away, that's a Craig Mullins painting. And when you see the shot in

which the Boa races toward the camera and the airport is underneath it, I painted that airport."

The jeep used by Deep Eyes, from wireframe to final rendered piece.

PROPS

In the virtual world of Final Fantasy, the line that separates sets and props is sometimes razor thin. Take, for example, the Zeus Cannon. In some scenes, the orbiting Cannon is a prop. In others, it is a set. "If it's an exterior, I would guess it would be a prop," says Steve Preeg. "If it's an interior, it's a set."

As they did with sets, the artists in Sets and Props created both low- and high-resolution models of props. The sometimes-set sometimes-prop Zeus Cannon exists much like the original Starship Enterprise from Star Trek. Sets and Props created a low-resolution model of the satellite-weapon's entire exterior. They also made separate sets based on its various rooms. What they did not make was a virtual Zeus Cannon model that could be explored inside and out.

"The Zeus Cannon was made very early on and got reworked," says Preeg. "The characters weren't ready for some of the early sequences, and we needed to do some shots with no characters in them. So we created what we call SSF and SSE, which stand for 'Space Station Firing' and 'Space Station Exploding.' We learned a lot between the time that we first started working on the movie to when we finished. A lot of the space station was reworked, remodeled, and retextured. When you see a close-up of a certain part of the Zeus station, the other parts don't even exist. We built sections of the Zeus just for that specific shot. Any time you see the exterior (of the Zeus Cannon), none of the interior exists. And any time you see the interior, none of the exterior exists."

> "If it's an exterior, I would guess it would be a prop.
> If it's an interior, it's a set. — STEVE PREEG,
> A TECHNICAL DIRECTOR OF SETS AND PROPS

The list of props created for the film includes vehicles, such as the damaged vehicle that Neil crashes into the station. This is entirely different than the model of the smashed jeep that lands on the other side. "Things like machinery, and the sorts of items that people handle, vehicles, and complex machinery, those come from Sets and Props," says Odaka. Some of the other props that were created include guns, telephones, and more. All of these props were delivered to Animation as lower-resolution models that had the exact same shape and size as the high-resolution models that appear in the final version of the movie. While this list of props encompasses guns and equipment, it does not include armor or items. "The eye pieces and helmets and armor was all done by Character (Section), and that's about where it ended. Everything else essentially went to us."

THE MAKING OF BATTLEFIELD WASTELAND (BFW)

Steve Preeg and General Hein have one thing in common: They spent their careers working up to the Zeus Cannon. But while Hein spent his entire life convincing the council to build that great weapon, Preeg only spent the early years of his career learning his craft so he could direct its construction.

"Before I came to Square, I worked for a company called Metropolis, and before that I did a lot of architectural freelancing and worked for a company in Los Angeles called Shock Wave Entertainment"

Actually, for Preeg, the Zeus Cannon did not even qualify as the pinnacle of the movie. For him and his team, the landscape outside of Tucson, with its twisted wreckages and armor-strewn fields, was the hardest task. "BFW (Battlefield Wasteland; see sidebar on Acronyms) was the most difficult set. There was just so much terrain; so many miles of terrain to build," remembers Preeg.

"There were certain shots that took one or two of our artists two months to complete. We eventually developed scripts to do things like place rocks and place things automatically. Then all the artists had to do was go back in and delete things that didn't fit."

Working on BFW was no small task—the battlefield was the virtual equivalent of 12 square miles of terrain. "Every shot had its own little chunk of ground, and everything was shot specific to that spot. We didn't have one model that was all the ground. That would have been enormous; it (the file) would have been hundreds of gigabytes," says Preeg. "There's pretty much a model for every shot in BFW exterior—probably 70 shots or so."

But Preeg's department played a double role in the creation of BFW. Along with the ground and wreckage that comprised the set, Sets and Props was also responsible for the armor from the fallen soldiers. "The bodies and the bones and the set-up were all done in the Character Department. I think they gave us five or six different dead-person poses and told us to place them. The problem was that the bodies worked great if you posed them on flat ground, but if you put a body on something that wasn't flat, all of a sudden he wouldn't fit. It took so much work to go back and tweak them that we probably should have done it ourselves."

THE BLACK BOA: A CASE STUDY IN CHANGING TECHNOLOGY

Because Square's artists, animators, and technicians had to use and create new technologies over time, they constantly had to make improvements and improvise as they worked. The work got easier as they mastered their new tools, but some of their early projects remained a challenge throughout the making of *Final Fantasy: The Spirits Within*. One of those challenges was Aki's space ship, the Black Boa.

"Aki's Black Boa... By the end of the movie, you've seen the interior, you've seen the wings opening, you've seen the cockpit, you've seen a close-up of the roof through which you could see Sid's head. You see all sorts of different angles," says Preeg. "The Black Boa was probably the first model built that was actually kept and used throughout the movie. So there were a lot of issues since it was shown so often and made so early."

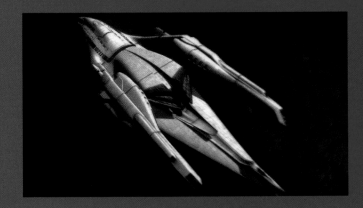

Some of the changes could not be helped. The Maya and Renderman 3rd software used to create the props, characters, and sets was upgraded several times during the four years that it took to make the film. Each time the software was upgraded, objects created in older versions had to be imported and fixed to work. "The Boa was the object in the movie that kept coming back, and I kept having to work on it, change it, and fix it. It never went away," says Preeg.

YOUR PERSONAL FFAP (FINAL FANTASY ACRONYM PRIMER)

The only way to fit in at Square USA is to become a master of Final Fantasy acronyms. The following is a brief FFAP. Don't even think about talking to anyone at Square USA without it.

AAA: Aki's Adventure Part A

AAB: Aki's Adventure Part B

AIA: The scene in which they drive the Jeep through the station

AIR: Airport; the sequence that begins with the jeep crash

BFW: Battlefield Wasteland

BCR: Barrier Control Room

CFR: Conference Room

ESC: Escape; the scene in which Aki and company escape prison

GON: Gondola

MCB: Military Cell Blocks (the prison)

PNC: Panic; the scene on a rooftop as people run to transports

SLA: Sid's Lab Part A

SLB: Sid's Lab Part B

SSE: Space Station Exploding

SSF: Space Station Firing

STR: Spiritual Treatment Room

BLACK BOA

Model #: MXOV-801

VTOL Self-Sustained, Empirically-Proven, Bi-Directional Cosmic Travel Concept Craft

POWER

Extended rocket engine (x1)

Linear aero-spike booster (x2)

Combined cycle engine (x2)

Acceleration position control booster (x4)

Expandable Payload

Payload can be expanded according to the mission.

Loads up to 4 Quatro-type armored vehicles.

Internal Payload

108

This craft was originally conceived as a large-scale transportation shuttle to be used in the construction of a space station for human habitation. The construction project was suspended after the first test shuttle was finished due to intensified combat. Also, the construction of the tactical space station "Zeus" was nearly completed by utilizing primarily the 600 series shuttles and as a result, the larger scale 800 series production plans were not nearly as advanced. As a result, only the first test shuttle currently exists.

As the Phantom/Gaia environmental research craft based on the outdated 500 series shuttle was retired, the military obtained the first test shuttle, renovated it by adding a scan radar system among other items and placed it into operation as a reconnaissance craft.

Its internal engine and fuel tank enable it to travel in and out of the atmosphere without any supporting external engines or fuel tanks. It is also capable of vertical lift-off and landing.

COPPERHEAD

Model #: MV-63B

VTOL Tactical Transport Assault Craft

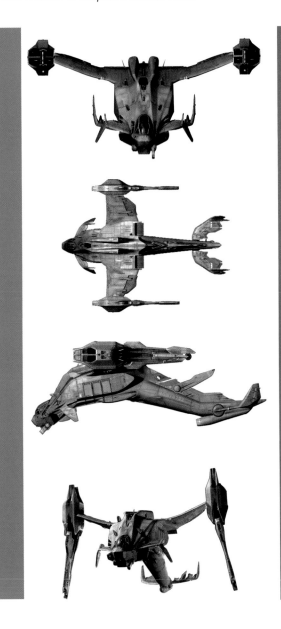

POWER

Allows transportation for up to 10 people:

> Heavily armored infantry (x6)
>
> Regular infantry (x4)
>
> Scramble descent unit (x6)

Maximum speed 720km, cruising speed 675km

Maximum continuous cruise distance 2200km

Mid-air refueling capability

Air turbo ram jet VCE (x2)

Turbo jet (x3)

PAYLOAD

Rear payload can accommodate up to eight 2000lb.-class, GPS guided spiritual warhead missiles or up to four large Seeker missiles.

As an option, up to four 2000lb-class spiritual warhead S-sonar image guided missiles can be loaded under the wing pylons.

Due to the weight increase of troops and armoring, the engine was upgraded in Block B to a split vertical fluctuation VCE to handle larger loads.

All-weather transport and assault craft. Originally developed as a small mobile transport craft. As combat intensified, it was modified to an offensive transport craft, Block-B type.

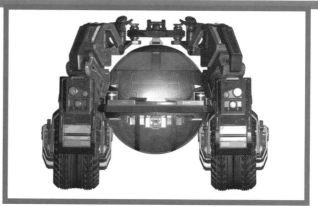

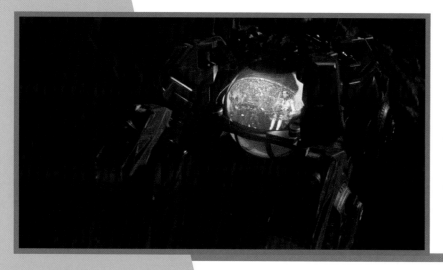

QUATRO

Model #: XR003B1

Reconnaissance S-Barrier Armored Vehicle

A very mobile transport device, capable of holding two soldiers. Used to investigate and explore small areas. Circular, glass front window provides excellent viewpoint.

JEEP (BANDID HUMMVY)

Model #: M2075A1

High Mobility, Multipurpose

Wheeled Vehicle

This high-mobility vehicle can travel across any type of terrain. It seats multiple people and comes equipped with lots of firepower.

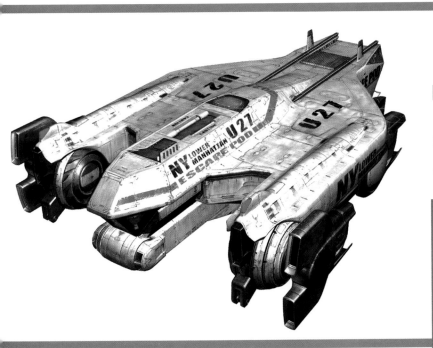

PENDULUM

Large transport device that serves as an escape vehicle.

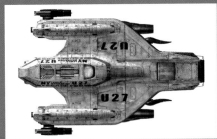

Large Emergency Escape Pod.

OLYMPIC-CLASS ASSAULT SPACE STATION
(ZEUS CANNON)

ABOUT THE ZEUS CANNON

Started construction in 2055, completed framework in 2061. Ongoing technical tests of the Zeus Cannon were still being conducted in 2065.

The cells have been cultured inside the OVO tank up to a launchable critical level.

Equipped with two heliotron devices; 6 million ampere class helical type nuclear fusion furnace as a power source. The heliotrons generate a 120 giga joule magnetic field inside the Zeus Cannon's barrel (acceleration chamber).

A 100km radius from the Zeus is a restricted area where unshielded shuttles and soldiers cannot enter, due to the risk of being exposed to radiation of nuclear/spiritual energy from the reactive nuclear thruster and giant OVO tank.

The habitat inside the space station is located within a magnetic field gauge. It has no contact points with the station frame, thus it is protected from the nuclear/spiritual energy emission shock.

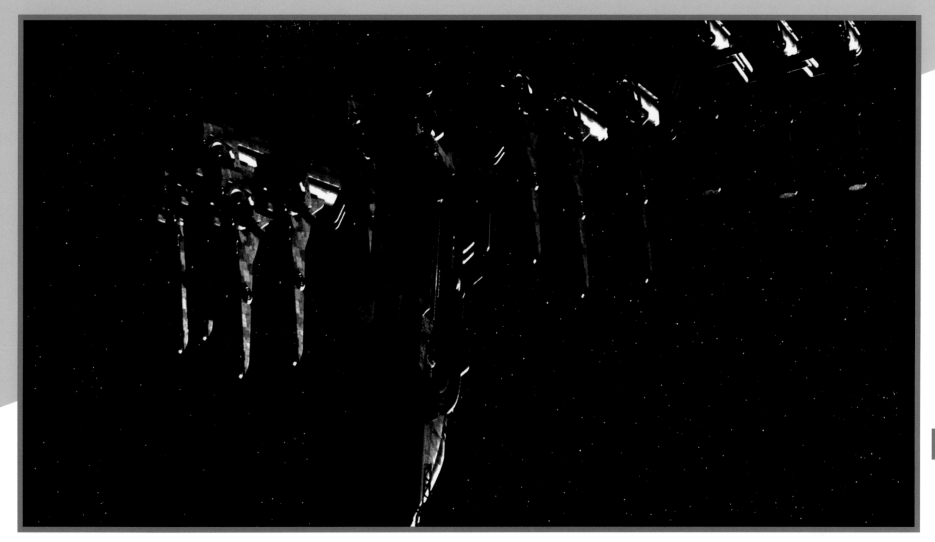

The original design concept was to have included consecutive firing capability up to 200 times. However, in the pre-critical launch test conducted in 2063, a series of malfunctions occurred (such as the expansion of material by heat inside the acceleration chamber, warping of the orbital path from the launch shock wave, numerous cracks on the cooling system pipeline, and coolant leaks).

The expansion of material caused by the difference of temperature inside the barrel, contraction rate, and launch shock wave were noted as substantial dangers capable of destroying the barrel itself with only a few launches.

WEAPONS & GEAR

AKI'S FLARE GUN

KIND (P-G02-B)
OERSTED INDUCED 5.66MM S SHORT RIFLE

A prototype gun currently being tested and developed to be light and compact. Due to the limited capacity of the loaded OVO pack, the number of bullets it can hold is reduced to approximately one fourth of the G300 series. For this reason, it is developed as a limited usage weapon, such as in-craft equipment rather than an assault weapon. It comes equipped with the S-flare grenade launcher as an option.

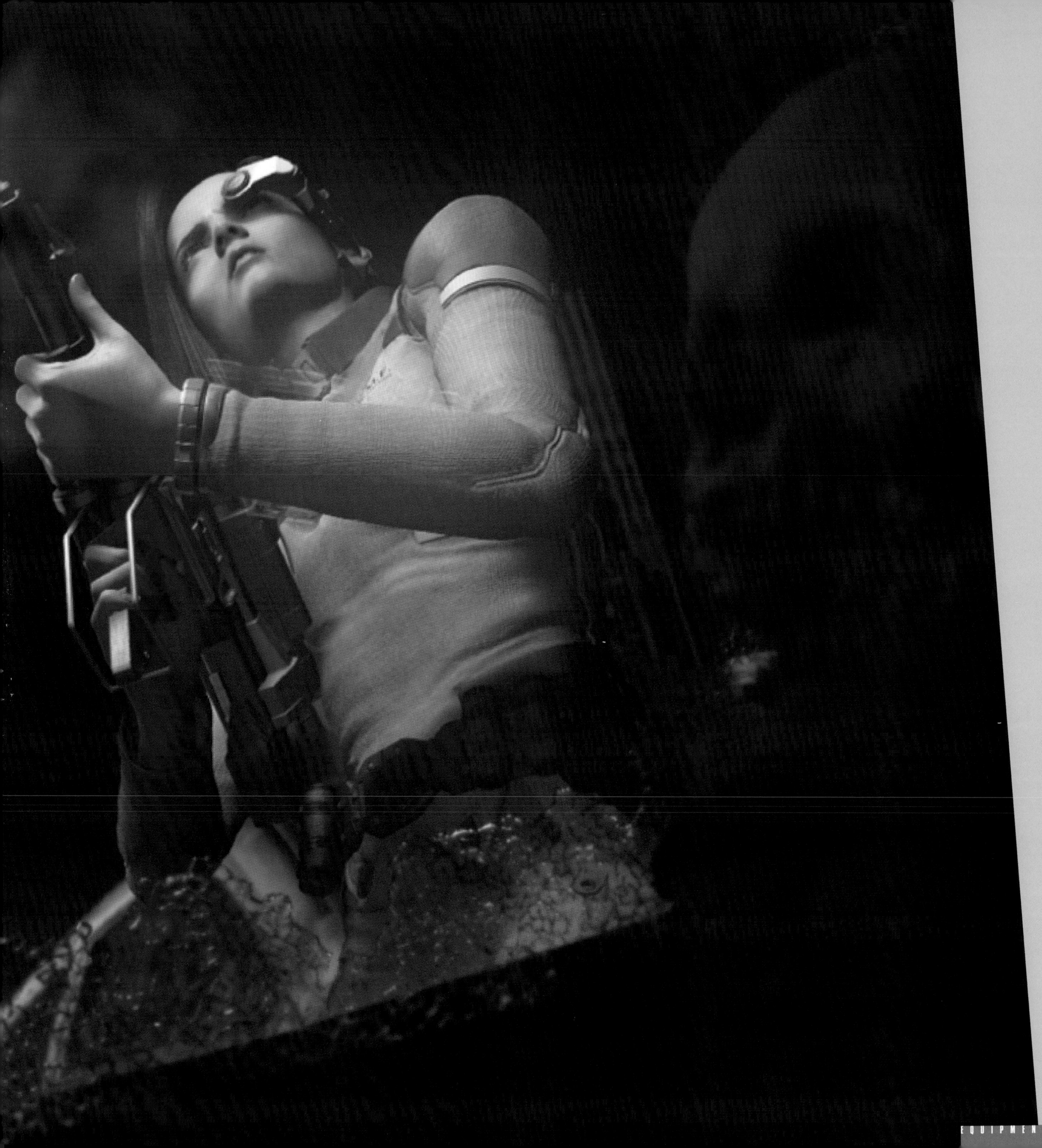

AKI'S SCOPE

CORONET (AN/SUS-X12A)
MONO-SCOPIC S-SCANNED RETINAL IMAGE PROJECTION EAR MOUNTED GOGGLE

The latest, state-of-the-art spiritual energy scanning goggle. Currently undergoing prototype testing, it has not been mass-produced or used in actual battle. Although its performance is near the same level as the 10 series, it is not suitable for extended operation due to lower battery capacity.

The X12B now being developed focuses on reducing power consumption and is expected to have longer operable hours.

AKI'S HOLO BRACELET

SPS HOLO-DISTANCE GAUGING DEVICE
(SPIRITUAL ENERGY POSITIONING SYSTEM)

A prototype holo-distance gauging device currently being tested. Equipped with a scanning scope with an approximate radius of 100 meters. The prototype model operates for only 25 minutes continuously, and the number of scan channels is still limited.

Scans for pre-programmed, specific spiritual energy by SE sonar. Furthermore, the micro SE sonar is difficult to develop, thus expected to take some time before mass production.

RIFLE

NOCTURNE (G302D-A)
OERSTED INDUCED 12 GAUGE S ASSAULT RIFLE

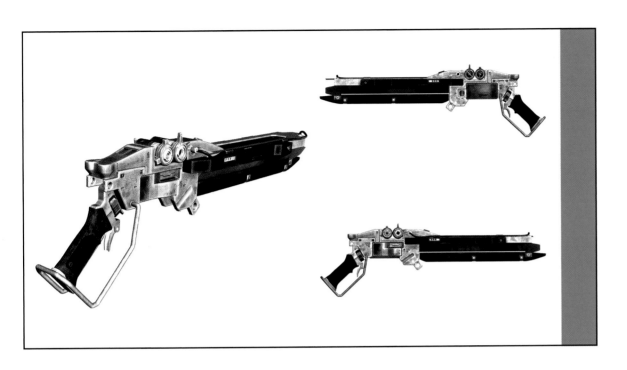

Discharges by having a magnetic flux barrel induce and accelerate spiritual energy. The variable energy shell can be fired as multiple low-energy shots or as a single high-energy shot.

Although its original model name was Serpent, it is said that the soldiers, seeing the dying Phantoms writhe as if they were dancing in a ballroom, maliciously began to call it Nocturne.

FULL HELMET

NIGHTMARE (AN/SUS-9C)
MULTI-SCOPIC S-SCANNED RETINAL IMAGE PROJECTION FULL FACE GOGGLE

Inputs the pulse data of spiritual entities directly into the brain and feeds the data back onto a built-in projector of the goggle, which projects the image directly on the retina.

The reason for this complex projection system is that a fully mechanical spiritual entity scanner, which does not pass through a human spiritual body, results in a very low precision image.

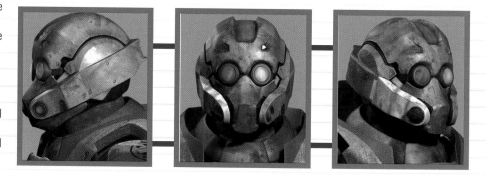

The Full Helmet was nicknamed "Nightmare" by the soldiers, denoting the horrific sight of the Phantoms seen through the goggles.

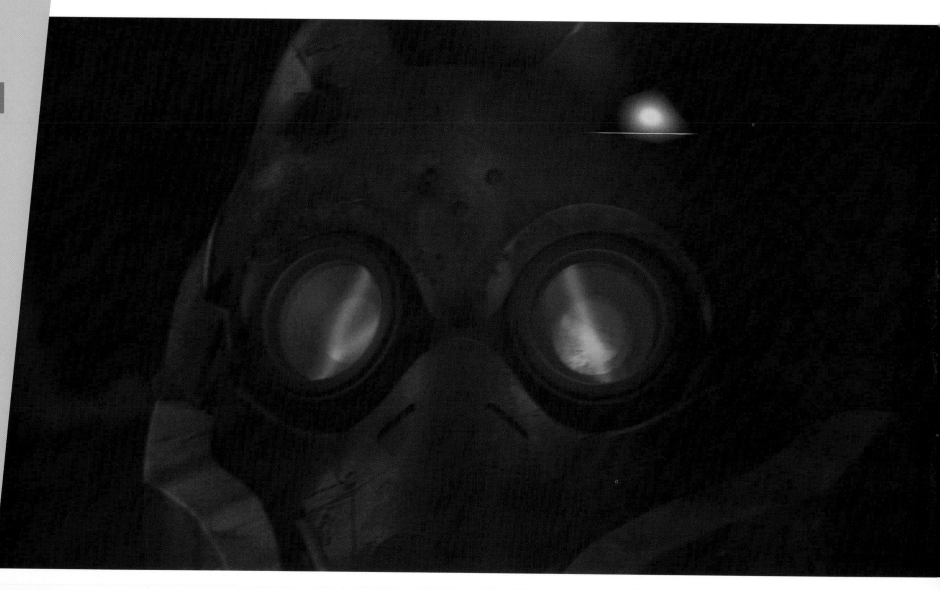

HALF HELMET

REVENANT (AN/SUS-10A)
MONO-SCOPIC S-SCANNED RETINAL IMAGE PROJECTION HALF FACE GOGGLE

In essence, this helmet is a simpler version of the 9 series. The difference is that this helmet has a simplified air filtration system and is not appropriate in chemically and/or biologically polluted areas.

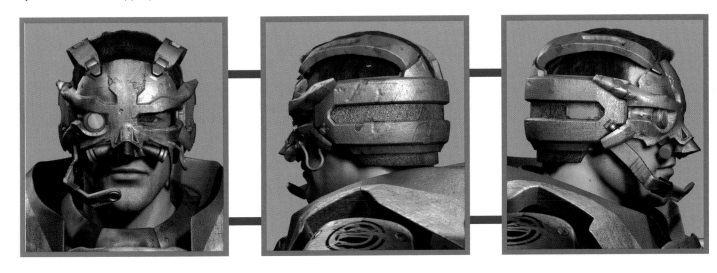

HEIN'S GUN

SONNET (HKMF-P325)
SEMI-AUTOMATIC PISTOL MANUFACTURED BY HKMF. AIR-PRESSURED, RECOILLESS GUN.

Caliber: 9mm x 19

Load: 17+1

Standard equipped with a folding grip.

Due to the increasing size of the space force within USMF (United States Military Forces), weapons capable of firing in zero G were required. One such weapon developed under this plan was the P-325 Sonnet, which was issued to the USMF general infantry in 2039.

OTHER PROPS

Here are some additional props used in the movie. Although this isn't an all-inclusive selection of every prop, it does provide some insight into what was created by the Sets and Props Section.

SID'S DIARY

ANESTHETIC GUN

Although this piece doesn't play a large role in the movie, it still comes across as a very dynamic prop.

HEADSET

OVO PACKS

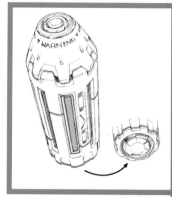
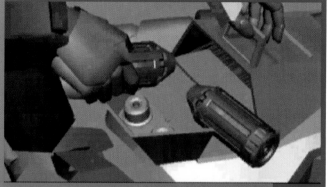

The first image, or the concept art, displays an early version. The last shot shows the rendered ovo pack.

PLANT

The first piece is early concept art of the plant, while the second piece shows it in its final form.

LASER SCALPEL

Here's a much more complicated piece that had to be created by Sets and Props. Notice all of the detail in the initial concept piece and how it was implemented into the final production piece.

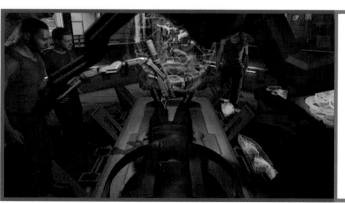
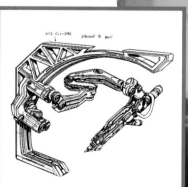

LAYOUT

LAYOUT

The jeep crash scene involving Ryan's injury.

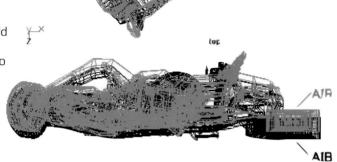

There were several stages within the making of *Final Fantasy: The Spirits Within*. First, the movie went through a conceptual stage that began with Hironobu Sakaguchi sketching a basic storyline and then fleshing it out with the help of professional script writers. The final part of this stage came as concept artists and storyboard illustrators created visual representations of the script.

The next phase of the process involved creating the various elements with which the movie would be created. This was the point at which rough models of sets, props, and characters merged to create a three-dimensional representation of the movie. In more familiar terms, this was the first draft of the movie—a version that bore a hazy resemblance to the final movie, but lacked all refinement.

"Basically, what layout does is to create a temporary image before the staff actually make the images," says Layout Supervisor Takashi Kubota. "There are three important steps in doing layout (deciding shots, making models, and monitoring data for consistency). You must initially decide what is to be shown in each shot. For example, if a certain shot only shows the upper half of a character's body, you don't have to do anything on the lower half of the body. And with landscape shots, if the camera does not move too much, we may opt to use a matte painting in the background instead of modeling the details."

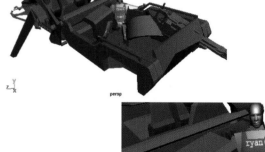

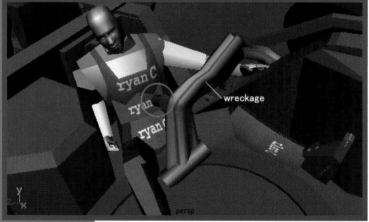

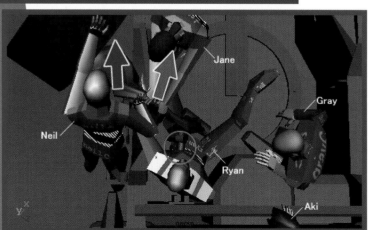

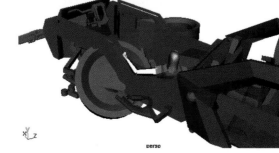

Creating an entirely computer-graphics motion picture requires both technical and artistic departments. Layout, like Rendering and Compositing, performs technical tasks. Selecting camera angles is more on the artistic side. "Camera angles are decided by the Director, Hironobu Sakaguchi, the Co-Director, Motonori Sakakibara, and sometimes Tani (Tani Kunitake, Staging Director) helps decide, as does Editorial." To help with the camera angle planning, Layout created crude models to plan out each scene. According to Kubota, while Sets and Props made many of the early models, Layout spearheaded these efforts.

These first-stage models are rough, even rougher than the simplified models that Sets and Props provides the Animation Section. "Working, staging, timing... We define all of them prior to production. We use very simple models to make the rendering faster."

125

"Basically, what layout does is to create a temporary image before the staff actually make the images." — TAKASHI KUBOTA, LAYOUT SUPERVISOR

TAKASHI KUBOTA, LAYOUT SUPERVISOR

Having begun his career in computer graphics animation working on the 1983 film *Lensman*, Takashi Kubota qualifies as one of the veterans of the industry.

As an established name in computer graphics, it was only natural that he would be familiar with Square, a company that had established itself as one of the pioneering companies in computer graphics as well as games. "I knew several people who worked for Square. They mentioned the movie to me and I wanted to come onboard."

That opportunity presented itself in 1996 when Kubota met with a Square employee at a SIGGRAPH (Special Interest Group for Computer Graphics) trade show. "SIGGRAPH is where we get most of our staff. I went to one of the parties at the show and somebody said, 'Hey, come check us out.' Later that year, I got a call from Mr. Sakaguchi and we went out for a drink. And that is how I came to Square."

Unlike Kubota, however, most of the Layout Section did not have a background in computer animation. In fact, the department's early work was slowed because of a lack of familiarity with computers. "When we first started, the problem was we had a certain percentage of Japanese artists who had worked in the traditional animation industry. They had virtually no computer graphics experience when they came to work for Square, so our first years were spent teaching them to work with computer animation."

"If you don't deal with computers much, things like naming files can become big issues," explains Kubota. "When you are working with upwards of 22,000 shots, you're bound to lose something somewhere."

According to Kubota, the models used for Sets and Props evolve. The models created in Layout are on the protozoa side of things, sort of the single-celled version of the much more sophisticated models to come. "The simplest models are called block models. These are light models that have a minimal amount of data," says Kubota. "That is what we use in the layout stage. In Animation, they are changed into rough models, and when they reach production, they become rendered."

Having delivered models, Layout moves into the next phase of its work—helping define the pace and time of the camera work. Considering the work done by the Storyboard Section, this may sound redundant. However, having block models gives Layout access to information not available in earlier production. "The Layout Team created a 3D storyboard," says Kubota. "In the story reel we receive from Tani, the objects are not defined in detail. Here in Layout, we put in the 3D element."

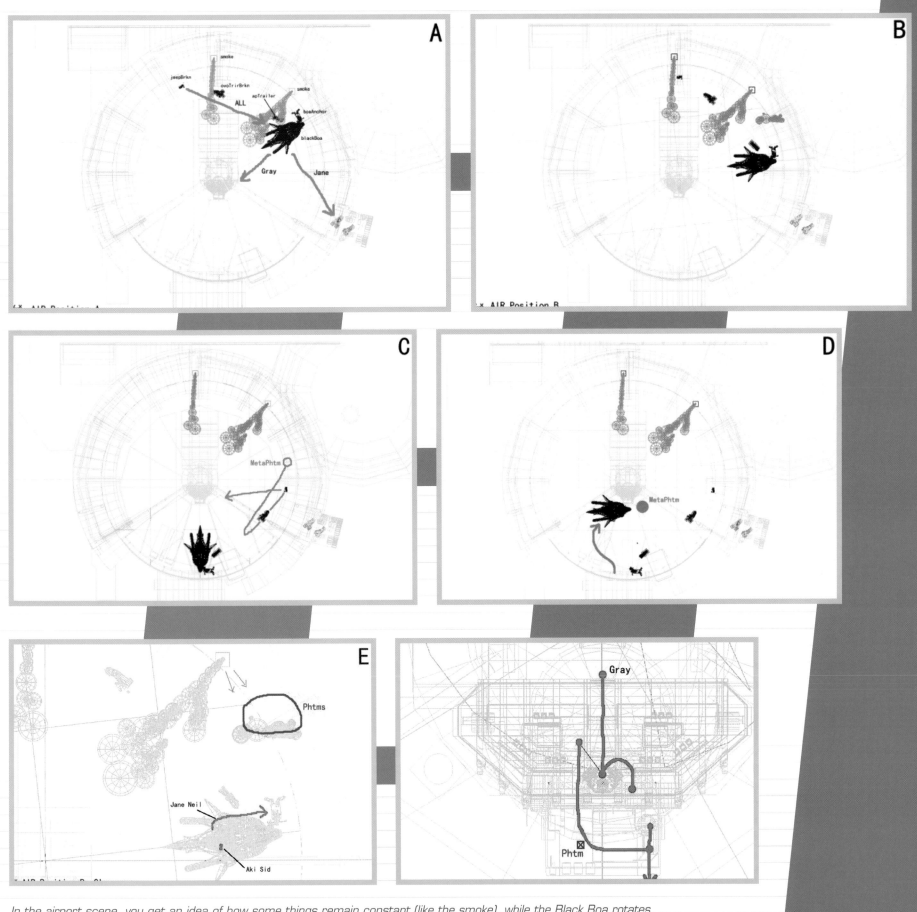

A

B

C

D

E

In the airport scene, you get an idea of how some things remain constant (like the smoke), while the Black Boa rotates on the platform. This provides a great visual of the layout process.

Kubota goes on to mention that after evaluating scenes Layout may suggest adding new shots, breaking up longer shots, or combining shorter shots into one larger shot.

And the responsibilities of the Layout Section do not stop there. Layout also monitors data used throughout the movie to ensure it remains consistent. Small changes in data, such as characters being moved slightly out of position, can have dire results during later stages of production. "Initially, it might not look too odd from certain camera (angles); however, as far as the data is concerned, the position of that character may be very obvious in the next shot. It causes problems if the character is standing here in one shot and standing over there in the next. In later stages of production like Lighting, this inconsistency can cause a blurring effect."

By the time Layout finished with Final Fantasy, the movie had sets, props, and direction. The visual images lacked all refinement, but the production was beginning to take shape and some of the hidden pitfalls were removed.

The finished scene as seen in the movie and illustrated on the previous page.

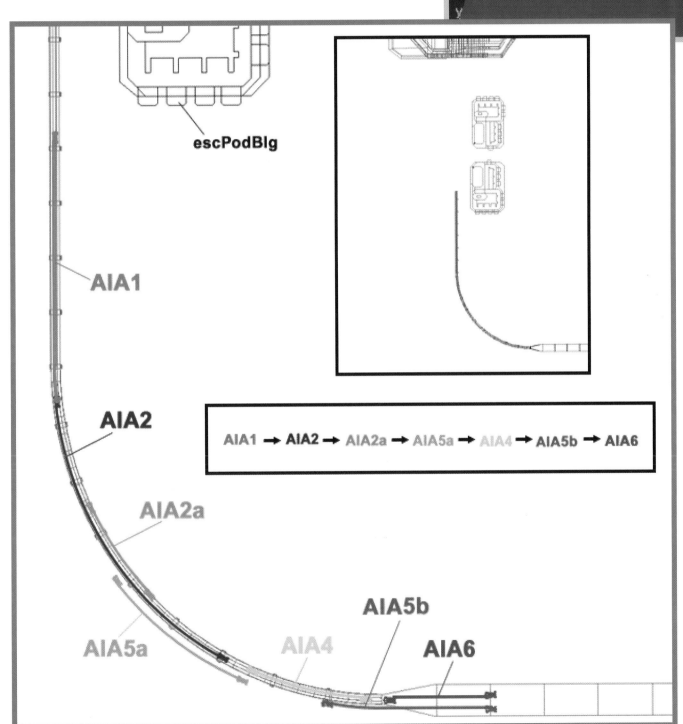

escPodBlg

AIA1

AIA2

AIA2a

AIA1 → AIA2 → AIA2a → AIA5a → AIA4 → AIA5b → AIA6

AIA5b

AIA5a   AIA4   AIA6

This diagram displays the jeep's path before its crash scene.

MOTION CAPTURE

MOTION CAPTURE

MOTION CAPTURE

Leonardo Da Vinci and Michelangelo Buonarroti may have mastered the art of creating characters that looked like real people, but they never had to make the subjects of their paintings move like real people. In his never-ending quest for knowledge, Da Vinci turned to actual human bodies to learn their secrets, paying thieves to bring him cadavers so that he might study the same way that modern medical students now learn their craft.

When the animators of *Final Fantasy: The Spirits Within* decided to fine-tune the way the characters in their movie look and move, they borrowed a page from Da Vinci's journal—looking to real humans to capture the grace and nuances of their motions.

Like so much of *Final Fantasy: The Spirits Within*, the motion capture process with which Square USA brought its virtual actors to life is a hybrid of art and science. Without using traditional photography or film, the technique of motion capture is a highly technical procedure that turns real movements into hard data that can then be used as a starting point to refine the movements of virtual bodies with lifelike results.

In the center of this part of the digital production were Motion Capture Directors Remington Scott, a veteran player in a relatively new field, Jack Fletcher, whose responsibilities included directing the voice recording sessions, co-directing the motion capture, and writing some of the dialog, and Animation Director Andy Jones.

Motion capture, like any other computer process, is hostage to the principle of garbage in-garbage out. In order for data to work, the captured movements had to be fluid and natural. Fletcher played an important role in finding movements that felt natural so that movement looked accurate and human when translated into data. For his part, Scott helped stage each scene to make sure that the staff translated the script into their pretended reality.

"My responsibility was to make sure that we could recreate all of the virtual scenes at the motion capture stage so that we could fill in specific elements, such as how the characters relate to each other and how they relate to the set and props," says Scott. "We had to carry that information back into the computer and make sure the characters are in the right place at the right time."

The motion capture for *Final Fantasy: The Spirits Within* was done in a 16,500-square foot warehouse that the Hawaii Film Studio uses as a sound stage, part of the same facility in which studio scenes from *Baywatch Hawaii* were filmed.

The outside of the facility in which all of the motion capture process was created.

■ JACK FLETCHER, MOTION CAPTURE DIRECTOR

Spend any time reading the Final Fantasy film credits, and you'll become very familiar with the name Jack Fletcher. Fletcher not only co-directed the motion capture, he also was involved in the voice casting, directed the voice recording, and wrote some of the movie's dialog. "A lot of what I was trying to do was keeping an eye on not sacrificing the humanity in the way that people behave under pressure or in any given situation."

According to Fletcher, wearing multiple hats was essential because Final Fantasy's blend of technology and art is a new frontier. "Once we started into motion capture, we had a fair amount of reels from the Layout Section, and everybody worked very hard and very conscientiously on how things were going to happen."

And as pioneers, Fletcher says, his team soon realized that none of the processes they worked with were etched in stone. Most of the motion capture scenes were done with unyielding precision, with movements and timing monitored to the tiniest degree. But other scenes came out better when Fletcher and Scott allowed the actors more breathing space.

"I know from a lot of experience in a lot of different areas in film and also theater that sometimes you lose the focus of a story when you are really concentrated on getting one thing to work," remembers Fletcher. "In the scene in the jail cell, for instance, we abandoned watching the clock and played the scene truthfully, realistically, and with a sense of urgency and momentum."

Scott managed a cast of live humans, directing them as they performed scenes from a script. It's important to note that Scott's staff performed on an all-black sound-stage wearing black body-stocking costumes.

Well, not entirely black. Each outfit was studded with 35 Ping-Pong ball-sized markers, silver balls designed to reflect light. This may sound like a drab setting; but to the video cameras surrounding the stage, the light reflecting off of those markers provided a wealth of information.

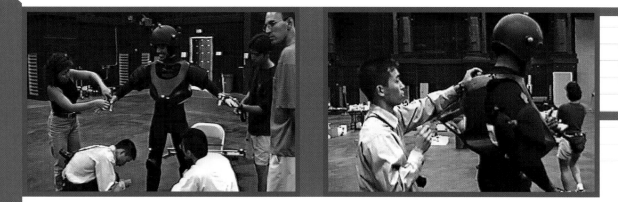

Prior to shooting any motion capture scene, a member of the staff goes through the process of having markers attached to a tight, black bodysuit.

"The motion capture stage has 16 optical cameras,"

says Scott, whose previous experience in the field of motion capture included making a Nintendo 64 game called *Turok the Dinosaur Hunter* for Long Island-based Acclaim Entertainment. "They record a visible red wavelength of light, the light that reflects off of the retro-flective markers they're wearing."

A close-up look at one of the motion capture cameras used during filming.

Positioned on 10-foot tripods with bright red lights mounted at their base, Scott's optical cameras are all but blind to the black-clad staffers. Instead of taping them, they track the movements of the reflections of their red lights that illuminate the markers. No matter how they turn or move, the cameras dutifully trace the markers and record their whereabouts in 3D space.

"Generally, each person would wear about 35 markers," says Scott. "Those things vary depending upon the setup of the character. If the person was going to fall on their back (in a specific scene), then we'd reposition several markers that we would normally put on his back so that they were on his stomach or chest."

Needless to say, this entire process depended on absolute pinpoint precision. If someone accidentally brushed against one of the cameras, the entire shoot had to be paused as technicians re-calibrated all 16 cameras. If one camera was even a fraction of an inch out of place, it could corrupt the data from an entire shoot.

The V-shaped bars serve as the outline for the window. We've included finished shots of the actual movie to show how this process translated to the big screen.

Not all scenes were easy to replicate, as some scenes even require mechanical assistance. Once this shot was motion captured, the data was flipped so that the person appeared to be jumping toward the other person.

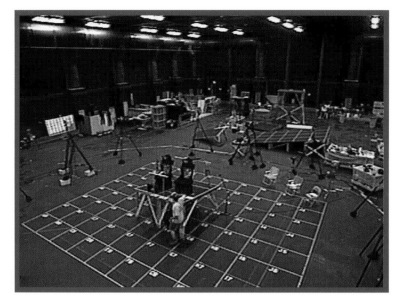

Here's an overview of the working environment. The object in the grid serves as the interior of the Quatro. The 3-D zone or grid acts as the place in which all of the action takes place.

But accurately tracking markers called for other considerations, too. Since every marker on every person had to be visible to at least one camera at any given moment, the stage area had to be clutter-free.

"The number of persons we used on each shot really varied on the proximity of each of the characters to each other," says Scott. "There were instances in which they were really close together, and we didn't want to have more than three people on the stage at one time. Any more than that, and the markers were obscured. One set of markers might start to shadow other markers when there were others close together. But in instances in which people were spread out, we were able to have up to six people on the stage."

And the human staff were not the only objects on the sound stage covered in marker-studded black. Stage props such as guns, armor, furniture, even mugs and cups can be found around the Diamond Head warehouse in which Scott, Jack Fletcher, Andy Jones and their associates did their work.

"We had to build something at the stage to stand in for anything that the staff touched..."

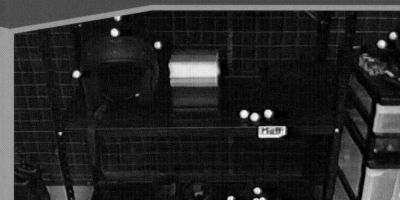

Even elements like weapons and gear must go through the motion capture procedure. The weapons are replicas carved out of wood; other elements, like the helmet seen on the shelf, also sport the motion capture markers.

Since everything was invisible to the motion capture digital sensors, accurate size and weight was important in their creation, not detailed looks. The futuristic plasma rifles that looked so powerful in the final movie were little more than wooden cutouts, weighted with steel so that they had the shape and weight of the guns in the script. But the motion capture guns did not have barrels, triggers, or circuitry.

The man primarily responsible for the creation of the vast majority of the set pros used during the motion capture process was Ron Perry.

The metal structure in the back prevents the motion capture staff from "stepping through" the vehicle during filming.

There is also some simplicity to a set, as this scene shows. There is not much detail to the chair and the metal stand to the right serves as a control mechanism on the Boa for the motion capture personnel.

When building these props, physical walls couldn't be built since they would obscure the markers; therefore, they took a minimalist approach. They simply built only the essentials. For example, when a scene takes place inside a vehicle, it must be constructed in such a way that nothing blocks the view of the markers on someone.

"We had to build something at the stage to stand in for anything that someone touched or with which they have any interaction," says Scott. "It didn't necessarily mean building something with the kind of high-resolution look that you see in the film, but we had to build something that would say to this particular person that this is the location and the height and, sometimes, generally the basic width or the area where they'd be putting their hands or their heads. If they picked up a canister, we needed to figure out which canister they were going to grab, and then design that canister and the compartment from which they grabbed it. The canister would be something simple like a Tupperware container that was filled with some weights." All of these were important considerations to ensure that the animators received the data that they needed in order to mimic human movement.

The props representing guns and armor sound primitive, but they were lavish compared to the landscapes created for these shots. Remember, people walk differently when they climb mountains than they do when they are moving across flat land. In settings such as the craterous battlefield outside of Tucson, Arizona, the motion was captured moving up and down sloped landscapes. So they had to shoot scenes walking along landscapes with the exact same slope. To do this, technicians had to build a series of ramps to exact specifications. The ramps were painted black, and the expansive virtual landscapes were born.

As it turns out, motion capture works better for the big picture than for the fine details. Before motion capture data can be sent to the Animation Department, it must be cleaned to remove flicker and other kinds of "noise," or bad data. Even cleaned data does not include facial, hands, or hair movements. Because these movements are too fine to be captured with any level of precision using Square's infrared technology, Square's animators do that work by hand.

A scene on the motion capture stage.

A discussion taking place with Animation Director, Andy Jones.

Though Square USA's artists eventually decided to animate a few scenes by hand, having motion captured footage of these scenes still provided a basis for understanding how the scenes should look. Additionally, motion capture also speeded up the animation process. The animators would use motion capture as a tool and fine-tune it to create the appropriate look.

The following section illustrates the process of a dramatic scene during a dream sequence.

In shot **A**, Animation Director Andy Jones discusses his take on how the scene should unfold. Shot **B** shows the action. Lastly, shot **C** captures the dramatic moment.

This shows the end result of this process.

REMINGTON SCOTT, MOTION CAPTURE DIRECTOR

One of the mainstays during the motion capture process was Remington Scott. Scott, who previously worked with Acclaim on such titles as Mortal Kombat and Turok, was in charge of supervising the production of the motion capture process.

While doing so, Scott relied upon many other departments to help him visualize the entire process. During a particular shot, he may utilize pieces of concept art or storyboards. On subsequent shots, Scott may refer to 3D layout examples to bring the scene to life.

While the motion capture data does not look like much on its own, when combined with the impressive models created by Square USA, it will produce virtual characters that nearly duplicate the look and movement of real human beings. Audiences may still be able to tell the difference between Square's virtual actors and the real ones used in live-action motion pictures.

If you were to examine Scott's role in the big picture, he was tasked with bridging the gap between the animation production and the motion capture production.

But motion capture data had to more than accurate, it had to be lifelike. Fletcher, whose past credits included working on MTV's Aeon Flux, scrutinized the shots to make sure they were convincing. "I made sure that people behaved in a real manner," says Fletcher. "It was a giant learning curve. The more work we did on the motion capture, the more we became aware of things that needed to be addressed to ensure that it would work for the overall story. Some scenes played too long, so I discussed it with the Animation Director (Andy Jones) and Storyboard Section (Tani Kunitake) that sometimes we were losing momentum because we were not dealing realistically in the physical space the way that people deal with each other.

The main purpose of motion capture at the end of the day is to provide the data to the animators for refinement, and the next trick was literally connecting the dots to turn this into useable data.

The two scenes to the right (A and B) show how the motion capture process translates into the finished scene.

Information recorded by the cameras is fed into computers that combine the data from the various cameras together, splice it to separate each marker and track it individually, then track the marker movements throughout the virtual 3D space. Those movements are then represented on a screen by images that resemble 35-point stellar constellations. These images can be flipped, rotated, and viewed from any angle. A motion-captured hunter may look no more detailed than the constellation Orion in the night sky, but that virtual image will move with all of the skill and grace of the person upon whom it is based.

The end result of the motion capture process may not look like much below the surface, but those dot figures comprise the skeletons over which skins of Aki, Gray, and Hein will eventually be laid.

ANIMATION

ANIMATION:
MAKING MEN AND MONSTERS

To create the dinosaurs in *Jurassic Park*, technicians at George Lucas's Industrial Light and Magic took a very anatomical route. First, they created skeletal frames for their terrible lizards, then they created webs of sinews to work the bones, and finally they covered their subjects with skins. Lengthy and detailed as this process may sound, it certainly resulted in dinosaurs with animation that was more than skin deep.

According to Jones, this may be the "best" way to create animated characters, but it is hardly the most efficient. "We had so many humans to do that it was more efficient for us to do less of an underlying muscle base structure and more on an artistic approach," says Jones. "A lot of people are creating actual muscles attached to bones, and then attaching skin on top of that. Even though that sounds great and it's probably the best way to do it, it wasn't the most efficient way to do it at the time (that Square began work on Final Fantasy). So we decided to go with more of an artistic based solution."

Jones, whose past credentials include high-profile work on the movie *Titanic*, is more concerned about final appearances than hidden effects. "It's a huge, tedious process to build all the muscles of the body, then use them to deform the outside skin. Ultimately, all you want to see is the skin anyway. If you can make sure that the skin looks right and moves right, and that the muscles feel like they're moving underneath the skin, then you've achieved your look."

In some ways, Square USA's Animation Section might better be named the "Alchemy Department." This was the section of the company where the real magic was performed; a place where wizards took the rough elements of block models and motion capture data and refined them into cinematic gold using new techniques that had to be created for unique situations.

The Animation Section brought together elements created by the Layout, Sets and Props, and Character Sections and wove them together. Overseeing the process was Animation Director Andy Jones, one of the busiest and most universally respected people at Square USA.

Jones' fingerprints permeate nearly every level of Final Fantasy's production. He helped the Storyboard Section devise the dramatic camera shots that gave General Hein's suicide attempt scene its climactic punch. Jones assisted in the motion capture process and attended voice recording sessions as well. He also oversaw the design of the characters.

While the majority of this section covers the animation process, that process could not begin until all of the building blocks were in place. Even after Sets and Props made its models and Motion Capture delivered its data, the work could not begin until the Character Section delivered the actors' virtual skins.

AKI

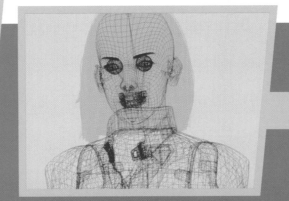

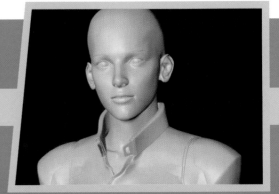

CHARACTER DEVELOPMENT

Designing the virtual people in *Final Fantasy: The Spirits Within* was a long and painstaking process that went through several evolutions. Square's first experiment in making movie-quality animation was titled "The Gray Project." Set in a science fiction world, this animated short film captured some of the mood and intensity of Final Fantasy, however, its animation quality lagged light years behind the final movie. The characters in "The Gray Project" had the same plastic-looking skin and hair that has plagued most computer-rendered humans.

Scenes from "The Gray Project."

Then, in 1998, there was a breakthrough named Charles. Charles was an old man with thinning white hair. His face was composed of over 50,000 individually placed and

textured polygons and his eyes, skin, and hair looked almost real. The only part of Charles' body that appeared in the demonstrations was his face. He stared out from a

dark screen with soft wind blowing his hair. But Charles' casting call did not include an appearance in the Final Fantasy movie. Instead, his

final appearance was in technology demonstrations for Square.

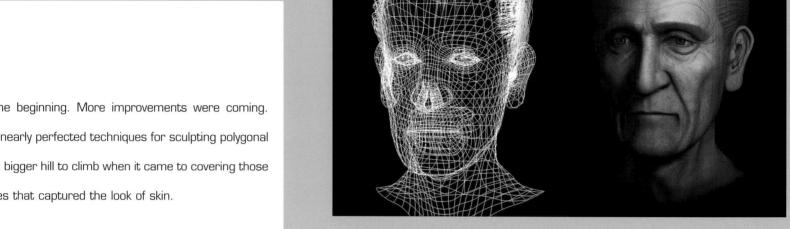

The transformation of Charles, the old man best known for his appearance as a demo for Square.

But this was only the beginning. More improvements were coming. Square's artists had nearly perfected techniques for sculpting polygonal faces, but they had a bigger hill to climb when it came to covering those polygons with textures that captured the look of skin.

"The basic frame for the faces is sort of like a thin chicken wire mesh

that gets shaded," says Lead Character Artist Steven Giesler. "Essentially, we're basically making a wire sculpture in the computer, so it's a bunch of

points which we call polygons that are connected together by edges. Each face has about 15,000 polygons that get subdivided, and the number goes

upwards of 70, 80, even 100,000 polygons. We determine how much we'll need to subdivide [the polygons] by the amount of complexity and detail we

need to achieve a certain result."

Just as Sets and Props used displacement maps as a way of achieving 3D results with mostly 2D backgrounds, Square's character artists sometimes

used the same technique. According to Giesler, 3D wrinkles were sometimes added to two-dimensional skin textures, giving the wizened Dr. Sid more

subdivided polygons than the smooth-skinned Aki Ross. "The texture for the skin was hand-created," says Giesler, "and it's different for each person."

GRAY

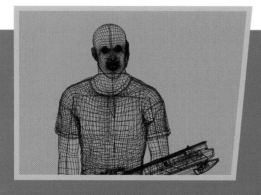

Lead Character Artist Steven Giesler at work.

One of the tricks to making convincing faces was adding details. Among Square's character artists, Dr. Sid is generally seen as having the most realistic face. General Hein, on the other hand, was purposely created to have a more "stylized" face. But one principle that ran through all of this character generation was that adding details like wrinkles, skin blemishes, age spots, and freckles made the characters more believable. "One of the things that helped Sid with his realism is the amount of detail they were able to add to his skin," says Animation Director Andy Jones. "Adding more detail, more age spots, more stuff like that makes characters look even more real. That's one of the reasons that Aki was one of the more difficult characters to make look real. We couldn't put a lot of age spots and things on her because we needed to keep her skin clean and attractive."

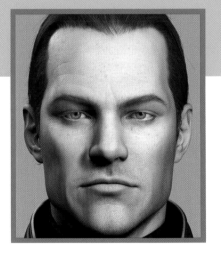

When placed side by side, the subtleties of Dr. Sid's face really come to light when compared to General Hein's.

"We gave her freckles, but it was difficult. We fought to get those in there. It was a battle between trying to make her look real and keeping her beauty. In a live-action film, they cover up a lot of blemishes. So where do we draw the line as far as reality is concerned? We were just trying to add detail to make the characters look more real."

In an eerie shadow of reality, the skins created by Square's character artists have some of the same supple qualities found in human skin. When forensic scientists perform autopsies, they cut an incision below their subject's scalp line, then peel back the skin of the face like an elastic sheet. The skins created by Square's artists have the same properties. Until they are attached to a character, the faces created by Square's character artists are fleshy, stretched sheets that adhere like a glove when attached to characters' heads.

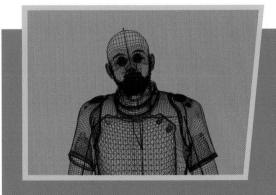

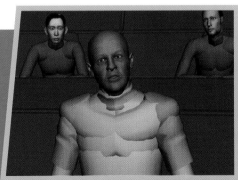

DR. SID

But there is more to creating a virtual actor than simply creating a "chicken wire" head and covering it with a skin. Faces like Aki's and Gray's must do more than look good; they need to emote. Their mouths need to work and they need to have lifelike eyes and expressions.

"Along with the artistic creation side, we integrated animation technology that is attached to the characters," says Jones. "There was a lot of orchestration by different people working together and implementing different things as we went through the pipeline."

Creating the controls required a blend of physiology and artistic license, according to Giesler. "It was sort of an artistic expression of some of the muscles, not literally the actual muscle. There are hundreds of muscles in the (human) face and we couldn't possibly replicate all of them because there are so many overlaps."

When it came to facial control, just as it was with blemishes, Dr. Sid was Final Fantasy's most complicated character. "Sid's animator, Louis Lefebvre, added some personal controls to help animate the face," says Character Artist Francisco Cortina. "Sid is my personal favorite, but he does have a few extra controls. With our system of facial animation set-up, we have the ability to add extra shapes or controls to do certain things. In Sid's case, there are a few more controls, such as jiggling, in his throat."

Most of the characters in *Final Fantasy: The Spirits Within* have approximately 100 control points, but more than one dozen additional controls were added to help with Sid. "We put in a lot of vibrations in the skin of his neck," says Jones. "Sid is a much older character. His skin is a lot looser. When Sid talks, we'd import the wave file of the speech itself and see how the wave form looks, and use that to drive the animation of his neck. You may notice that when Donald Sutherland (the voice actor for Dr. Sid) speaks, his neck kind of vibrates a little based on his vocal cords. Little things like that are what make Sid look so real—that along with Louis' (Character Animator Louis Lefebvre) attention to facial details, such as lips and eye movements."

RYAN

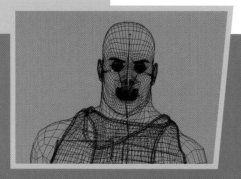

LET THERE BE LIFE

The number of artists working in the Animation Section fluctuated throughout the project. During its peak, there were 22 people on the team. Team members included people like Lead Animator Roy Sato, who jokingly refers to himself as "lead Aki animator." A Hawaii native, Sato worked at Disney Studios for nearly five years. His credits include the cartoon series "Dark Wing Duck."

During a typical workday, Sato might go through a scene with Aki, with a rough version of her face filling his computer monitor and a smaller window showing Ming-Na in the top-right corner of his screen. "What we get (from Layout) is a really rough-looking Aki, what we would call a 'block model'," says Sato. "It's attached to the motion capture data, so you can see her walking around in her 3D scenes. From there, I have to move her to the right place in front of the camera. On top of that "block model Aki," I have to place the animation model of Aki so that I can start animating her face and her fingers."

"Lead Aki Animator" Roy Sato.

Before finishing with Aki, Sato must review the quality of her motion-captured movements to ensure they are fluid. He will have to animate her hair, hands, lip synch, and expression using tools from Character. "To do shots in which Aki is talking, I bring up video footage of Ming-Na and start lip synching her," says Sato. "I usually start with the face first, going frame by frame using animation controls that our programmers built for us. I shape her mouth and move her eyes and do all of the details that motion capture leaves out."

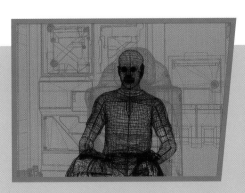

THE HAIRY SIDE OF CHARACTER CREATION

It doesn't matter whether you're talking about Gray's curly main, Hein's overly-moussed solid sheet of hair, or Aki's silky locks. The characters in *Final Fantasy: The Spirits Within* all received their hair the old fashioned way: they grew it using a process that Character Artist Francisco Cortina compares to growing sprouts on a Chia Pet.

A clean-shaven Dr. Sid.

A normal view of Dr. Sid.

Dr. Sid in need of a haircut.

"It's not all that far from the truth," jokes Cortina, "because their hair does grow that way. It starts out at the root. A mass of hair starts growing from the scalp, then we use tools to tell it how to grow. The guides are these little wires or curves in space that I move around to style different elements of the hair. I can use the guides to control how far the hair goes out, how much it grows, etc. It does essentially grow like a Chia Pet."

And about Hein, Cortina says that the greased-down rug on his head is composed of individual strands. "Hein? Oh, Hein has got a complete head of hair. He's got layers of hair. He had more of a slicked back, tight kind of moussed look; but if you look closely, you can see layers inside of it."

Knowing that most of the final touches in animation would be done by hand, Andy Jones purposely chose animators who would add a bit of themselves into the way they interpreted their characters. "In the beginning, I chose the lead animators for each character based on their personalities and what they would be able to put from their personalities into their characters," says Jones. "If you met Louis (Lefebvre), you'd know that he is reserved. He is very proper and he sits very straight just like Sid would, even though Louis is only about 30 years old. And a lot of Roy's personality is in Aki, too. His little idiosyncrasies—the timing of how Roy says things and the way he looks at people when he talks to them, it's very similar to the way Aki does it."

But along with the interpretive work of creating personalities, character animators must oversee thousands of meticulous details. If not executed properly, audiences will ultimately be reminded that they are not watching live actors. Sato, for instance, had tools for animating Aki's hair one strand at a time.

Of course, the Animation Section's responsibilities went beyond bringing characters to life. "We had seven or eight people doing phantom animation. They were 'the phantom team' that did the running and fighting and even some of the effects throughout the film," says Jones. "The rest of it was ships flying and stuff like that." Asked if space ships were supposed to be handled by Sets and Props, Jones just smiled and said: "They built it, we animated it."

JANE

CLOTHING: WELL-TAILORED SUITS

There's a reason why people pay more money for Armani—it wears well. Well-made clothes not only fit better, they look better. And that goes for virtual clothing, too.

Don't bother looking for guys in cheap suits while watching this movie. Having gone to all the trouble and expense of creating realistic models with motion-captured movements, the creative minds at Square USA were not about to hide their great animation work behind inexpensive clothes. "We actually went out and bought pieces of clothing and ripped them apart at the seams so we could see the patterns," says Character Technical Director Kevin Ochs. "My background is in physics. I've never sewn in my life, but yet it came to a point that I had to understand the basic principles of tailoring. One thing we quickly realized is if you did not tailor it properly in the computer, then when the simulation dynamics got a hold of it, it looked like a poorly tailored suit on the screen. We were forced to make high-quality clothing."

Ochs' clothing simulations were actual simulations with each kind of material having unique properties. "We needed to be very versatile to make things like Hein's jacket, which obviously weighs several pounds. Everyone is an expert on leather. Everyone seems to have a leather jacket somewhere in the closet. They all know how it looks, and especially how it wrinkles. That was a key factor on all the clothing in the movie. If it didn't wrinkle the way you would think it would, your eyes were immediately drawn to it."

"We had to come up with different waves and techniques to get everything from t-shirts—very light, flimsy pieces of wool—to a leather jacket with shoulder pads to wrinkle and move the way people would expect."

To do this, artists made dynamic calculations for every kind of cloth that appears in the movie. "We had to come up with its properties. With t-shirts and pants, it was an absolute necessity to have them bend and flex like they would in normal life. There's a couple of shots in the movie in which you actually see the clothing, particularly Gray's clothing, being blown by the wind. You can see his pants flapping in the wind and his shirt pressed up against his body. We made all those calculations—wind resistance, gravity and stuff like that."

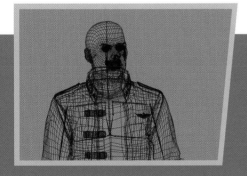

GENERAL HEIN

DR. AKI ROSS

Age: 27

Weight: 56kg

Height: 170cm

Date of Birth: October 7, 2038

Birthplace: San Francisco

Specialty: Biotechnology; Aerospace Training

Already infected by the Phantoms, Aki must use her scientific intellect to find means to combat the alien predators. As she searches for an answer to the Earth's plight, Aki works simultaneously to reveal her enemies' purpose. She remains true to her optimistic nature despite the fact that time is dwindling for the Earth and herself. Possessing unwavering determination, Aki battles to overcome earth-shattering obstacles in her efforts to save mankind.

153

Ming-Na lent her voice talents to Disney's *Mulan*. Her other feature film credits include *One Night Stand*, *Street Fighter*, and *The Joy Luck Club*. She currently stars as Dr. Deb Chen on the popular NBC series *ER*.

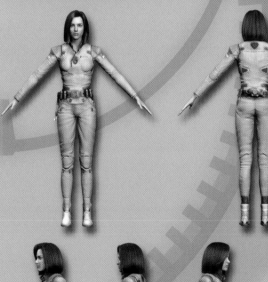

ANIMATOR: ROY SATO

156

Aki examines the sixth spirit.

Aki struggles to understand her recurring dreams.

GRAY EDWARDS

Age: 31

Weight: 82kg

Height: 184cm

Date of Birth: April 15, 2034

Birthplace: Chicago

Specialty: Tactical; Special Forces

A military captain and leader of the elite Deep Eyes squadron, Gray confronts enemies and allies alike—head on. Gray's reputation for loyalty and trustworthiness earns him the unquestioning support of his troops, leading them into battle with unhesitating courage and determination. Yet the biggest challenge he faces may be his devotion to a woman.

mrsav

edwards

159

DEEPEYES
SEARCH AND DELETE SQUAD

Gray joins Aki in her dream sequence and experiences it firsthand. It's at this point in the movie that Aki and Gray's relationship grows even stronger.

VOICE TALENT: ALEC BALDWIN

Gray helplessly watches the phantoms as they move in on the Deep Eyes.

161

ANIMATORS: TOBY HARUNO & BEN RUSH

DR. SID

Age: 70

Weight: 72kg

Height: 170cm

Date of Birth: June 16, 1995

Birthplace: Toronto

Specialty: Biochemistry

The genius behind the wave theory, Dr. Sid possesses a facile mind as well as a compassionate heart. As he guides his protégé, Aki, towards a final solution, he imparts both scientific principles and fatherly advice. The Earth's fate depends on his innovative and unprecedented scientific vision.

162

dr.SYN

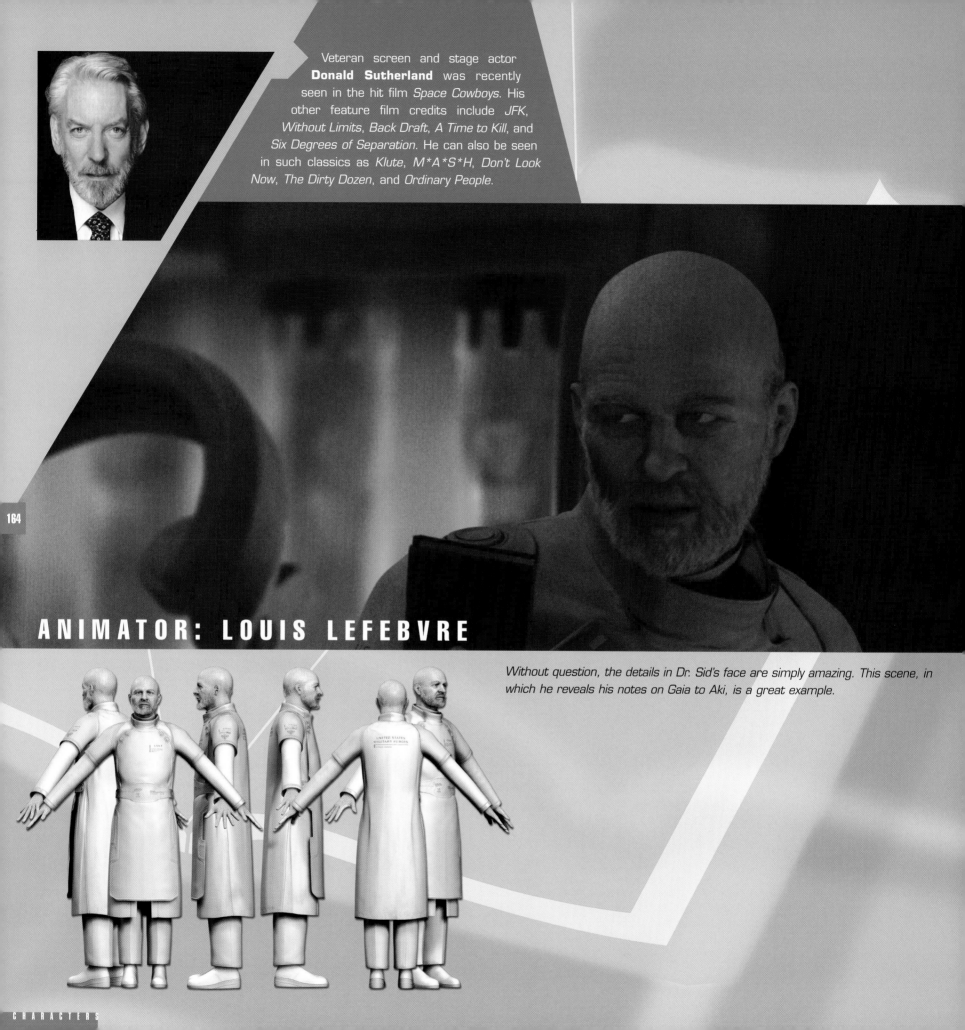

Veteran screen and stage actor **Donald Sutherland** was recently seen in the hit film *Space Cowboys*. His other feature film credits include *JFK*, *Without Limits*, *Back Draft*, *A Time to Kill*, and *Six Degrees of Separation*. He can also be seen in such classics as *Klute*, *M*A*S*H*, *Don't Look Now*, *The Dirty Dozen*, and *Ordinary People*.

ANIMATOR: LOUIS LEFEBVRE

Without question, the details in Dr. Sid's face are simply amazing. This scene, in which he reveals his notes on Gaia to Aki, is a great example.

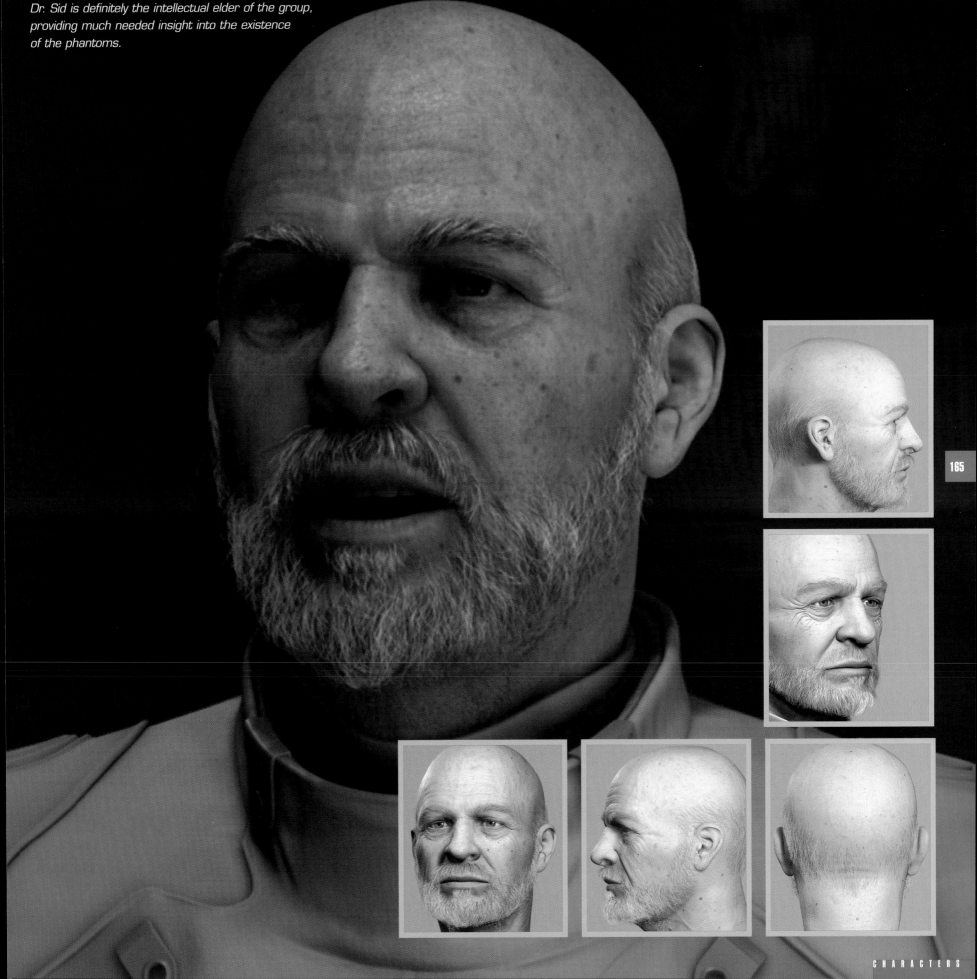

Dr. Sid is definitely the intellectual elder of the group, providing much needed insight into the existence of the phantoms.

RYAN WHITTAKER

Age: 30

Weight: 105kg

Height: 188cm

Date of Birth: July 11, 2035

Birthplace: New York

Specialty: Tactical; Infantry

The Deep Eyes squadron's sergeant and second in command, Ryan displays a relentless dedication to his team and their cause. His selflessness and courage set an example for his fellow soldiers. Irreverent at times, Ryan recognizes his duty to his superior and best friend Gray Edwards. Ryan will seek victory until he, or his opposition, is defeated.

166

ryan whittaker

167

Ryan places his life on the line as he fights off one of Hein's men as he returns from Battlefield Wasteland.

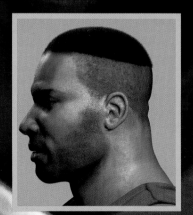
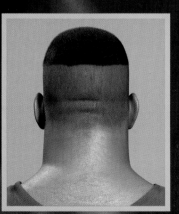

ANIMATOR: CHRISTOPHER ERIN WALSH

Ryan's deep and powerful voice is supplied by **VING RHAMES**. He earned acclaim for his performance as Don King in HBO's "*Don King: Only in America*". His feature film credits include *Mission: Impossible 2, Entrapment, Out of Sight, Con Air, Rosewood, Striptease, Mission: Impossible, Kiss of Death*, and *Pulp Fiction*. He was most recently seen in *Baby Boy*. Future projects include *Undisputed* and *Plague Season*.

169

An imposing figure, the members of Deep Eyes look to Ryan in times of need. In this scene, he leads the troops through a vast wasteland.

NEIL FLEMING

The mechanical guru of the Deep Eyes squadron, Neil applies mental and physical fortitude to challenge the alien predators. Possessing a sarcastic sense of humor that belies his intellectual pessimism, Neil is an integral and reliable component of the force.

Age: 27

Weight: 68kg

Height: 174cm

Date of Birth: February 23, 2038

Birthplace: New York

Specialty: Tactical;
Mechanic

170

neil
fleming

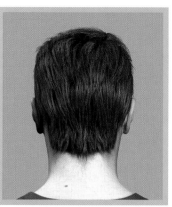

Neil serves as comic relief for the Deep Eyes. Well respected, Neil is the team's premier pilot and mechanic. Here, Neil pilots the Deep Eyes out of impending danger.

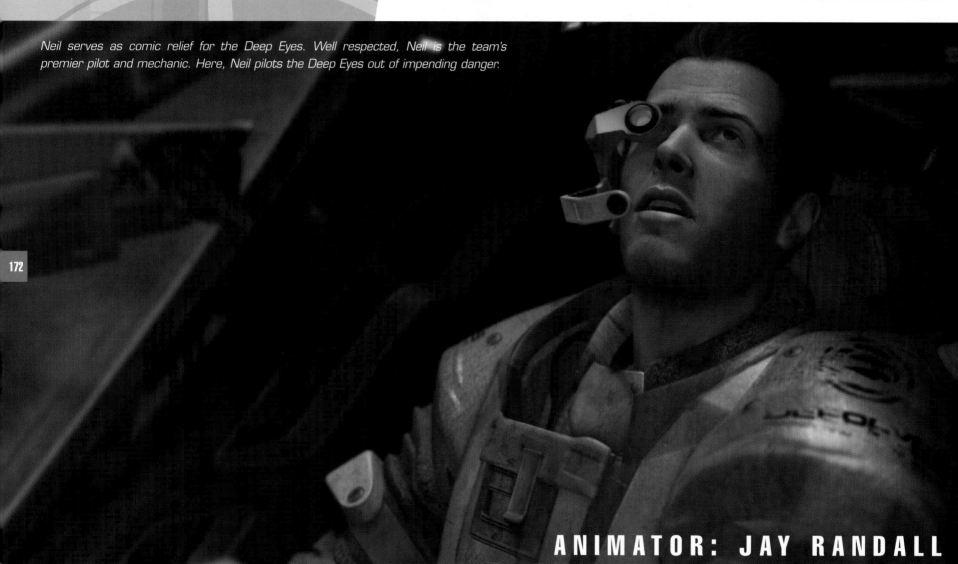

172

ANIMATOR: JAY RANDALL

VOICE TALENT: STEVE BUSCEMI

Once again, the incredible lighting effects from above illuminate Neil's face as he struggles to free the Black Boa.

173

JANE PROUDFOOT

Age: 28

Weight: 63kg

Height: 175cm

Date of Birth: January 18, 2037

Birthplace: Houston

Specialty: Tactical; Artillery

The slayer of all misogynistic stereotypes, Jane meshes good looks with even greater courage and athleticism. An imposing soldier, she charges bravely into battle, regardless of the risk. Fueled by honor and a short fuse, Jane often butts heads with her sarcastic team member, Neil, although her direct nature ensures she wastes no time with either fellow soldiers or her opposition.

jane proudfoot

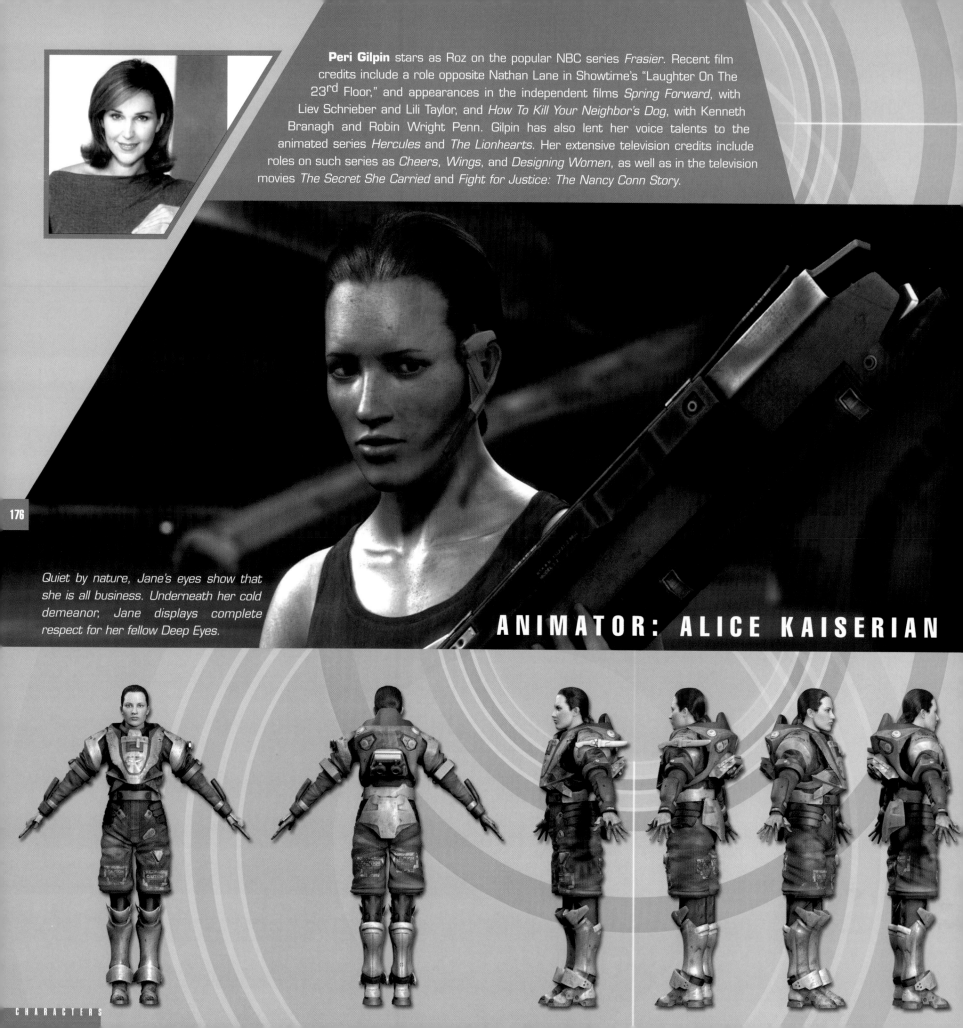

Peri Gilpin stars as Roz on the popular NBC series *Frasier*. Recent film credits include a role opposite Nathan Lane in Showtime's "Laughter On The 23rd Floor," and appearances in the independent films *Spring Forward*, with Liev Schrieber and Lili Taylor, and *How To Kill Your Neighbor's Dog*, with Kenneth Branagh and Robin Wright Penn. Gilpin has also lent her voice talents to the animated series *Hercules* and *The Lionhearts*. Her extensive television credits include roles on such series as *Cheers*, *Wings*, and *Designing Women*, as well as in the television movies *The Secret She Carried* and *Fight for Justice: The Nancy Conn Story*.

Quiet by nature, Jane's eyes show that she is all business. Underneath her cold demeanor, Jane displays complete respect for her fellow Deep Eyes.

ANIMATOR: ALICE KAISERIAN

This scene showcases a great view of the Deep Eyes' battle suits. Note the complete head gear, armor, and the impressive weapon.

GENERAL HEIN

Age: 35

Weight: 78kg

Height: 180cm

Date of Birth: October 25, 2030

Birthplace: San Francisco

Specialty: Tactical; Artillery

Driven by a hero complex and a desire for vengeance, General Douglas Hein seeks a quick and violent end to the alien invasion. Hein, a military strategist, clearly shows skill, yet his ego overshadows his wisdom. Determined to avenge the death of his family at the hands of predators, General Hein will take whatever course necessary to destroy both the enemy and Aki's alternative strategies. However, his stubbornness and hatred may be a greater threat to the Earth than the aliens.

178

general
hero

179

As his plan begins to fail him, General Hein lets loose in an angry tirade.

180

The voice of General Hein is performed by **JAMES WOODS**. Woods is a two-time Academy Award nominee for *Salvador* (Best Actor, 1987) and *Ghosts of Mississippi* (Best Supporting Actor, 1997). His recent feature credits include *Scary Movie 2*, *Any Given Sunday*, *The General's Daughter*, *True Crime*, *The Virgin Suicides*, *John Carpenter's Vampires*, the Disney animated feature *Hercules*, *Another Day in Paradise*, and *Contact*.

180

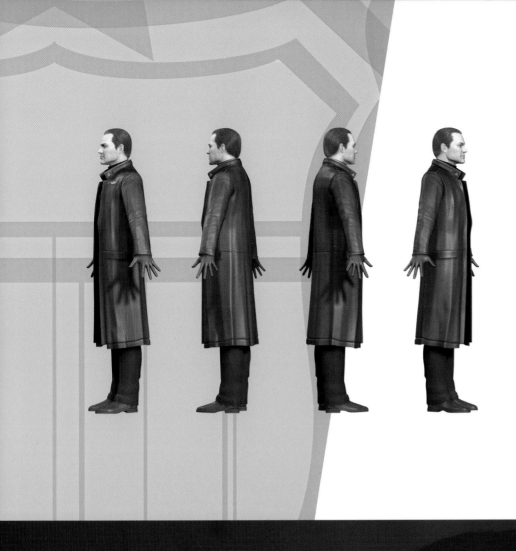

The look on General Hein's face epitomizes his overall demeanor. He's clearly a man seeking to fulfill his egotistical desires, wickedly on display here.

ANIMATOR: MATTHEW HACKETT

PHANTOMS: GHOSTLY SPACE INVADERS

What exactly are the Phantoms? Mankind fears them, General Hein hates them, Aki dreams about them, and the Deep Eyes vaporize them. There are Phantoms of all shapes and sizes. You have your humanoid Phantoms, flying snake-like Phantoms, and enormous Meta Phantoms. The two things all of them have in common are a ghostly translucent appearance and a genuine craving for the taste of human spirits. Originally conceived by Director Hironobu Sakaguchi, the ghostly phantoms were fleshed out and given form by Phantom Supervisor Takao Noguchi.

"We were given an initial concept of what these Phantoms were supposed to look like and given vague ideas such as sometimes they would be transparent and ghostlike and sometimes they would have armor," says Noguchi. "Then after that, the artwork came from Mr. Yasushi Nirasawa, a famous creature designer in Japan who did the design for the Phantoms. So we received the design from Mr. Nirasawa, and based on that, my team recreated the ideas in 3D."

An array of Phantom concept art.

Only its back is seen.

Even elements like weapons and ships were devised at the concept stage.

Rendering these ideas into 3D images became a bit more confusing, as there were six types of Phantoms in total: the common humanoid variety, snake Phantoms, flying "Meta" Phantoms, gigantic "Proto" Phantoms, bird Phantoms and whale Phantoms. Adding to this confusion was the small detail that the humanoid Phantoms appear in flesh and bony armor in Aki's re-occurring dream.

Of all the Phantoms, the "bi-pedal" humanoid variety was of the most concern. These were the foot soldiers of the invading army, and director Hironobu Sakaguchi wanted them to have human features and a completely alien appearance. Audiences will get their best glimpse of these creatures during the dream sequences, when the camera closes in on the eye of one of the living Phantoms.

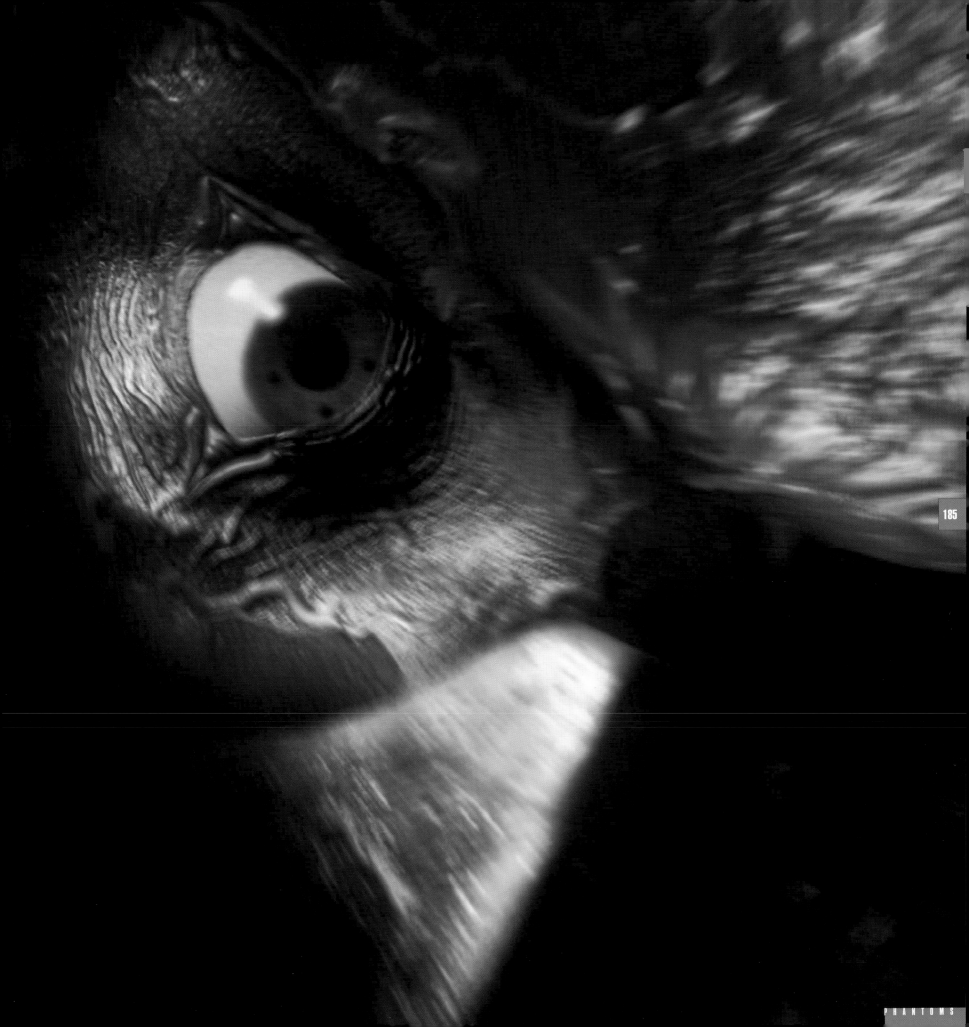

TAKAO NOGUCHI, PHANTOM SUPERVISOR

Photo by: Anna Johnson Photography

During scenes such as Aki's unauthorized excursion to Times Square, bi-pedal Phantoms walked through walls and even rose from the ground. Having such abilities, according to Phantom Supervisor Takao Noguchi, should allow them to move around as freely as their flying Phantom comrades. But this does not seem to be the case. Instead, they marched in a ponderous and relentless pursuit of Aki and her Deep Eyes rescuers. Trying to rectify this incongruity caused Noguchi to perform a little Phantom psychoanalysis so that he could get into the Phantoms' heads and come up with a theory about why they marched.

"You see them walking, but they really have no reason to," says Noguchi. "They don't exist, and they can go through walls. The explanation behind that is that the two-legged humanoid ones were essentially the spirits that carried the memory of their past life. They walked when they were alive, and the residual memory caused them to walk around with two legs even though they don't need to."

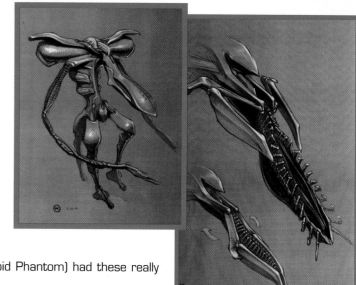

"Initially, that Phantom (the humanoid Phantom) had these really bug(-like) eyes that did not look human at all," says Noguchi. "With those eyes it did not quite look like the intelligent life-forms that Mr. Sakaguchi wanted, so he requested that their eyes, look more human." Based on that request, Noguchi devised an eyeball buffet, providing Sakaguchi a choice of 20 different eyes from which to choose.

As the project continued, the humanoid Phantoms took on a logic of their own. In the dream sequences, they wore armor which they opened to reveal their eyes. Judging by their silhouettes, the invading ghostly Phantoms wore the exact same armor. Since armor-plated ghosts seemed a bit oxy-moronic, Noguchi decided that their armor must have been a bio-evolutionary development.

187

LIGHTING

Make no mistake, lighting the sets of *Final Fantasy: The Spirits Within* was not simply a case of turning up a simple set of gamma controls. The movie may take place in virtual space, but the techniques used to illuminate its sets were completely based on techniques used in making live-action movies.

Then again, lighting the sets was only a small part of the job that the Lighting Section performed. Lighting was where all of the elements of the movie came together. This was the place where layout's "block model Aki" was replaced with the virtual starlet that the character team created and Roy Sato animated. Lighting was where simplified models of sets, characters, and props were replaced with the fully textured final images that appeared in the movie.

"If you think of it strictly as what is delivered from one department to the next, Lighting receives 3D geometry and animation, then delivers it as 2D images to Compositing," says David Seager, who, as the Head of the Lighting Section, was both a Sequence Supervisor and the Lighting Supervisor on the film. "There's a lot of trade-off between Compositing and Lighting because certain things are easier to do in 3D and others are easier to do in 2D. So we're constantly in communication."

"Rendering software does not completely simulate the way light behaves, so we have to make our own little cheats."

—DAVID SEAGER, LIGHTING SUPERVISOR

The Lighting Section begins its work by assembling every scene from the movie. Until it reached the lighting artist's hands, Aki and Gray were pretty much floating in space and kissing the air until Lighting put them together inside the compartment of the Boa. The room and any objects they touched all existed independently.

By the time images reach Lighting, they should be completely refined and consistent throughout the film. Parts cannot be added or removed once the lighting process begins without tremendous difficulty. "By the time we receive the characters, the sets, and the animation, everything has been approved so that we can just run with it," says Seager. "If those things need to be changed and we've already started, that's a problem because we will need to start over again in certain cases. There always comes a point when you are locked in. Once the image is approved and lit, you've locked down the elements that create that image."

The role of the Lighting Section is best exemplified by this series of shots. Notice the subtle lighting effects from shot 1 to shot 3 and what a difference each effect makes. The key lighting source to this scene came from Jane's muzzle flash.

DAVID SEAGER, LIGHTING SUPERVISOR

Every member of the Final Fantasy team has a favorite scene, a moment that really highlights their work. For David Seager, that scene is the Barrier Control Room.

"I'm biased because I had the role of Sequence Supervisor, so there were five sequences that I was in charge of. The last one that I dealt with was the Barrier Control Room, which was when Hein finally crosses the line and decides to dim the power to the barriers."

"There are a couple of reasons I really like that sequence. The artistic design, the way they created the sets and props, it's a very cool-looking room. I like this sequence because it has everything. It has Phantoms. It has visual effects. It has holograms. It has the soldiers and this great combination of the key things in our film and they're all put together in a very action-packed dramatic scene."

"It was the last scene we handled in Lighting. We were able to apply all the lessons we had learned, but at the same time, we had pretty much saved one of the most difficult scenes for last. At one point, we had the entire Lighting Section working on the Barrier Control Room, so it stands out in my mind. Again, it's hard to know if I'm looking at it completely unbiased. I was very involved with it and the Lighting team really came together to pull off a very powerful sequence."

Once scenes are assembled, the next task is to light them. As anyone who has ever had a studio sitting with a professional photographer or watched a "making of" documentary can attest, lighting a movie is a lot more complex than simply flipping on a switch. Single-source lighting may be fine for real life, but in movies light is used for dramatic effect. Like the lighting staff of a live-action studio, the staff at Square USA uses multiple light sources and other tools to highlight some parts of the shot while diminishing others.

"Where that (single-source lighting) starts to break down is in the tools that we have to do lighting," says Seager. "Rendering software does not completely simulate the way light behaves, so we have to make our own little cheats."

Lighting would not have needed to invent "little cheats" if this movie were like a David Mamet movie with characters sitting around holding long conversations. Instead, it is an action movie with characters running through dramatically-lit environments, explosions giving off flares, and all kinds of light sources creating their own forms of illumination noise.

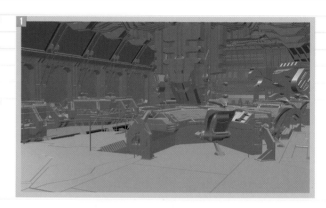

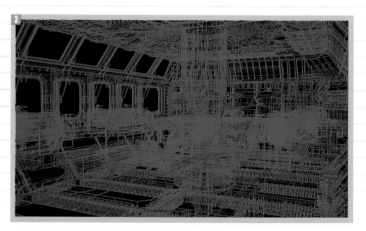

The lighting effects in the Barrier Control Room.

"We have what we think of as light rigs," says Seager. "They don't really have the tuning and support structure that is required in the real world, but essentially it's the same kind of thing—a light positioned in various locations about the character that is used to fill certain areas or create highlights. We've often found that when characters move, the shots are often more difficult. If we are just dealing with a space and we have positioned lights, they do pretty much what lights do in the real world. But shots like SCN (the scene in which Aki saves Gray from Phantom infestation) are rather difficult because the characters are moving through all these different light sources, light rigs. When they're moving and they're mixing together as they're walking along, it increases the complexity of the shot."

193

Fortunately, working in a virtual space enabled the Lighting Section to bend a few rules with movable lighting sources and other tricks that are not available in the real world. Knowing a few good tricks became especially important with the Phantoms, characters that acted as their own sources of illumination.

"For half the movie, the Phantoms were kind of invisible," says Seager. "But when they interacted more closely, and they were maybe only a couple of feet away, it was like they were lighting up the whole room. At those times, we would attach point lights to their joints—like their elbow and their wrist and their shoulder and so forth—and just animate them moving through an environment. There were really only a couple of cases when we did that, and in those cases we were able to get away with it."

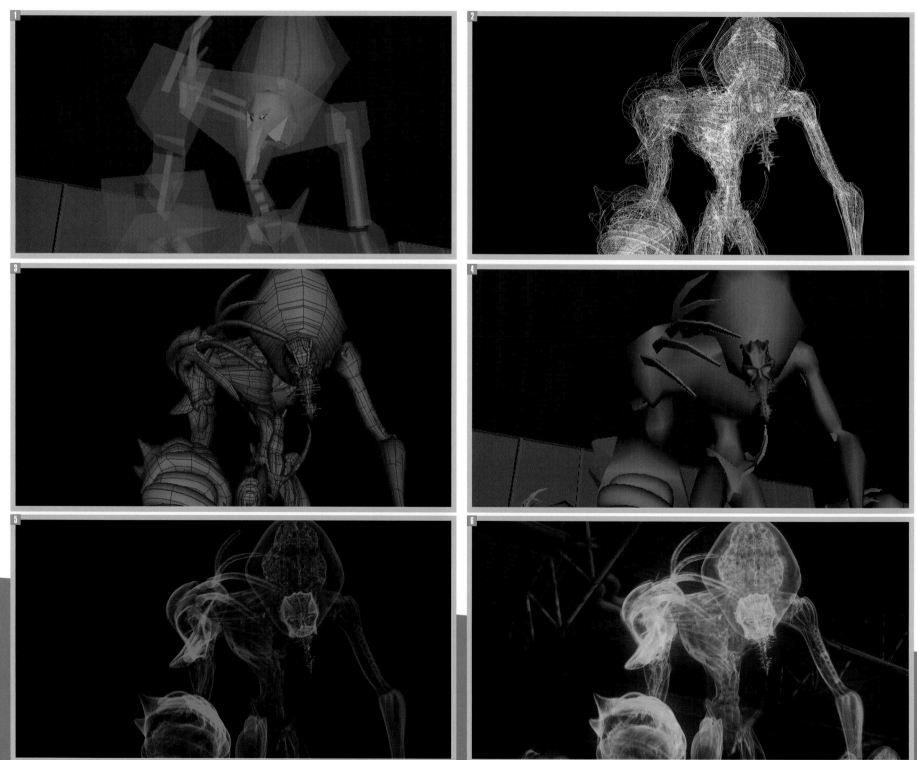

A perfect example of Phantom lighting.

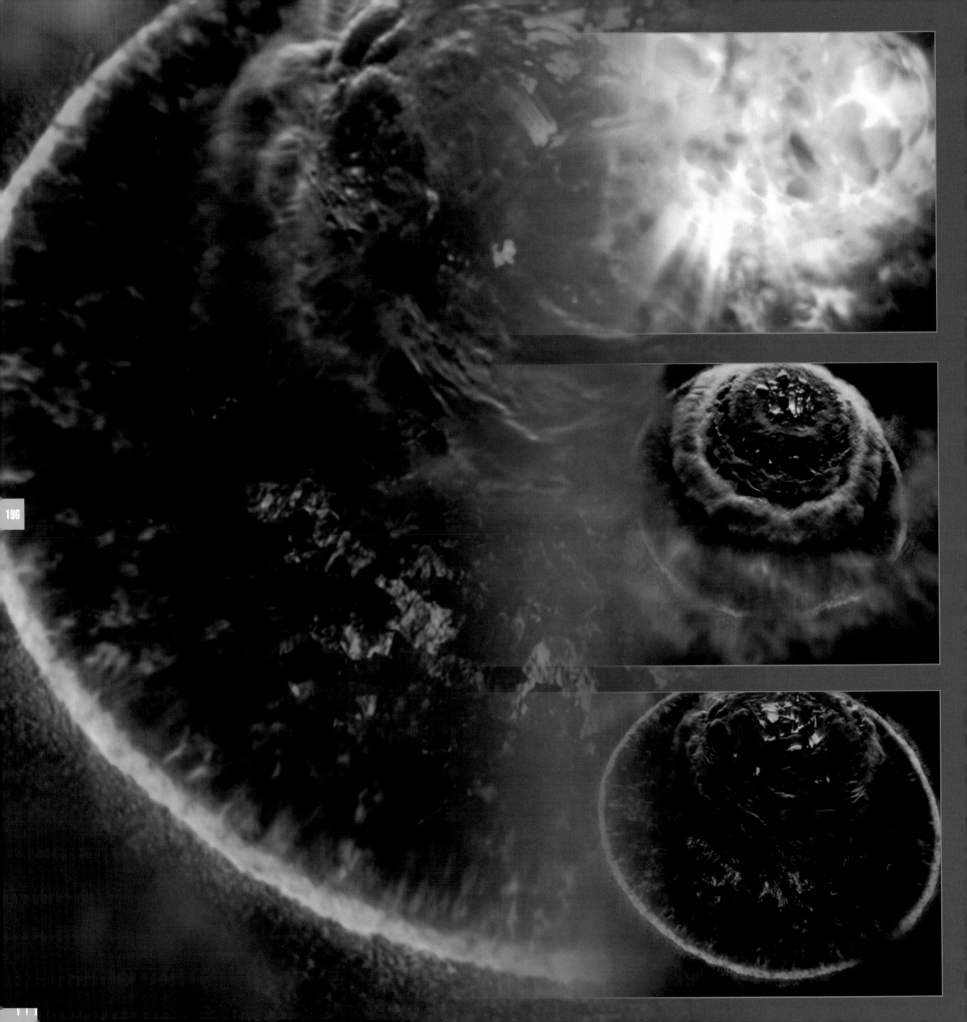

VISUAL EFFECTS

VISUAL EFFECTS: FLAMES, FLARES, AND FINISHING TOUCHES

When Sets and Props finished modeling Aki's Black Boa space transport, it had wings, windows, and a solid-looking shell. Then Animation took it, placed in three-dimensional sets, and gave it the illusion of motion. Now it hovered over the tarmac in the airport and soared past Phantoms on its way into space. But it did these amazing feats no more realistically than a plastic toy rocket in the hands of a five-year-old boy. Sure, the model of the Boa looked good, but the model that came from Animation only moved. It had none of the trimmings that help audiences suspend their disbelief.

That would all change when Aki's Boa landed in the Visual Effects (VFX) Section. This is the department that put the fiery plume in the jets on the back of the Boa. It was VFX who put the muzzle flares on the Deep Eyes' guns and the fireballs in the explosions.

"In this movie, visual effects refers to explosions, fire, debris... We even blow up a whole planet," says VFX Supervisor Remo Balcells. "We did all of the natural phenomena (referring to explosions and phenomena that occur in the world as we know it) and fictional phenomena such as barrier shields and rays. We mostly (made) a lot of explosions, debris flying up, and dust—lots of dust. One of my artists referred to us as 'the Dust Bunnies.' It all has been done digitally."

But Square USA also took serious risks. Many of the visual effects that appear in the movie were made using untested technologies. Hironobu Sakaguchi, the film's director, expressed reservations about trying this early on, but expressed confidence in Balcells's judgment and let him proceed as he thought best.

"There was an interesting moment in which we needed to make a lot of fire and a lot of explosions, and the director questioned whether we should do it digitally or with natural fire," says Balcells. "I asked for the opportunity to try to make digital fire and digital explosions at one of our meetings. In the beginning, there was a certain degree of skepticism; but they gave us about a month, and we presented our research. It looked good enough that the director said, 'Okay, we're going to go with digital fire.'"

"As far as I know, and I have not done any research on this, I don't think any other studio has ever approached this in this scale. Some of the explosions cover the full screen."

So with his team of 15 artists (which swelled to 25 artists near the end of the film), Balcells directed their work. What they discovered was that there are a lot of ways to go wrong when creating huge effects. "There are a few shots in which you see the big fireball coming towards the camera. We risked making a cheesy explosion in those shots. We, as humans, are very familiar with fire, and it is very easy (for audiences) to catch anything that is wrong with fire. Fire and explosions have very complex dynamics, and fooling the eyes is very tricky."

GODS OF SMOKE AND FIRE

Balcells divided the VFX Section into teams of five or six artists, and then assigned each team certain tasks. Visual Effects Artist Mach Kobayashi led the team that created the core technology at the heart of the movie's explosions. "I created a shader, which is a mini-program that would actually take spheres and then generate clouds with them. The first part of the process was to write a program that we could use whenever we needed to create that effect. And we used it for all the regular-looking explosions, for some of the smoke, and for some of the fires. I just kept on adding options to it and trying it out on different things."

Kobayashi's shader created swarms of rotating, volumetric spheres that could be covered with smoke, fire, dust, or other textures. "The last (part of the) process was to do color correction—add a bit of a glow to it to make it red or brown. For example, the nuclear explosion on the Phantom planet is primarily dust colored. It's brownish, and the top has these fiery highlights. That was all done in the post process by the Compositing Section."

"The planet was challenging," Balcells agrees. "It was a very artistic explosion. It was not very realistic. The director wanted it that way."

"Usually, when you see planets blowing up, you see this big bang and this big flash, and maybe some shockwaves going toward the camera. We decided that since the explosion was caused by the war, they wouldn't have that much power. So what we did was create this chain reaction of nuclear explosions that causes the planet to crack into big pieces... hemispheres. The planet doesn't boom, it cracks like a small rock. It was beautiful, because you could see the detail of the surface and everything blowing up. It wasn't covered up by a big white flash."

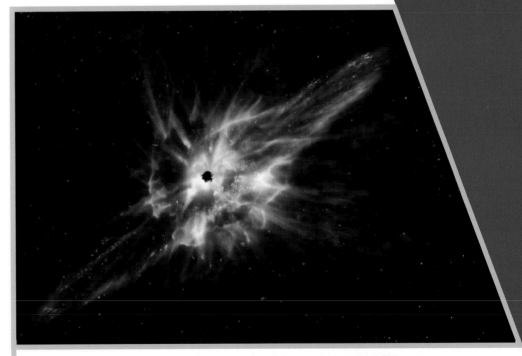

This planet exploding is just one fine example of the work done by VFX.

But not all of the special effects were of a planet-splitting magnitude. In another scene, a spaceship kicks up an enormous cloud of dust. Stripped to its digital bones, that cloud of dust has the same DNA as the explosions on the Phantom planet and the columns of smoke around the ruins of Barrier City New York. Under carefully selected textures, all of those effects were generated using the volumetric spheres in Mach Kobayashi's shader.

There is, however, more to creating convincing effects than having new technologies. Balcells, Kobayashi, and the rest of the VFX team took their inspiration from a number of sources.

"I looked at pictures of many, many, many different explosions," says Kobayashi. "Lots of nuclear explosions and also some footage from some of the early atomic bomb tests. I watched footage of the Bikini Island test. It's pretty impressive and a little daunting to see something like that and realize that it actually happened."

Inspiration for a different effect—the dust trails left by the living Phantoms in Aki's dreams—came to Balcells from a far less technical source. "When we started, our artists were putting dust trails right behind their footsteps. For some reason, one night I watched *Dances With Wolves*, and I noticed during the stampede you could see the buffalo running at full-speed, but the dust would not kick in until about six feet behind them. So we moved the dust plumes about six feet behind the soldiers, and it looked a little more natural."

"We have all sorts of references from NASA. We have tons of NASA footage and disaster footage. We have medical books, films, you name it."

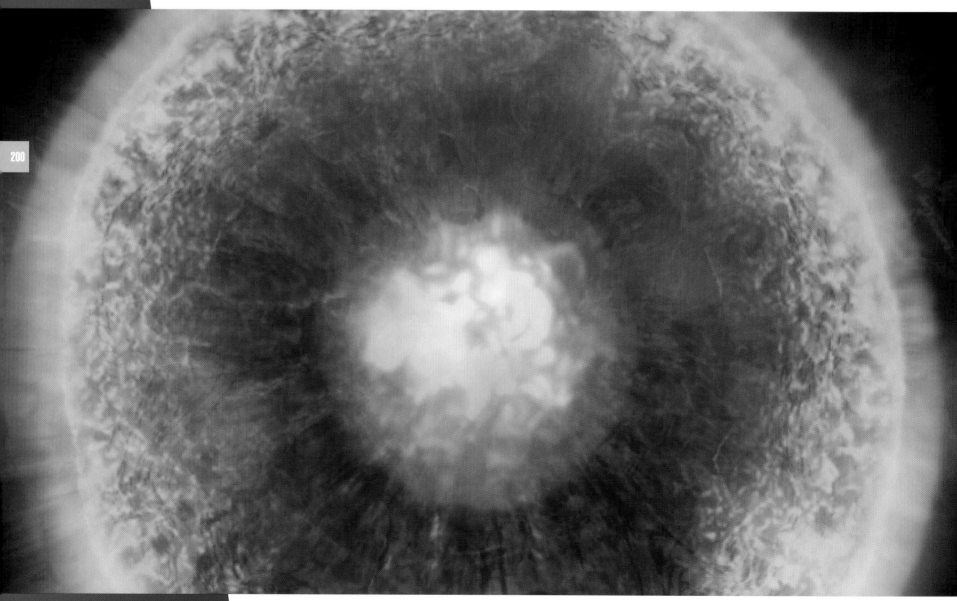

By researching realistic explosions, the VFX Department was able to capture the realism in this crater explosion.

> "You can make an explosion, but with computer graphics you need to know what reacts to what and how."

—REMO BALCELLS, VFX SUPERVISOR

But there were times when research and good tools were not enough. The VFX Section could not begin work on scenes until the Sets and Props and Animation Sections finished their work. "We came pretty late in the game because we couldn't start effects until we knew where the camera was going to be, where the objects were going to be, and where the actors were going to be," says Balcells. "You can make an explosion, but with computer graphics you need to know what reacts to what and how. So we were pretty much at the end of the pipeline."

"Sometimes this caused problems for us because we would be pretty far along on production and then they would have a camera reposition or they would change an object's position or one actor would be put in a different place, and we would have to reshuffle things. One of the things I requested from other supervisors was to have a locked shot where they could not move things anymore. In the end, however, the VFX Section finished its work a full month ahead of schedule. "This was very odd," admits Balcells. "If you would have asked me last fall if we were going to finish on time, I would have said, "No, I am sure we are not going to finish on time. This film will not be released in July." Then something magical happened, and the machine caught momentum, and everything finished on time."

The matte painting.

Highlights the terrain blocks actually caving in.

The above sequence shows the steps involved in creating the explosion.

REMO BALCELLS, VFX SUPERVISOR

Before joining Square USA, VFX Supervisor Remo Balcells worked at special effects studio Digital Domain, where his former projects included *The Fifth Element* and *T2 3D* (the Terminator 2 3D ride at Universal Studios). "I made the mercury head," says Balcells. He also worked on the movie *Titanic* during his tenure at Digital Domain. During this time, he learned quite a bit about scenes with splashy special effects that he refers to as "money shots." For Balcells, the final scene in *Final Fantasy: The Spirits Within* was one of the movie's most challenging money shots.

"You see a close-up of the crater as the ground caves in. That one was very challenging," says Balcells. "I remember that was difficult because it was going to be so big on the screen."

"We tried it with displacement maps in the beginning to push the geometry." (Map displacement is a technique in which artists build three-dimensional objects on top of a 2D picture to give it depth.) "We created a flat surface, and with the displacement texture we created a hole and bumps. But I could tell that it was not going to work out, so I requested my artist to create geometry—boulders that would collide and give the impression of caving in. The director insisted that we give the sensation that the ground was caving in. So we built hundreds of blocks and made them collapse in a natural way."

Photo by: Arna Johnson Photography

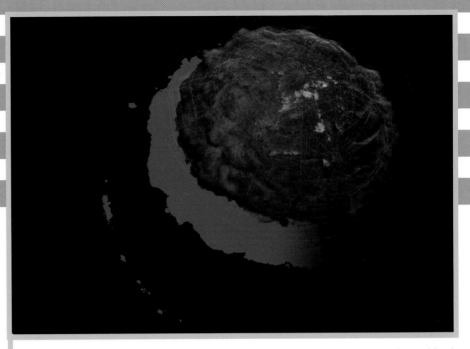

Shows the particle system used to make the fire shockwave and smoke expansion.

Animated wireframe spheres used to generate the nuclear explosion with the Renderman 3rd volumetric shader.

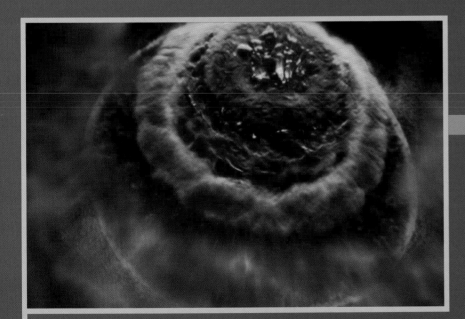

Here's how the scene unfolded in the movie.

204

COMPOSITING

COMPOSITING: THE COMING TOGETHER

One of the universal experiences of going to grade school is looking through a moldy old encyclopedia and discovering overlay transparencies demonstrating human anatomy with a "visible man." These are the layered sheets, the first of which shows the insides of organs such as the heart, lungs, and stomach. Pull the second page over the first, and you magically seal the organs. The next transparency overlays the sinew and the front of the rib cage over the organs. And if there is an additional transparency, it wraps skin over your two-dimensional cadaver.

Simplified to an extreme, the work performed by the Compositing Section is very similar to that "visible man." Compositing's job is to take the sets, props, and characters rendered by other sections and merge them with the work created in the Lighting and VFX Sections in a highly complex 16-plate overlay. "Compositing is the end process," says Compositing Supervisor James Rogers. "We're dealing with such large amounts of 3D data that we need a process like compositing to put it all together."

In many ways, compositing was the most traditional process used during the making of *Final Fantasy: The Spirits Within*. Traditional cartoons are made by overlaying images of characters over backgrounds in animation cells. A cartoon may feature a hand-drawn character on one layer, overlayed on a drawing of a bicycle, placed over a hand-painted background of a busy street. Of course, with Final Fantasy, nothing was hand-painted.

These scenes (numbered 1-10) provide a great example of the Compositing Section's role in this film. In some of the early shots shown here, not much changes. However, as the process goes further along, the changes are quite noticeable. For purposes of this illustration, only a small percentage of the shots that actually went into this scene's production are shown.

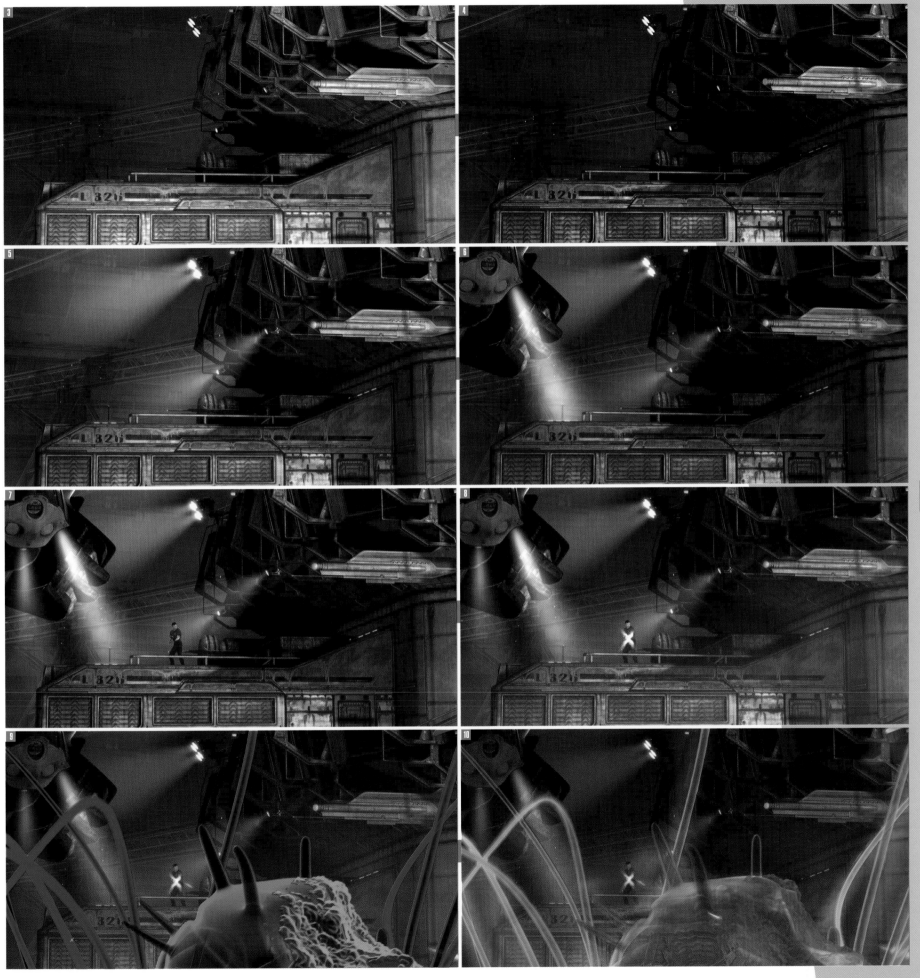

JAMES ROGERS, COMPOSITING SUPERVISOR

While the Compositing Section's main task was assembling the movie, there were other responsibilities. Compositing also adds final touches on scenes. "On top of everything else, we're also required to simulate a real-life camera and make the whole show look like it was actually shot through a real lens," says Compositing Supervisor James Rogers.

Strangely enough, improving shots often means making them less perfect. "Sometimes we have to sort of dirty things up a little to make them look real. It's kind of ironic. We take pristine images and spoil them to make them look right. We'll do things like add depth-of-field, which is basically to focus on an object in the foreground so that everything else sort of gets blurred. If someone reaches towards the camera, for example, his face and body is actually in focus and everything behind him should be out of focus."

"If you can imagine, in a live-action film you have people who make sure the lead character is in focus. Because we're working digitally, we have to animate that camera focus, and we have to animate it for every single layer. The further a layer is from the camera spatially, the more amount of blur it has."

Working in a world in which he sees what goes on behind the curtains, Rogers knows the technology that goes into the smoke and mirrors of movie making. Asked if perhaps his work affects the way he watches movies, Rogers shrugs jokingly. "My wife hates me. Oh well, I guess you do the same thing if you're an editor when you're reading a book."

"When you paint textures into 3D models, you basically have to take pictures of them (to see the final product), which is known as 'rendering,'" says Rogers. "Rendering takes them from being abstract 3D numbers to being less abstract 2D images; but there is so much detail and data in the models that you have to render them in different layers. So, for one scene, we'll render each character separately. We'll render the background and everything else in the scene separately, too, so that we may end up with 16 different layers. Then we take those images into Compositing and we layer them. It's pretty much the same as you do in traditional animation."

But many of the layers that Compositing placed were more subtle. Along with characters and objects, Compositing also dealt with layers of light and dust. The shots where the Deep Eyes walked through moody settings in tight formations, those beams of ambient light through which they walked were an additional layer. So were the muzzle flashes from their guns.

Compositing, by the way, is not limited to cartoons and computer graphic movies. Robert Zemeckis did not cut off Gary Sinise's legs in the making of *Forrest Gump*. The scene in which the legless Sinise jumps off the Bubba Gump fishing boat was created through the magic of compositing. So were many of the more memorable scenes in the *Star Wars* movies.

"They say they did 2,000 composites in the last *Star Wars* film," says Rogers. "We did about 1,315 composites, one for each shot in Final Fantasy. But we had an average of 16 layers per composite. The team that did *Star Wars* counted any light and any touch-up or dust removal as a composite, so the level of intensity that we worked with was sky high."

Another visual example of Compositing's role, this one from Gray's encounter with the Phantom in the airport. Although some of the changes from scene to scene may go unnoticed to the untrained eye, each one of the pictures above has at least one change from the previous one. Note that in the particular sequence shown here, only a small fraction of scenes were shown compared to the actual number done by the Compositing Section.

209

Here's the final scene as witnessed in the movie.

BRINGING IT ALL TOGETHER

AIR: WHERE ALL THINGS COMBINED

If there was one scene in *Final Fantasy: The Spirits Within* in which the work of Storyboard, Animation, and VFX all came together, it was AIR (the airport scene). This is the scene that begins with Neil crashing the jeep through the station, and ends with Aki picking up Gray and leaving the ruins of Barrier City New York.

JEEP TRICKS FROM STORYBOARD

"AIR was a more complex scene from the beginning to the end of the process," says Staging Director Tani Kunitake. "That's the sequence in the airport in which they're trying to escape the city, and they go through this intense sequence with the jeep and they crash through a barrier and jump through the station...We orchestrated the whole crash; but the difficult part about that sequence was actually the next part when they discover that Ryan's injured."

"We aborted this scene a few times. A lot of things were awkward. We got all the way to the motion capture stage, started blocking it out, and decided that it was not working. Then we'd go back to the storyboard stage, do it again, get back into the motion capture stage, and it still wasn't working. We finally found that since it was not working, the problem must be in the script and dialogue, so we went back. This was late in the game, after half of the movie was done and we were getting a little nervous. The schedule was getting really crunched."

Part of the problem was that AIR included a full-compliment of characters—

Gray's entire team of Deep Eyes, plus Aki and Dr. Sid, all crammed into a jeep. "We had

so many characters, so many blocking issues. When you talk about replicating something on

stage, everything had been attached to computer models and some of the ergonomics weren't correct.

So everything had to be really forced to work along the way."

One of the problems turned out to be the jeep. The physical prop used in the motion capture studio turned out to be considerably

smaller than the virtual jeep in the film. What looked like a tight fit with the crew looked loose with their virtual counterparts. "When we got

the staff in the jeep, we found out that the model in the virtual environment was about 30% bigger and you could fit a couple of extra people in it.

When we changed all the schematics to scale, we found out that we couldn't fit all those people in there. So we had to do a lot of clever blocking and redressing

of cameras to hide those weaknesses in the shot."

But changing the jeep did not repair problems with the dialogue. "Andy [Animation Director Andy Jones] and Jack [Voice and Motion Capture Director Jack Fletcher] worked

with us very closely because we were changing dialogue. Originally, the scene played really cold, and then in the next stage it felt really stiff. Finally, it started to warm up. So

AIR is one of the few scenes that came alive."

VFX'S SHATTERING MOMENT

Like so many scenes in the film, AIR was literally peppered with visual effects; but one of the most impressive effects in this scene might go unnoticed.

After crashing the jeep, the team splits up on multiple missions as they prepare to evacuate the city. Gray heads into a building on his own, and then must exit in a hurry. Discovering that the quickest way out is through a solid pane of glass, Gray fires four bullets into the window and then crashes through the glass. Not surprisingly, this scene could not be created with motion-captured data.

"Toby Haruno was the animator who animated Gray for that, and it was all done by hand because the motion capture didn't really work. They couldn't give the sense of someone hitting something; there was nothing there for anyone to hit," says Lead Visual Effects Artist Spencer Knapp. "Knowing in advance that we were going to be using Gray's body as a collision object, I wanted to make sure that Gray traveled through the pane of glass at the same rate that the glass broke. The animation was done so that he smashes the butt of his gun and his knee through the glass first."

Now that Knapp had his virtual stuntman, the next step was creating the ill-fated window. "Once the animation was done, we asked Sets and Props to create a clean pane of glass. He shoots the glass four times with his rifle. So we had a pane of glass with one bullet hole, one with two bullet holes, three bullet holes, and four bullet holes. Each time he shot the glass, we'd switch from one model to the next giving the illusion of him putting bullet holes in it."

Then came the big hit—when Gray jumped through the pane of glass.

"We took the model from Sets and Props that had all the puzzle pieces of glass and turned those into active rigid bodies. We turned Gray into a passive rigid body. We basically told the computer that we want these objects to collide with each other and it figured out all the appropriate rotational values for the difference in velocity between the pieces of glass. Glass that he broke with his gun would have different velocities than pieces that hit his chest. They would have less acceleration. So you'll see two regions—where his knee and the barrel of the gun are—where glass is really flying out. The remaining glass gets pushed out with less velocity."

According to Knapp, VFX did not cheat by adding particles of glass to this scene. Watch the collision carefully, and you should be able to see that the pieces will fit together to create a single pane of glass. But working with a single pane of glass and real collision physics led to its own wacky problem.

"If we just use Gray as a collision object, we would have ended up with a lot of pieces of glass that are still sitting in the window, kind of like the outline Daffy Duck leaves when he's crashing through glass. It looks really 'cartoony.' The model did not have the illusion of surface tension that real glass has. Real glass bows out before it breaks."

"The software doesn't quite work that way. You have control over physical properties of the glass, but it doesn't take into account these adjacent pieces of glass all being from a single pane. The model is a clean sheet when it's unbroken because all of the pieces don't reveal themselves until he actually hits it. Once he hits the piece, on the first frame where he hits the barrel of the gun to the glass, we swap that model out again and then you can start to see all the broken pieces."

S C R I P T

It should be noted that this script is not the final draft, therefore what is written here may have changed at the time of the movie's release.

FINAL FANTASY: THE SPIRITS WITHIN
Editorial Script

1   EXT. AN ALIEN LANDSCAPE—DREAM [DRA]

A scarred and barren wasteland. Two suns and a moon shine through the thick dusty sky. AKI is standing here, as if waiting for something.

AKI'S POV Eerily overturned rocks form a jagged horizon in the distance. AKI watches as if expecting to see something. There is nothing there.

AKI waits. Then she hears a faint sound far in the distance. It gradually grows louder. The rumbling of something big approaching.

AKI'S POV It draws closer. AKI feels the impact of the rumbling. The horizon itself seems to shake as the rumbling grows louder—deafening.

AKI stares transfixed at the horizon.

2.   INT. BLACK BOA—DAY [BOA]

AKI wakes, [W1 AKI] short of breath. Looking as if she had seen a nightmare.

AKI blinks a few times. She reaches for the holographic control panel floating before her. Running her fingers over the controls, the holograph display reads "DREAM FILE SAVED" "12/13/2065."

The hologram disappears. The scanning device retracts into its housing. With a click her chair's magnetic connectors deactivate. AKI floats up out of the chair, she is in a zero-grav state.

AKI pushes away from the chair with her legs, floating across a high-tech laboratory. She grabs a handhold at the window, and stares out at the blue earth.

> 1. AKI (V.O.) [PENDING]
>
> The dream is always the same. I'm standing, waiting for something. It's over the horizon—coming for me—and then it's over. If the council knew about these dreams, they'd shut our research down. But I need to know what the dreams mean. I think the answer may lie down there. The question is will I be in time to save the earth.

3.   EXT. SPACE—BLACK BOA—DAY [BBB]

The space shuttle Black Boa orbits above the Atlantic toward North America.

The Black Boa slowly descends. Flames engulf its hull as it enters the atmosphere.

4.   EXT. N.Y. TIMES SQUARE—NIGHT [AAA]

Times Square is enveloped in darkness. Crumbling buildings loom over scattered piles of burnt cars. The scene looks like the aftermath of a World War. There is no trace of life anywhere.

The Boa's light shines through the array of run down buildings.

Dust and debris are churned upward as the Black Boa lands.

A passenger lift descends from the hatch. AKI steps on to it and is lowered down. A gun hangs from her hip. She turns on the scanner over her left eye, it beeps in response, the lens begins to move.

AKI'S POV Everything is still. A world immersed in darkness.

AKI raises her pistol and fires into the air. A flare arches over Times Square bathing the city in an eerie glow. Sparks of light float to the ground like snowflakes.

AKI'S POV The scanner shows no life forms in the area.

> 2. AKI
>
> Where are you?

She lowers her gun and turns on a bracelet scanner. The compass' beacon light on the inner side of the bracelet begins to blink and beep at fixed intervals.

> INSERT—HOLOGRAPH DISPLAY
>
> which reads "SCANNING FOR SIXTH SPIRIT"

She points the scanner in one direction, then another. The beeps intensify. AKI raises her gun with both hands and starts off. (She continues to monitor the compass on her left arm.)

AKI walks through the ruins. There is no other sound but the beeping.

AKI'S POV She searches piles of stone and metal, but finds nothing. The sound of beeping. Lifting the gun over her head, AKI fires again sending sparks arching over the square. But now...

Barely visible in the darkness, faint outlines of some life form react to the flare sparks.

AKI'S POV Something in the darkness moves, like animals emerging from their hiding places. Grossly asymmetric creatures, translucent, with enormous heads and tentacle arms. They are strange ghost-like apparitions—Phantoms.

AKI'S POV As she turns, she sees the last sparks from the flare outline Phantoms standing between her and Black Boa. There are almost a dozen of them.

AKI suddenly looks afraid, she slowly begins to back up. As she does, she scans the area around her. Something is lurking everywhere.

She turns back around again and takes off running. Checking her scanner once again, she darts through the ruins in search of her target.

Trapped in the ruins, AKI finds herself alone in a deadly situation. A phantom appears out of the alleyway AKI tried to enter. Backing up, she hears a rumbling noise above and turns her attention to it.

6.   EXT. TROOP TRANSPORT—NIGHT

The DEEP EYES hang from the bottom of the troop transport high above the city. One-by-one they descend through the buildings to the street below. On their way down, they launch their gel pacs.

7.   EXT. N.Y. TIMES SQUARE—NIGHT [AAB]

High-density gas pellets strike the ground in front of the bewildered AKI. Reacting like a liquid, the gas spreads forming a cushion throughout the area to break the DEEP EYES fall. After the soldiers have risen, that gel evaporates into the air.

The point Deep Eye suddenly fires and the others join in. Another Deep Eyes member fires towards the rear.

When the energy from the guns penetrates a Phantom, it diffuses inside it creating an electrical discharge making the Phantoms visible to the naked eye for an instant. This results in a structural breakdown causing them to vaporize into red sparks.

The LEADER of the DEEP EYES shouts.

> 3. LEADER
>
> This is a restricted area! Do not move!
>
> 3A. RYAN
>
> What's she doing here, Captain?
>
> 3B. LEADER
>
> I don't know, but we're getting her out.
>
> 3C. LEADER
>
> You're coming with us.

AKI notices another phantom.

> 4. AKI
>
> Behind you!

The Deep Eyes blast that phantom to pieces. She bolts toward a crumbling building.

> 5. LEADER
>
> HALT! I said HALT!
>
> 6. LEADER
>
> Dammit! Let's move, people!
>
> 6A. RYAN
>
> Two coming through the east wall!
>
> 6B-1. NEIL
>
> Sarge, hold your fire. Those tanks are flammable

The Deep Eyes run after AKI. (Keep spotlight and roar of the overhead transport until this point.)

8.   INT. RUINED BUILDING—NIGHT

(The roar of the transport is goin, all is silent.)

Ryan notices something.

RYAN'S POV We see two very ugly phantoms.

Cut back to CU of Ryan.

Ryan fires at them, hitting the phantoms along with accidentally hitting a combustible oil barrel. It explodes.

> 6B. RYAN
>
> (grunt)
>
> 6E. NEIL
>
> Oumph!

As Neil runs up behind Ryan...

> 6D. LEADER
>
> Ryan, Neil, let's go.

AKI points the scanner around the hollow interior of what used to be a building. The beeping intensifies. Suddenly, the DEEP EYES leader catches her, yanking her arm.

> 7. LEADER
>
> Just what the hell do you think you're doing?
>
> 8. AKI
>
> (desperately)
>
> There's a life form in here!
>
> 9. LEADER
>
> There hasn't been life here in years.
>
> 10. AKI
>
> But there is now.
>
> 11. LEADER
>
> Life form or not, I'm taking you in.
>
> 12. AKI
>
> Fine. Take me, I don't care. But not until I extract this life form!

AKI pulls away from the Leader's grip and leaves.

> 12A. RYAN
>
> It's gonna be one of those days.

AKI continues into the building. The Deep Eyes watch her in disbelief, then follow her.

AKI follows the beeping through the rubble. The LEADER follows, shining the lift from his armor on the path ahead of her.

AKI'S POV Her gaze searches down from the top of a fountain and she fixes upon something small at the base.

> 12B-1. JANE
>
> Captain, the transport is not going to wait for us much longer.

12B-2. LEADER

I understand that.

AKI sees something. Judging from her expression, it is something wonderful. She kneels. The Deep Eyes shine light from behind her.

CLOSE UP of a weed growing up from a crack in the floor.

The scanner stops beeping.

12B-3. AKI

It's in bad shape.

13. RYAN

Oh, please... Tell me we're not risking our necks for this plant!

14. JANE

I wouldn't even call it a plant. It's a weed.

15. NEIL

I wouldn't even call it a weed.

15A. AKI

I need a minute to extract it.

15C. NEIL

Miss... That's a minute we do not have.

15B. RYAN

I'm afraid he's right about that ma'am.

Neil looks around.

NEIL'S POV—SCANNER IMAGE. The CAMERA ZOOMS IN through several walls to FOCUS on several Phantoms passing through the walls approaching this way. (scanners have a zoom function)

AKI carefully lifts the plant out of the ground. The other three DEEP EYES walk over to the LEADER.

16. NEIL

Phantoms. We have incoming.

The DEEP EYES get into position.

16A. RYAN

(worried)

Uh, Captain, we need to get moving.

16E. LEADER

Understood, Sergeant.

16C. JANE

We've got a lot of phantoms here.

AKI carefully places the plant in a container. Gunfire illuminates the area.

16D. RYAN

We need to get outta here.

16A-1. RYAN

Could you hurry please miss.

16C-1. AKI

Done.

16F. NEIL

Capain...

16G. LEADER

Yes, Neil.

16H. NEIL

... just so you know, I agree with the let's get outta here thing.

The Deep Eyes have their backs to the fountain when a Phantom rises out of it in front of Aki. Noticing, the Leader steps in, aims...

16I. LEADER

Duly noted.

... and fires, destroying it.

The fountain also breaks into pieces as the phantom is destroyed.

17. JANE

Can I have this please? Thank you.

Jane reaches over to Aki and grabs one of the flare guns attached to Aki's waist. She jams it into her rifle and fires. She fires the flare gun at the floor. It bounces off the floor and phantoms, now visible, slowly close in on the group.

17A. RYAN

I hate to say 'I told you so'...

(Aki gasps)

The DEEP EYES look for a way out.

18. AKI

We're surrounded!

19. JANE

No shit!

19A. LEADER

(breath)

Alright everybody. Just relax.

Suddenly! A light glares down upon the group. They all look up at what is left of the building's ceiling.

19B. JANE

Captain, we gotta get to higher ground.

They move toward a staircase, firing at phantoms, which continue to emerge as they move. The leader protects the rear.

20. LEADER

(looking up at the stairs)

Go, go, go!

Everyone is up the stairs. The Leader notices phantoms through his scope. The others finish climbing a rubble pile, but the Leader is still at the base.

20A. NEIL

Up here!

The Leader proceeds to climb the pile when a phantom emerges in his way. He blasts it away. The rubble pile begins to crumble and he is thrown backward, and drops his weapon.

22. JANE

Captain!

21. RYAN

They're right behind you!

22E. JANE

Captain, come on!

21A. RYAN

You can make it, keep moving Captain!

The Leader climbs, but his foot slips just one more step before the top. Jane grabs his hand just in time and pulls him up.

22A. JANE

I've got you...

22B. JANE

You okay?

22C. LEADER

Yeah.

22D. NEIL

All right everybody. Here they come.

The DEEP EYES open fire on the ascending phantoms. Escape lines extend down from the transport. The DEEP EYES attach the hooks to their armor. The LEADER holds AKI and they barely manage to rise through the phantom tentacles up into the transport.

They disappear inside and the transport flies off into the darkness.

9   INT TROOP TRANSPORT—NIGHT [UNV]

The three DEEP EYES sit across from each other. AKI is in the front. One sits next to AKI. The LEADER sits in the seat furthest away and diagonal from her.

The DEEP EYES remove their helmets. The LEADER does not remove his helmet.

AKI looks at her rescuers RYAN and JANE. Their faces look vulnerably human in contrast to the cold metallic helmets. They watch AKI. She looks a bit shaken.

24A. RYAN

You okay?

Aki shoots an awkward look and faint smile in Ryan's direction.

24B. RYAN

You're gonna be alright.

25. LEADER

Can you give me one good reason why I shouldn't arrest you?

Aki stiffens, facing down the armored LEADER.

26. AKI

I am Doctor Aki Ross. I have clearance to be here.

27. LEADER

Not unlimited clearance, and not without authorization.

27A. AKI

Listen Captain, I don't have time for this.

27B. LEADER

Do you realize you've just risked the lives of my squad and me?

AKI steps to the counter, and checks the readings on the plant's container using her bracelet.

28. AKI

(interrupts him)

Look, I don't want to talk about it. The fact of the matter is, it was worth the lives of you and your men!

An awkward silence as RYAN, JANE, and NEIL look at each other.

28A. JANE

(under her breath)

You and your men?

29. RYAN

She thinks you're a man.

29A. JANE

I think she's an idiot.

30. NEIL

I know you're not a man.

31. RYAN

I think you're an idiot too.

32. LEADER

(to AKI)

Well, I do wanna talk about it. Did it ever occur to you that maybe we would have volunteered to risk our lives. Had we been given a choice?!

-8-

---

33. AKI

Well nobody asked you to save me!

34. LEADER

I don't believe this. You have not changed a bit

AKI turns to the LEADER. The LEADER removes his helmet, revealing that he is GRAY.

36. AKI

(surprised)

Gray?

AKI looks like she doesn't know what to say.

GRAY looks down placing his helmet on his lap. He looks back up at AKI.

37. GRAY

Yeah. Nice to see you too.

10   EXT. BARRIER CITY—NIGHT [TCB]

The transport flies toward the barrier city which is visible in the distance. The barrier covering old New York sparkles in the night. The transport flies around the exterior of the barrier and descends onto the airport runway.

11   INT. SCANNING CHAMBER—NIGHT [SCN]

AKI and the DEEP EYES step into a high-tech chamber looking like a cross between a hospital and an airlock. A technician monitors them from the other side of the glass.

38. TECHNICIAN

Welcome back, Captain.

GRAY nods. He appears upset having AKI next to him.

39. GRAY

We're clean.

The technician smiles back, but his tone is stern.

40. TECHNICIAN

Let's make sure of that, shall we?

[W2 RYAN, JANE, NEIL]

RYAN, JANE, and NEIL grumble in unison, until GRAY turns around.

40A. NEIL

I hate gettin' scanned.

41. RYAN

These scanners are probably worse for us than the Phantoms.

42. NEIL

No probably about it, Captain. These machines are suspected of causing sterility and I wanna have a little Neil Jr. calling me 'Daddy' someday.

42A. JANE

That's a spooky thought.

42B. NEIL

Why are you always bustin' my chops?

43. GRAY

People, let's just do this thing, all right?

44. DEEP EYES

Yes, sir!

RYAN steps onto the platform and is scanned. His spirit appears on screen on the other side of the glass, like a heat wave, only blue. The technician watches.

45. TECHNICIAN

Ok... Next.

RYAN steps off, looking bored. JANE steps on next.

-6-

SCRIPT

46. NEIL

Looks like you've gained some weight.

47. JANE

It's called upper body strength, Neil. Get a girlfriend.

48. NEIL

I'm working on it.

AKI watches the procedure nervously. She turns to GRAY, who tries to ignore her.

49. AKI

You know, my security rating allows me to bypass this.

GRAY frowns a little. He doesn't look directly at AKI.

51. GRAY

Not today it doesn't.

The technician examines JANE'S spirit and nods. JANE steps off. NEIL steps on. The technician examines NEIL'S spirit and nods.

Jane and Ryan stand in the room outside of the scanning chamber.

52. JANE

Something's not right.

53. RYAN

About this mission, or that woman?

54. JANE

Both.

50. TECHNICIAN

Next.

GRAY moves toward the platform but AKI stops him.

55. AKI

Listen, Captain I think we...

GRAY steps onto the platform.

56. GRAY
(interrupting)

I don't care what you think, Doctor.
You're getting scanned just like everybody else.

An alarm sounds. Startled, Aki looks at the Technician's holograph. GRAY looks around in disbelief. The other DEEP EYES run up to the glass. On the other side of the glass GRAY'S spirit shows infestation.

Before GRAY realizes what is happening, a cylinder drops from the ceiling surrounding him. (The cylinder functions to both restrain him and monitor him.) GRAY places his hands against the inside of the cylinder.

57. RYAN

Ah, shit!

57A. JANE

Captain!

57B. NEIL

They got him!

58. GRAY
(suddenly worried)

There must be a mistake—

59. TECHNICIAN

You came in contact with a Phantom, sir. Please remain calm. Administering treatment shield.

AKI steps up to the glass, looking at the data.

60. AKI

What level is he?

–7–

61. TECHNICIAN

Blue. It'll be code red in three-and-a-half minutes.

AKI intensely examines the room and notices something in the back.

62. AKI

We have to treat him now.

63. TECHNICIAN

I'm sorry, but that's impossible. We'll transfer him to the Treatment Center.

Ignoring him, AKI turns to the other DEEP EYES.

64. AKI
(interrupting)

There's no time for that.

The DEEP EYES hesitate for a moment, then rush to the cylinder holding GRAY. AKI runs to the wall and pulls a lever. The cylinder rises toward the ceiling.

The DEEP EYES help GRAY over and onto the operating table. AKI operates the holograph controls on the side of the table.

65. GRAY

Aki, there's something I need to say.

AKI puts the anesthesia gun to his neck.

66. AKI
(calmly)

Don't try to speak.

She injects the anesthesia. GRAY closes his eyes.

AKI activates the operating table. The DEEP EYES stand aside looking worriedly at their Captain.

A holograph of GRAY'S body is visible. That holo then disappears and in its place, one area of his blue spirit is shown on a spherical holo. Inside, it is infested with what looks like a red tentacle.

INSERT—HOLOGRAPH DISPLAY

which reads "PHANTOM PARTICLES."

The infested area is magnified on the holograph. Tentacles writhe grotesquely turning the blue particles around them red. They gradually spread.

67. NEIL

Jesus, look at that thing.

68. AKI

How much more time?

INSERT—HOLOGRAPH DISPLAY

which reads 2 minutes 50 seconds.

69. TECHNICIAN (SPEAKER)

Not enough. When he reaches code red, the treatment shield won't be able to hold the alien particles.

The holograph displays the time remaining until code red.
The DEEP EYES look at the display. Less than 3 minutes remaining.

AKI activates the laser scalpel. It beams down onto GRAY'S chest. The holograph shows the Phantom particles being burnt out by the laser beam.

The holograph display. One remaining tentacle disappears. AKI waits for it to settle, glancing at the display.

A sign appears indicating that one piece has been missed.

70. RYAN

What's going on?

71. JANE
(to AKI)

Where'd it go?

71A. RYAN

What the hell is going on?!?

AKI generates another holograph and chases the last remaining phantom fragment.
GRAY'S eyes roll back into his head and he lapses into convulsions.

–8–

71B. TECHNICIAN

We've lost contact. Infestation is moving deeper.

71C. AKI

Tracking...

71D. TECHNICIAN

There's no time.

71E. AKI

Tracking...

71F. TECHNICIAN

There's no time! You're gonna lose him.

GRAY'S spirit writhes in agony on the display. Twisting as if insane, the holo shows his spirit contort and wrench into a picture of terror.

72. TECHNICIAN (SPEAKER)

His treatment shield is falling!

72A. AKI

Found it!

73. RYAN
(growling)

Come onnn!

The DEEP EYES watch AKI work. She calmly continues her search and ...

AKI burns out the last particle. At that very instant, the clock strikes zero.

A disappointed RYAN. NEIL taps him on the shoulder an he turns toward AKI.

AKI'S expression.

GRAY regains consciousness. He slowly opens his eyes.

GRAY'S POV A distorted image turns clear.

RYAN is looking down at him and helps GRAY to slowly sit up. GRAY cannot stop shaking.

AKI looks at GRAY calmly. Her expression changes, looking as if she wants to comfort him, but she regains her composure.

75. AKI

It's alright...

Aki looks as if she is holding something back.

77. AKI

...don't worry. You'll be back to normal in no time.

AKI picks up the plant container and begins to leave the room.

78. TECHNICIAN
(interrupting)

Ah, we need to scan you for infestation.

AKI hesitates toward the technician.

We HEAR the sound of a door opening. A man speaks.

79. MALE VOICE (SID)

That won't be necessary. I'll take responsibility.

AKI turns in his direction. SID and AKI look at each other. Her hand instinctively reaches for the container hanging from her waist containing the plant. She is sending SID a message.

The DEEP EYES look at AKI gratefully.

80. RYAN

Hey doc...
(pause)
...thanks for saving him.

AKI nods in acknowledgment, but says nothing. She follows Dr. SID out of the room.

522B. SID

Are you alright?

–9–

80. AKI

The military's impounded my ship.

The DEEP EYES watch them leave the room. There is silence for a moment.

81. JANE

What's with her?

82. RYAN

What's with her and the Captain?

83. NEIL

What's with her and that stupid plant?

Jane and Ryan walk up behind Neil as they continue to follow Aki's movements off camera. Jane and Ryan look at Neil. Neil looks back at Ryan and Jane.

83A. NEIL

What?

12 **INT. SPIRIT RESEARCH FACILITY—SID'S LAB—NIGHT [SLA]**

The CAMERA FOLLOWS the small plant discovered in the ruined building. It is put into a machine and analyzed.

AKI and Dr. SID monitor the data expectantly.

Dr. SID instructs his aides.

84. SID

Forward me the Phantom data and everything regarding the five spirits collected so far.

84A. AIDE (FEMALE)

Yes, Doctor.

85. AKI

Spirits? I thought we weren't supposed to use the 'S' word?

86. SID
(laughs)

Don't get smart with me.
(Aki giggles)
Now let's see if that plant does the trick.

Five energy fields combine. The spiritual energy extracted from the plant is added to this. They work intensely.

SID operates the holograph console merging the plant's energy wave with those extracted from the other five spirits.

AKI watches the plant's wave merge with the others forming a near perfect opposite of a Phantom wave. Nearly, but not quite complete.

AKI watches Dr. SID expectantly. No longer able to wait.

88. AKI

It's a match! We've found it.

89. SID

Yes. The sixth spirit.

AKI looks pleased for the first time.

90. SID

Your little scene today broke nearly every protocol.

She walks over to the plant. SID follows her. AKI lifts the pod housing the plant out of the machine with the greatest of care.

91. AKI
(as she moves plant)

How long do you think this would have survived outside the barrier?

92. SID

Aki, you know there are elements in the council and military just waiting for an excuse to shut us down.

93. AKI
(as she continues working)

Look, twenty years ago, who discovered this energy in the phantom? You. And who proved the same energy source existed in humand and every life form? You.
(stops working, looks at Sid)
You made it possible to harness that energy for ovo-pacs, scanners, even the barrier, the council knows that. They trust you. Doctor, we're so close to proving it...

95. SID

We still need...
(pointing on the holograph)
...this part and this one here.

96. AKI

Exactly! Two more pieces and we've solved the puzzle.

SID nods.

96A. SID

And we need to be free to find those pieces. I want to show you something, Aki.

He hands her a small, linen bound book. She studies it.

96B. AKI

What is this?

She opens to a page marked by a dried leaf.

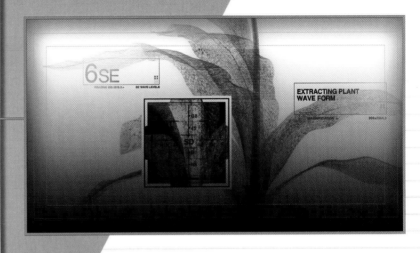

EXTRACTING PLANT WAVE FORM

6SE

—10—

96C. SID

Read.

96D. AKI

"All life is born of Gaia and each life has a spirit. Each new spirit is housed in a physical body"- Doctor...

96E. SID

Go on.

96F. AKI

Through their experiences on Earth, each spirit matures and grows. When the physical body dies, the mature spirit enriched by it's life on earth, returns to Gaia, bringing with it the experiences—enabling Gaia to live and grow.

96G. SID

It's my old diary. I wrote that forty-three years ago when I was the age you are now.

He burns the book.

96H. AKI

Doctor Sid!

96I. SID

Remember what happened to Galileo? They threw him in jail because he said the Earth was not the center of the universe. That could happen to us. Our ideas are unpopular, Aki. If you have any notes or records that could be used against you, destroy them. Keep them up here.

Sid points to his head.

99B. AKI

"Right."

Aki starts to leave.

99A. SID

And stay away from your friend, the Captain.

She stops, looks at Sid with an 'Excuse me?' look.

100. SID
(sing-songy)

He saves your life—you save his life, this leads to that... I was young once, too, you know.

101. AKI

Doctor, there is a war going on.

Aki turns and walks out the door.

102. AKI (CONT'D.)

No one's young anymore.

13 **EXT. ALIEN LANDSCAPE—DREAM [DRB]**

A scarred and barren wasteland. Through the thick dusty sky, two suns and a moon shine. AKI stands here, as if waiting for something.

AKI'S POV Eerily overturned rocks form a jagged horizon in the distnce. AKI watches as if expecting to see something.

AKI feels the impact of the rumbling. It draws closer. The horizon itself seems to shake as the rumbling grows louder—deafening.

An alien army charges over the horizon toward the solitary AKI. Hundreds of screaming Phantoms.

AKI hears another sound. Another rumbling. Turning to the opposite horizon, she sees a second Phantom army hurling itself toward the first.

AKI stands between the two attacking alien armies. The screaming is unearthly. AKI is terrified.

The two armies collide in battle...

14 **INT. SLEEP CHAMBER—MORING [ASC]**

AKI wakes from her nightmare. **[W3 AKI]** Panicked breathing.

103. HEIN

Ladies and gentlemen of the council...

15 **INT. COUNCIL HALL—DAY [CFR]**

103. HEIN (CONT'D)

... could you please explain why?!

HEIN stands up, shouting at the eight-member council of top-level government officials. The Space Station and earth are displayed on the holograph between HEIN and the other members.

104. HEIN

Zeus was completed a month ago. If we attack the meteor with this, we will eliminate the Phantoms at their source.

The holograph displays a beam fired from the Space Station. The beam blasts the meteor in the crater, eliminating it effortlessly.

One older member of the Assembly speaks.

105. COUNCIL MEMBER 1

General Hein calm down. At our last meeting we voted 6 to 2 to postpone using the Zeus cannon to attack the Leonid Meteor. We have reconvened today to vote on that very issue again.
(beat)
Now I'd like to ask the Director of the Bio-Etheric Center to speak. Dr. Sid, please.

SID sits a slight distance away from HEIN, facing the council. AKI is beside him.

—11—

SID stands and a holograph control panel appears 50cm above the table. (Automatically adjusting to SID'S height.) HEIN glares at it for an instant. AKI notices this, then sees GRAY sitting among the dozen or so military officers behind HEIN.
SID operates the controls projecting an image in the center. Phantoms are being spawned from the meteor.

106. SID
(clears throat)
Thank you. As you all know, the Phantoms' nest is in the Leonid Meteor that landed here thirty-four years ago.
A 2D image is superimposed on top of the holograph.

107A. SID
What you see now are the records of every assault on the meteor to date. Physical attacks have had utterly no effect.
Images of the meteor being bombed. Finally, a 2D image of a nuclear attack is displayed.

108A SID (CONT'D.)
This scene took place three months ago during a full-scale bombardment.
A missile is fired from a remote base. Concentrated fire from a Bio-Etheric beam.
The Phantoms are destroyed one after another.
HEIN smiles.

109. SID (CONT.)
Now, please note, the Phantoms outside the meteor are indeed destroyed. However, inside many that were dormant come to life and, as you see, overall phantom density remains the same. The newly risen aliens respond to the attacks by burrowing even deeper into the Earth.
An attack begins from above. Images of phantoms being destroyed and of those burying themselves deeper into the earth.

109A. COUNCIL MEMBER 2
Now this is very interesting to me Doctor Sid, because we see the same thing during surgery when using Bio-Etheric lasers on Phantom particles, do we not?

110. SID
Yes, indeed we do! You see, the injured particles escape, burying or digging themselves deeper into a patient's body. And when we increase the laser power to destroy these deeper particles, we have had incidents resulting in further injury to a patient and in some cases, death.
Inside the meteor, a group of Phantom particles head toward Gaia. Then, a powerful beam from a bomber overhead violently pierces through the earth injuring the Gaia.

111. COUNCIL MEMBER 1
And what exactly does that mean, Doctor?

112. SID
It means there's a very good chance the beam from the Zeus cannon will burn the Phantoms in the meteor.

112A. HEIN
Exactly! Thank you.

112B. SID
Now, however, it also means that the beam energy may be too strong, injuring the earth.

113. COUNCIL MEMBER 2
Injure the earth? You mean the Gaia?

114B. SID
I mean...

114A. COUNCIL MEMBER 2
You mean the spirit of the earth.

114. SID
Yes. The spirit of the earth.
The room stirs a rather large flurry. Council members cock their heads. **[W4 AUDIENCE] Vocal hubbub.** HEIN sees this as the COUNCIL MEMBER asks for order to be restored.

114D. AKI
(emphatic whisper to Doctor Sid)
What are you doing?

114E. SID
I know what I'm doing and whatever you do, keep your mouth shut!

115. HEIN
(snickers)
This is ridiculous! Doctor, with all due respect, did ou come here just to talk about some Gaia theory? To tell us that the planet is... alive? That it has a... spirit? That's a fairy tale Doctor, and I'm sorry, but we don't have time for that.

116. SID
It is not a fairy tale. It is true.
Forming his hand like a gun, HEIN points to the floor.

117. HEIN
Ah, oh, so if I point a gun at the earth and fire, I'm not just making a hole in the ground, I'm killing the planet?
Many of the **[W5 AUDIENCE] audience members laugh while others voice pleas for respect and order.** COUNCIL MEMBER 1 again asks for order.

118. COUNCIL MEMBER 1
Dr. Sid, the Gaia theory has not been proven.

119. COUNCIL MEMBER 2 (FEMALE)
Even if Gaia does exist, won't we still have to remove the Phantoms? I think if there is any chance of success we should take it, don't you agree?

120. SID
Well, uh, of course I do, but there is an alternative to the space cannon.

121. COUNCIL MEMBER 2

—12—

Another method?

122. SID
Yes. A means of disabling the phantoms.

122A. COUNCIL MEMBER 2
Please.
SID displays the holograph he and AKI examined in the lab.

123. SID (CONT.)
Ah, as we know, the aliens display a distinct energy pattern. Now it is a fact that two opposing bio-etheric waves placed one over the other will cancel each other out. It is theoretically possible to construct a wave pattern in direct opposition to the phantom energy.

123. SID
We are currently...

123C. HEIN
...Doctor...

123. SID (CONT.)
...assembling such a wave and are nearing completion.
The Phantom particles on the holograph disappear.

124. HEIN
(beat)
Members of the council, gathering plants and animals from around the world to fight the Phantoms is utter nonsense.
The 'Zeus Cannon' is a proven, effective weapon, it will kill Phantoms. Can we afford to wait for some crazy invention, some army of touch-feely plants and animals. An invention that offers no solid evidence that it will destroy the aliens?
AKI rises from her chair.

126. AKI
There is evidence!
SID tries to stop her, but AKI continues.

127. AKI
Our partially completed energy wave has successfully stopped Phantom particles from spreading through a terminally-infected patient.
[W6 AUDIENCE] The entire hall is stunned. It is a moment before the council quiets down.

128. COUNCIL MEMBER 1
Doctor, do you claim to have evidence that a terminal patient has been cured?

129. AKI
Not cured. The wave is not complete. But we've succeeded in containing the particles safely inside the patient.
[W7 AUDIENCE] Another commotion.

130. HEIN
Aah, my... Where is the proof?

131. AKI
Here!
Opening her tunic, AKI reveals her chest encased in a strange metallic device. General HEIN looks at her repulsed. In the back of the room, GRAY looks shocked. AKI pushes a switch on the device displaying the Phantom particles inside of her on a holograph.
Something grotesque is writhing. (Shoot it wide enough so we can't tell what it is.)
AKI operates the holograph controls and adjusts the desk controls.
The image in the center of the conference room is magnified.
Her body is full of writhing Phantom infestation.
Everyone stares in stunned silence.
In the midst of the others, GRAY keeps his composure and looks at AKI.

15A INT. COUNCIL HALL—HALLWAY
[W8 AUDIENCE] Council Hall noises are heard in the background.
SID and AKI walk quickly down a hallway away from the Council Meeting Hall. Arguing can still be heard. SID is in front of AKI. AKI calls after him.

131K. SID
You may have bought us some time, Aki, but I wonder—at what cost?

131L. AKI
Doctor, I can't keep hiding in the background while you protect me. I want what life I have left to mean something.
Sid stops and looks at her deeply and directly.

131H. SID
You listen to me. When we find the seventh and eighth spirits...

131I. AKI
If we find them. What we need now is some luck.

131J. SID
Luck has nothing to do with it.
(he begins walking again)
Faith and hard work, girl. 'Cause I'll be damned if you're going to die before me!

—13—

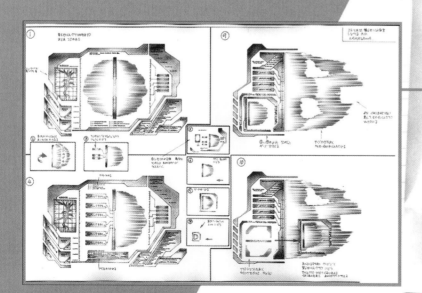

15B   EXT. BARRIER GONDOLA—NIGHT [GON]

Establishing exterior shot.

16   INT. BARRIER GONDOLA—NIGHT

The interior looks like a cable car filled with beeping and blinking high-tech equipment. AKI enters with another device, sets it in place, and turns it on.

GRAY comes to the doorway as AKI works the device.

132. GRAY

The council decided to postpone firing the Zeus Cannon.

AKI turns, but doesn't look at GRAY. She continues operating the panel.

133. AKI

I guess I put on a good show.

GRAY looks around inside, he glances at AKI.

134. GRAY

Mind if I tag along?

135. AKI

You'll probably get bored.

GRAY steps on as the doors slide shut. The cabin shakes slightly.

17   EXT. BARRIER GONDOLA—NIGHT

The gondola leaves the platform moving up toward the barrier covering New York. (They RISE INTO FRAME. The CAMERA FOLLOWS them for the rest of the shot.)

18   INT. BARRIER GONDOLA—NIGHT

AKI busily moves about in the device-packed room not even noticing GRAY. She doesn't even try to step around him.

136. GRAY

So, what are you doing?

AKI almost bumps into GRAY. They are so close they nearly touch. GRAY looks glad AKI is near. AKI doesn't answer his questions. GRAY follows her, peaking at a device over her shoulder.

138. GRAY

Oh, I see, you are giving me the silent treatment.

AKI goes about her business.

She sighs and standing up bumps right into GRAY. It takes her a moment to recover. GRAY does not move out of her way.

139. AKI

I'm scanning the city for the seventh spirit.

She moves past him to the other side of the gondola.

19   EXT. BARRIER GONDOLA—NIGHT

The gondola is high above the city. The view is tremendous. The Bio-Etheric energy from sprinklers attached to the supporting pillars of the barrier behind them glows orange. This barrier protects the city from the Phantoms, bathing it in eternal twilight.

21   EXT. GONDOLA PLATFORM—NIGHT

A simple scanner like the one AKI was wearing in Times Square. RYAN is wearing it as he looks up at the maintenance gondola diagonally above him.

RYAN adjusts the scanner.

RYAN'S POV. AKI and GRAY'S spirits in the gondola.

JANE discovers RYAN and NEIL. NEIL fiddles with the wiring in the control panel.

139A. RYAN

Hurry up, Neil.

139B. NEIL

Relax Sarge. I've almost got it.

141. JANE
(to NEIL)

What do you think you're doing?

142. NEIL

We're just gonna strand 'em for a while. Hey, don't look at me, it was his idea.

143. JANE

This was your idea?

144. RYAN

We're just helping the Captain out a little.

145. NEIL

Yeah, come on Jane, where's your sense of romance?

146. RYAN

You've seen how the Captain looks at her.

Sparks fly from the wires NEIL is fooling with. The gondola comes to a halt.

147. NEIL
(to JANE)

It's amore, baby!

22   INT. BARRIER GONDOLA—NIGHT

AKI checks the inside of the gondola.

148. AKI (O.S.)

What's going on?

149. GRAY

It's probably just a glitch.

GRAY watches AKI monitor the scanners. He thinks a bit.

149A. GRAY

Listen Aki...

149B. AKI

Ah, I'm still mad at you.

149C. GRAY

You're mad at me?

149D. AKI

Leaving your helmet on? Not telling me who you were? Th-that doesn't seem a little childish?

150. GRAY

Hey, well I was just a little upset when you just packed up and left for the Zeus Station without saying a word.

151. AKI

Well, now you know what was going on, all right?

152. GRAY

Yeah, now I know.

152A. AKI

My operation had to be done in zero-grav, okay?

152B. GRAY

Fine... and how about the fact that I was sent there on a job and you wouldn't even see me...

153. AKI

I was probably helping Doctor Sid collect spirit waves.

153A. GRAY

Well, now I know.

153B. AKI

So I'm sorry.

—15—

153C. GRAY

Well, me too! So... we're both sorry.

153D. AKI
(Sighs.)

153E. GRAY
(Sighs.)

154. GRAY

So... will you tell me about them?

155. AKI

About what?

156. GRAY

About the spirits you've collected.

For a moment, AKI doesn't know where to begin. She speaks in a calm voice, as if she were talking about the weather. She continues manipulating the device.

157. AKI

I was infected by a Phantom during an experiment. Normally, no one could have survived.

158. GRAY

How did you?

159. AKI

Dr. Sid created a membrane around the infection, keeping me alive. So the first spirit wave was me.

AKI gazes at the holograph display.

160. AKI

The second, was a fish.

161. GRAY

A fish?

GRAY nods, listening. AKI doesn't look at him.

162. AKI

The third was a deer I found in a wildlife preserve outside Moscow. The fourth was a bird.

164. AKI

Ever tried to track a sparrow from outer space? It's no fun... what am I saying? You probably would love that.

164A. GRAY

You're right, I probably would.

164B. AKI

And then there was that, um, plant I collected from Times Square.

165. GRAY

I thought that was number six?

166. AKI

What?

167. GRAY

You skipped one.

AKI looks up at GRAY for the first time.

168. AKI
(sigh)

The fifth was a little girl, dying in a hospital emergency room. I retrieved the sample in time but she, uh... I told her everything had a spirit. Dogs, cats, trees, little girls, even the Earth. I told her that she wasn't dying—just returning to the Earth's spirit, to Gaia.

AKI'S voice begins to tremble.

169. AKI (CONT.)

She told me that she was ready to die. She said I didn't have to make up stories to make her feel better.
(beat)
... Only seven years old, and ready to die.

GRAY tries to comfort AKI. He moves to put his hand on her shoulder.

—16—

170. GRAY
I'm sorry.

AKI quickly returns to her device, avoiding his touch.

171. AKI
I have work to do. I have to find the seventh and eighth spirits.

AKI stops working, unable to continue. GRAY extends his hand. AKI has her back to him, but senses his presence.

172. AKI
Don't, please...

GRAY moves his hand away, but remains next to her.

173. AKI
(accusingly)
You don't believe any of this, do you?

174. GRAY
You're asking me if I believe that all life, even the Earth itself, has a living spirit, and that we are all born from, and return to this Gaia? I just... don't know, Aki.

GRAY gently pulls her close.
Part of her chest plate is visible. GRAY runs his fingers over the metal, then her neck. Aki closes her eyes at his gentle touch.

179. GRAY
Is this why you shut me out? You should have told me.

182. AKI
I don't know how much time I have left.

183. GRAY
Who does?

GRAY moves in to kiss her. AKI hesitates.
Their lips almost meet... the gondola jolts.
Using this as an excuse, AKI returns to her research equipment.

184. AKI
Uh, I better get back to scanning.

23 EXT. BARRIER GONDOLA—NIGHT
The gondola moves high above the city skyline.

24 INT. A MILITARY OFFICE—DAY [MOA]
GRAY walks up to the desk and salutes. A somber MAJOR returns his salute. General HEIN stands off to the side looking out a window. The MAJOR clears his throat.

185. MAJOR
(clears throat)
Captain Edwards. You extracted a Doctor Ross from old New York several days ago, did you not?

186. GRAY
Yes, sir.

187. MAJOR
What were your impressions of Dr. Ross?

188. GRAY
She seemed very capable and determined, sir.

189. MAJOR
You and the Deep Eyes are being temporarily re-assigned. You will guard Dr. Ross when she re-enters the wasteland.

190. GRAY
Understood, sir.

191. HEIN (O.S.)
You don't understand yet, Captain.

192. HEIN
Report and aberrant behavior in Doctor Ross to the Major immediately.

193. GRAY
Aberrant behavior, sir?

HEIN turns around toward GRAY.

194. HEIN
The woman carries an alien infestation, Captain. We don't know what it may be doing to her. The alien presence could be affecting her judgement. They may be manipulating the Doctor for their very own purposes.

195. GRAY
Is the General suggesting that Dr. Ross is a spy?

195A. HEIN
(laughs)
The General is wondering why he's explaining himself to a Captain.

General HEIN squints. He looks GRAY over trying to determine his true motives. The MAJOR interjects.

196. MAJOR
She's had prolonged exposure to Phantom tissue. If this begins to manifest itself, in any way, Doctor Ross is to be placed under arrest and transported here for observation.

197. HEIN
(unconvincing)
It is in fact for her own good, Captain.

198. GRAY
Of course, sir.

They salute. GRAY turns and walks toward the door.

198A. HEIN
Major, send some of our men to keep an eye on the good Captain.

25 EXT. ALIEN LANDSCAPE—DREAM [DRC]
An alien army charges over the horizon toward the solitary AKI. Hundreds of screaming Phantoms.
Aki hears another sound. Another rumbling. Turning to the opposite horizon, she sees a second Phantom army hurling itself toward the first.
AKI is caught between two attacking alien armies.
The two armies collide, AKI finds herself in the midst of the battle. Unharmed, she watches the carnage unfold as they destroy one another.
Suddenly, the Phantoms stop fighting as if a pause button had been pushed. They all turn toward AKI.
AKI stands there confused. Then she hears an unearthly sound. The aliens are not staring at AKI... but behind her.
AKI turns and looks [W9 AKI] She screams.

27 EXT. BATTLEFIELD RUINS—DAY [BFW]
The landscape resembles her dreams—pock marked and ravaged. Shadows of twisted metal vehicles and ravaged tree trunks dot the horizon.
A transport ship races through the battlefield.

200. AKI (V.O.)
I'm convinced that these dreams are some for of communication. The message still eludes me, but the dream is coming faster now and that can only mean one thing...

28 INT. TRANSPORT SHIP—DAY
AKI sits inside of the dark claustrophobic transport.

201. AKI (V.O.)
The Phantoms inside me are beginning to win.

GRAY and the DEEP EYES are in their armor with only their faces uncovered. GRAY turns to JANE who is seated in front of a holograph next to him. JANE operates the holograph controls; it responds to her commands.

202. JANE
Our target is 50 klicks west of Tucson.

-18-

NEIL is in the cockpit flying the transport. The cargo room is displayed on a very small holograph. Next to it, another small holograph displays JANE'S data.

203. NEIL
Roger.

The cargo room. Looking at the display, GRAY asks JANE.

204. GRAY
Phantom concentration?

JANE gives GRAY a sickly look. GRAY nods. AKI sits next to GRAY, waiting for the word. GRAY stares straight ahead.

205. JANE
Not good. We've got big meta's everywhere.

206. RYAN
So it's gonna be a real picnic.

207A. GRAY
Basic fire ineffective. Build up your charges and make them count.

GRAY turns and looks at her. He tries to smile.

208. GRAY (CONT'D)
Stick close to me. No heroics today, OK? Everything by the book.

AKI nods, a slight teasing smile floats to her lips.

209. AKI
By the book. Right.

A rough map of their destination appears on the screen with a blip in the center. JANE manipulates the controls. She points out locations on the screen to GRAY.

215. JANE
If we drop energy buoys here, here, and here... we should be able to land, acquire the target, and get out before the Phantoms even know we were there.

216. AKI
... and the buoys will attract the Phantoms?

217. JANE
Yeah.

Short pause.

218. GRAY
For a while.

RYAN sits between THREE NEW SOLDIERS wearing full-masks.

210. RYAN
So, you're from the 307s, right? Under General Hein? Yo man. Ever done any wasteland re-con before? It can get pretty ugly.

The soldiers remain silent. Aki is sitting. Silence. The soldiers just sit there.

29 EXT. BATTLEFIELD RUINS—DAY
The transport skims over the wasteland and drops an energy buoy. Turning abruptly, it drops another, and another. The buoys strike the ground and transform, revealing the ovo cells inside them through the glass.
A snake-like phantom approaches the buoy.

30 INT. TRANSPORT SHIP—DAY
NEIL pilots the ship skimming over the landscape.

31 EXT. TRANSPORT SHIP—DAY
The transport lands in the middle of what once must have been a fearsome battle. Tanks and air ships litter the land, making it a twisted metal graveyard. Bodies are everywhere.
The transport lands and everyone emerges down out of the hatch.

-19-

EXT. BATTLEFIELD RUINS—DAY

Everyone begins to walk. **Breathing noises for everyone.** AKI turns around and gazes at the swarm of phantoms now rendered visible by the ovo buoy. [W10]

220A. GRAY

Looks like they've taken the bait.

The Phantom approaches the buoy spewing energy into the air. In the distance, more Phantoms of different shapes appear. They all converge on the buoys.

Mixed among the Phantoms are smaller animal-shaped Phantoms. Together they look like countless whales and dolphins jumping up in a vast ocean.

GRAY raises his arm, signals, and they move out.

AKI is on point. GRAY is immediately after her. The others fall in behind. She follows the beeping of her scanner as she proceeds.

221. AKI

The seventh spirit should be just beyond that line of wreckage.

222. GRAY

I don't see how any living thing could survive out here.

223. AKI

We'll find out soon enough.

They cross the rough landscape, carefully but steadily.

DEEP EYES' POV Suddenly, a vast field of male and female soldiers unfolds before them. Their armored bodies are twisted and broken. It sends chills through them. The carnage is endless.

Rusted tanks and the remains of huge ovo-pacs used to bait Phantoms are scattered among the corpses.

For a while they all stand stunned, unable to move.

224/226. RYAN

This was the "Phantom Cleansing" mission. It was supposed to end the war. My father's in here somewhere.

The group looks out over the wasteland with a moment of silence, grazing at their surroundings as they walk.

AKI raises her scanner and it beeps.

226B. GRAY

Alright, let's move out, people.

The group begins to descend down the hillside into the wasteland.

AKI checks her monitor. She looks up. The Deep Eyes notice and do the same. In the sky, a single hawk glides majestically.

226B-2. RYAN

I'll be damned.

226B-3. AKI

A survivor.

226B-4. GRAY

What's it doing out here?

226B-5. AKI

Hoping for life to return.

226B-6. RYAN

Is that our spirit, Doc?

226B-7. AKI

No.

POV They pass fallen soldiers, arms frozen reaching for the sky. The Phantoms are visible in the distance.

226C. AKI

We're closing in on the life-form.

226D. GRAY

Distance?

AKI moves the handheld scanner. The beeping intensifies.

226E. AKI

Hard to say...
(Aki pauses briefly, discreetly hugging her chestplate)
We're very close.

226F. GRAY

I don't see anything.

They approach the body of a soldier lying face down on the ground. Aki hesitates, as if momentarily confused, looking from her scanner to the body. Gray steps up beside her.

227. GRAY

You're not gonna tell me it's him?

AKI doesn't answer, obviously thinking.

229. RYAN

That's impossible.

230. JANE
(skeptical)
Yeah.

GRAY turns the body over and a skull is visible under the helmet. Parts of his skeleton fall free as the armor breaks away in pieces. **[W12-G, W12-R, W12-J, W12-N] The Deep Eyes are a little startled** as GRAY drops the body.

The scanner is still beeping.

AKI adjusts the scope over her left eye and the ovo-pac on the soldier's back appears.

231. AKI

It's not the soldier. It's his ovo-pac.

232. GRAY

How do you explain that? The pacs power our weapons, the barrier cities... I mean it's just Bio-etheric energy.

233. AKI

And to create that energy we use living tissue. Single cell organisms!

234. GRAY

You're telling me his backpack is the seventh spirit?

235. AKI

Yes.

A communication comes in for GRAY.

237. NEIL'S VOICE

We have incoming. Captain, do you read me? Captain...

He turns away, straining to hear NEIL'S voice over the radio static.

236/236B. GRAY

What? Say again.

237A. NEIL'S VOICE (RADIO)

Do you read me... Captain? We have incoming.

GRAY turns pale. He looks around, searching in every direction.

GRAY'S POV Phantoms approach from all sides. They cross the ruins like enormous monsters.

GRAY'S POV **[W13 SOLDIER] One of the 307s screams.** Looking in his direction, GRAY sees a Phantom emerging from the ground attacking the soldier.

The Phantom rips out the soldier's spirit. Superimposed over the Phantom, the spirit discharges electricity making the Phantom visible.

Everyone watches with their guns raised.

The Phantom and the soldier's spirit diffuse into light particles.

The soldiers begin firing at phantoms.

237B. GRAY

Ryan, get the soldier's pack!

Ryan moves to the corpse to retrieve the ovo-pack.

246A. JANE

I need a hand here!

238. AKI

Those buoys?

239. GRAY

Yeah.

240. AKI

They're not working.

241. GRAY

Thank you.

And then GRAY looks at her. He frowns noticing AKI looks ill. She is sweating and pale.

242. GRAY

Are you alright?

243. AKI
(vaguely)
Of course I am.

Ryan has the ovo-pack.

246. GRAY

Let's get the hell outta here!

GRAY'S POV Another phantom attacks.

JANE and GRAY both fire.

247. JANE

Something's not right. This shouldn't be happening!

The DEP EYES **[W14 DEEP EYES&AKI] run back through the field,** JANE is carrying the dead man's ovo-pac. Everyone runs at top speed. AKI nearly stumbles.

248. RYAN

Something's attracting them!

JANE'S POV through her scope looking at AKI running in front of her.

GRAY turns around, defensive.

AKI suddenly stops running. She looks about to pass out. Gray stops beside here and takes her arm.

251A. GRAY

Aki.

They look into each others eyes, fear and understanding on their faces.

Then, Aki passes out falling into his arms.

251B. JANE

They're right on us, sir... closing in fast!

252A. GRAY

Jane, take the lead!

GRAY bends down and picks up her limp body. Looking over his shoulder, he takes one last look at the Phantoms. They are above the clearing, GRAY holds AKI tightly to his chest and runs.

A phantom is on the heels of the soldiers in the rear. It is about to attack when at the last minute, the soldier who is in front of him turns around...

> 252B. JANE
> Fire in the hole!
> ... and blows it to pieces. Everyone manages to reach and board the transport. The transport ascends.

33 INT. TRANSPORT SHIP—DAY

> 253. GRAY
> Get us out of here, Neil!
> 256. NEIL (V.O.)
> Sir? I would love to but I...
> 257. GRAY
> (to the cockpit)
> Just DO IT!

34 EXT. BATTLEFIELD RUINS—DAY

The transport begins to ascend further and is blocked by a huge phantom about to envelop the ship.

35 INT. TRANSPORT SHIP COCKPIT—DAY

The transport just manages to fly away from the huge encroaching phantom, when it is faced with another phantom flying in from the front. The transport tilts and passes just inches away from the side of the phantom. The force causes a wing of the transport to scrape along the side of the rock wall which crumbles down. The cockpit shakes from the shock.

36 INT. TRANSPORT SHIP—DAY

GRAY lays AKI down and looks at her. She looks bad.

NEIL thinks for a moment, then grabs the controls, and pulls.

38 INT. TRANSPORT SHIP—DAY

AKI'S internal organs are displayed on a holograph. GRAY'S expression reflects her worsening infection.

39 EXT. BATTLEFIELD RUINS—DAY

The transport races along, flying through the cracks of the cliffs.

40 INT. TRANSPORT SHIP—DAY

GRAY watches AKI'S holo helplessly. He doesn't know what to do.

> 258. GRAY
> We have to get her to a hospital.
> 259. SOLDIER
> You have your orders, sir.

GRAY snaps for an instant. He turns toward the voice.

The two new soldiers sit with their guns aimed at him. They are expressionless, and look dangerous.

> 260. GRAY
> What the hell's going on here?
> 261. SOLDIER
> Doctor Ross is to be taken into custody now, sir.

The transport continues to fly along the bottom of a narrow valley.

> CUT TO:

Nervously, NEIL glances backwards from the cockpit to see what is going on. When he returns his attention to piloting, he sees a phantom approaching head on. Startled, he immediately grabs the handle and averts the phantom by a hair.

But there is another phantom in this direction as well.

> BACK TO SCENE

The two soldiers aim their guns at the DEEP EYES. RYAN and JANE try to resist but then freeze.

> 263A. GRAY
> Lower your weapons. That's an order!
> 263B. SOLDIER
> I'm sorry, sir. We have no choice but to relieve you of your command.

42 INT. TRANSPORT SHIP—DAY

NEIL tries to steer the ship and look over his shoulder at the same time. GRAY and the DEEP EYES face off with the three new soldiers.

GRAY stands, the soldiers have him at gunpoint. A tense situation.

> 266B. GRAY
> I won't let you do this, soldier. You're going to have to shoot me.
> 267. SOLDIER
> (shouting)
> Stand Down, Captain!

The DEEP EYES are coiled and ready to attack but the gun barrels pointed at them keep them at bay.

A tense RYAN and JANE.

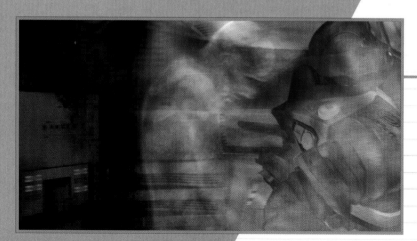

AKI begins dreaming.

43 EXT. ALIEN LANDSCAPE—DREAM [DRD]

The two Phantom armies stare at AKI. They do nothing, only stare. AKI looks confused. And then she hears a sound from behind her. It is an unearthly sound. She turns.

AKI'S POV A wall of fire approaches, burning everything in its path. The sound is deafening.

The wall of fire descends on AKI.

44 INT. TRANSPORT SHIP—DAY [BFW CONT'D]

AKI suddenly sits straight up. She opens her eyes wide, and **[W15 AKI] lets out a scream.**

Startled, the lead soldier fires. AKI is thrown back by the impact.

In that one unguarded moment, JANE slips her body up onto the chair and whips her leg out kicking the gun away. She then roundhouses the soldier and sends him flying backwards. As she does, the second soldier sticks his gun in her face.

RYAN stands and tries to snatch the gun away from the soldier. The soldier fires in the struggle.

> 267B. GRAY
> (when Aki gets shot)
> AKI!

RYAN'S metallic arm protects him and he manages to seem to grab the gun.

But the soldier who shot AKI stands, aiming his gun at JANE and RYAN...

Intensely, NEIL grabs the pilot lever.

45 EXT. BATTLEFIELD RUINS—DAY

The transport weaves and dips inside the wreckage.

46 INT. TRANSPORT SHIP—DAY

Inside the cockpit, NEIL fights to keep the ship steady.

NEIL'S POV Looking out through the nose of the craft. The ship nears the mouth of the wreck, and it looks clear. Then a Phantom blocks the way.

47 EXT. BATTLEFIELD RUINS—DAY

The transport exits the wreckage and turns sharply.

48 INT. TRANSPORT SHIP—DAY

As everyone is thrown as the ship pitches, a gun slides in front of the soldier. He aims it at GRAY.

> 267C. SOLDIER
> That's enough. Hands where I can see them. Everyone! Now!

49 EXT. BATTLEFIELD RUINS—DAY

The transport tries to avoid the Phantom but can't. The cockpit of the ship passes through the Phantom's legs. NEIL slams the lever down and manages to slip by.

50 INT. TRANSPORT SHIP—DAY

GRAY is staring down a gun barrel when part of the Phantom comes through the wall sweeping everything from one side to the other. Part of that phantom passes right through the soldier holding the gun.

Then, as quickly as it appeared, it's gone. The soldier stands there for a moment, like a vertical corpse, and then crumples to the floor.

51 EXT. BATTLEFIELD RUINS—DAY

The transport regains its course and flies away.

52 INT. TRANSPORT SHIP—DAY

GRAY runs to Aki and feels her vitals. Her chest plate is still translucent, showing the infestation inside her. Gray works the controls, and the chest plate looks solid again. A smashed bullet is visible imbedded in the metal.

Gray turns toward the cockpit.

> 267A. GRAY
> Neil, get us back to New York—fast!

57A INT—GENERAL HEIN'S OFFICE—DAY [MOA CONT'D]

GENERAL HEIN looks up from his desk as MAJOR ELLIOT steps up.

> 276A. MAJOR
> The Deep Eyes are returning from the wasteland, sir. Apparently there was an incident.
> (HEIN: "um-hmmm.")
> It would seem the phantoms were attracted to Dr. Ross. The crew barely escaped with their lives. And Sir, Captain Edwards is still in command.
> 278A. HEIN
> Issue an order. I want Edwards and Dr. Ross placed under arrest. All research materials pertaining to Dr. Sid's wave theory are to be confiscated immediately.

279A. MAJOR

That might not go over too well with the council, sir.

Hein rises to his feet.

279B. HEIN

Ah, what a tragedy that would be. No. This is what I've been waiting for. The good Captain has opened the door for us. By tomorrow morning, the council will be at our feet, thanking us for exposing the traitors in our midst... and imploring us to save them from the phantoms.

63A INT.—SPIRITUAL TREATMENT CENTER—DAY [STR]

Gray and the Deep Eyes rush into the treatment center. Gray is carrying Aki. They are met by Dr. Sid and his assistants.

GRAY and Sid hurry to the operating table and gently set Aki down. They both lean down over her body as Sid examines her.

Gray watches Sid work. Then can't help himself:

271A. GRAY
(impatiently, emotionally)

How is she, Doctor?

Sid looks up into Gray's eyes, with a grave look on his face.

271B. SID

She is dying.

271C. GRAY

But there must be something you can do.

Sid begins to push back her tunic revealing the chest device.

271D. SID

Aki is fighting with only six of the eight spirits. We'll have to implant the seventh directly into her chest-plate.

271E. GRAY

It took a bullet. I think it might be damaged.

Sid sees the bullet and the damaged panel. His face reacts, obviously worried, but recovering fast:

271F. SID

We have to repair this panel quickly.

Gray looks ready to act.

Sid pulls him aside.

Gray looks worried, concentrating on Aki. Sid looks at read-outs, then gestures to his assistants, not letting Gray go, turning to explain.

271G. SID

Her vital signs are dropping. Aki is slipping away from us. She nees a sympathetic spirit to help hold her in this world and I can think of no spirit better suited for that than yours, Captain.

Before Gray can respond, the Assistants Sid summoned take hold of Gray and start to maneuver him onto the operating table. Gray lets them, but is clearly confused.

271H. GRAY

I don't understand.

Dr. Sid lays a hand on his shoulder to reassure him.

271I. SID

You don't have to understand. You just be with her now. You keep her here with us.

They share a look, and then Gray nods. Sid hrries off and joins his assistants scurrying frantically around the table.

Gray lies back. He turns and looks at Aki lying beside him.

Very gently, Gray moves his hand on top of hers. They both lie there together on the operating table...

64 EXT. ALIEN LANDSCAPE—DREAM [DRE]

[W-16 GRAY] Slight gasp. As GRAY finds himself on the scarred and barren surface, he looks up at the two suns and moon.

Turning, GRAY finds AKI standing beside him.

312. GRAY

Aki. Where are we?

313. AKI
(matter of factly)

On an alien planet.

314. GRAY

How is that possible?

315. AKI

I'm not entirely sure.

316. GRAY

You seem pretty calm.

317. AKI

I've been having this dream every night for months.

318. GRAY

Dream?

319. AKI

Well, whatever it is...
(realizing)

You're really here, aren't' you? What's happening to me?

320. GRAY

Dr. Sid is implanting the seventh spirit directly into your body.

AKI looks at him. Her face lights up. She looks very happy.

321. AKI

Then you're my spiritual support? Gray, how sweet of you!

322. GRAY

Look, I don't think you realize how serious this situation is.

58 INT. DR. SID'S LABORATORY—DAY [SLB]

General HEIN watches as soldiers ransack the laboratory. A soldier activates a holograph on Sid's desk and Major Elliot calls out.

295. MAJOR

Something you should see here, sir.

The MAJOR and General Hein turn to look at a holograph on Dr. Sid's desk. The images from AKI'S dreams are projected on the screen. Images of a barren alien planet.

296. HEIN

And I am watching what, Major?

INSERT—DISPLAY
Which reads "DREAM FILE."
BACK TO SCENE:

297. MAJOR

It seems Doctor Ross has been recording her dreams.

298. HEIN

and why would I be interested in her dreams...
(beat.)
This is it! This is our evidence. She's under the influence of the Phantoms!

General HEIN turns around. He looks almost ravenous. Noticing something he walks to the spirit containment tank. The waves appear on the tank's display.

General HEIN turns to leave. The MAJOR gestures toward a group of soldiers. They watch the General walk out the door. The soldiers line up in front of the tank, raise their weapons and fire. The spirit containment tank is destroyed.

59 INT. A CORRIDOR—DAY

General HEIN and the MAJOR hurry down a corridor.

303. MAJOR

Dr. Ross' dreams should be all the council needs to authorize the firing of the Zeus Cannon.

304. HEIN

The council is content to hide cowering inside this barrier, while the world dies a little more every day. I believe they need a push in the right direction, Major.

306. HEIN

Get together a group of your most trusted men.

65 INT. TREATMENT ROOM—DAY [STR CONT'D]

Aki and Gray lie on two treatment tables in the treatment room, Sid is running the operation. Ryan, Neil and Jane look on with worried looks on their faces.

Their spiritual bodies are displayed on the holograph. They start to change and look as if their spiritual bodies are fusing.

Neil looks at the holograph communication on his arm. Jane looks at the phantom particles inside of the holograph of Aki. The particles are wriggling eerily.

66 EXT. ALIEN LANDSCAPE—DREAM [DRE CONT'D]

An alien army charges over the horizon at them. GRAY looks stunned. GRAY grabs AKI and starts to run.

GRAY looks at AKI. She doesn't look afraid.

A second alien army appears, attacking the first. AKI and GRAY stand between two Phantom armies screaming at each other. The armies collide in combat. The two watch the battle rage around them.

Suddenly the Phantoms stop fighting, they stare at GRAY and AKI. Hundreds of alien faces, looking like ghosts.

325. GRAY

W-what are they doing? Why are they staring at us?

AKI turns around, and gestures.

325A. AKI

Not at us.

GRAY turns. A wall of fire sweeps over the surface of the alien planet burning everything in its path. The roar is deafening. The wall of fire rushes closer and the Phantom armies are vaporized in their tracks. Nothing remains but their dust.

AKI and GRAY are alone again in the field. AKI points. GRAY turns toward the horizon.

AKI and GRAY'S POV The planet is self-destructing. Great upheavals in the planet's crust grow closer, like fiery volcanoes rushing forward across the surface.

67 EXT. OUTER SPACE—DREAM

The alien planet explodes, spewing matter deep into space.

All of the cursed spirits are absorbed into the largest meteor. The meteor hurtles in the distance.

68 INT. SPIRITUAL TREATMENT ROOM—DAY [STR CONT'D]

GRAY opens his eyes suddenly. As if awaking from a nightmare.

GRAY'S POV Dr. SID smiles down at him.

329. SID

Welcome back Captain.

GRAY sits up, and looks next to him. He sees AKI beside him.

330. GRAY

Is it over? How is she, Doctor?

331. SID

She's gonna be fine. But this is only temporary. We'll need to find the eighth and final spirit to cure her.

GRAY nods, concentrating on AKI. He leans over and gently touches her cheek. Looking for a sign,

332. GRAY

Aki? Can you hear me?

Slowly AKI begins to stir. She opens her eyes and looks up at GRAY. AKI smiles weakly, but brightly.

333. AKI

I finished it. I know what it means. I know what the phantoms really are.

Suddenly doors in the front and rear of the room fly open and Hein's MP's in full battle gear charge into the room, weapons raised at the Deep Eyes, Sid and the others.

334. MILITARY POLICEMAN

Nobody move! You are all under arrest!

69 INT. GENERAL HEIN'S ROOM—NIGHT [MOA CONT'D]

HEIN sits at his desk, the MAJOR and a small group of soldiers are in front of him. (They are not wearing helmets.)

The MAJOR turns off the communicator he was using.

335. MAJOR

We have them, sir.

The MAJOR expects a great response. But he gets nothing.

336. MAJOR

Sir?

337. HEIN

My wife and daughter were killed by Phantoms when the San Francisco Barrier city was attacked. Did I ever tell you that?

The MAJOR glances at HEIN. He grows upset.

339. HEIN

I try to imagine what that must've been like, seeing everyone around you fall over dead for no apparent reason. And then, at the end, feeling something next to you, invisible, touching you, reaching inside your body and...
(beat. He thinks)
You've lost family, haven't you?

339A. MAJOR

Y-yes, sir.

General HEIN stands and watches the city as it passes by the window. He turns to the squad.

340. HEIN

That's why I trust you, all of you. You know what must be done.

70A INT. BARRIER GENERATOR FACILITY—NIGHT [BCR]

Hein, Major Elliott and a small squad of soldiers descend on the elevator lift down into the Barrier Generator Facility, a massive sculpture of complex and heavy machinery. Glowing green ovo pipes lead to the core of the facility.

The troops, led by Hein, descend to the security door leading into the Barrier Control Room. One of the soldiers swipes the key card and punches in the security pass code allowing Hein entrance.

71 INT. BARRIER CONTROL ROOM—NIGHT [BCR]

The large metal facility doors open. Hein enters followed by the soldiers.

340B. HEIN

Major, arrest these men!

The soldiers approach and arrest the facility workers and escort them out of the control room.

The remaining soldiers fill the workers chairs and begin operating the facility.

Hein stands in the center of the room as the last technician is escorted from the facility. The large metal doors close behind him. Hein orders the Major.

341. HEIN

Reduce power to Sector 31.

341A. MAJOR

Sir... you do realize that the phantoms will...?

341B. HEIN

What I realize, Major, is that we must force the council to take action against the enemy.

One of the Soldiers sits in front of the main control unit and descends to where the central ovo tanks are visible.

342A. SOLDIER 1

25% of energy pipe alpha redirected.

342B. SOLDIER 2

Lowering power output to Sector 31.

Hein watches as the barrier holo map shuts down sector 31.

An alarm sounds in the control center. The Major scans the holo of the city and reports nervously on the phantom activity.

354. MAJOR

Barrier breach in sector 31, General. They're coming through now.

Hein addresses the Major, quite please that his actions in an attempt to force the council will be a success.

355. HEIN

Oh, I think we can easily handle a few Phantoms in a contained space. Relax, major. When this night's over, you're going to be a hero.

75   INT. A MILITARY CELL BLOCK—NIGHT [MCB]

The voices of Aki and Gray travel down through the long corridor of cells. Gray, Aki and Sid sit in one cell facing the Deep Eyes.

355O. GRAY

Aki, I don't think...

355P. AKI

You were in my dream, Gray. You saw it.

355Q. GRAY

That's just it. I'm not sure what I saw. How can you be?

355F. SID

Captain, please, let her continue.

356A. AKI

Alright, why do you think we've never been able to determine a relationship between the human-sized phantoms and the giant ones roaming the wastelands.

357A. NEIL

Excuse me, Doc, but what friggin' relationship, I mean you got your human-sized Phantoms, a-a-and your creepy caterpillar Phantoms, and your flying phantoms, and let's not forget my personal favorite, the big fat giant Phantoms!

358. JANE

Down boy.

357A. RYAN

He's right. If you've spent as much time in the field as we have, you know there is no relationship—it's like a zoo out there.

357C. AKI

Precisely. I think those giant ones are like our whales or elephants.

361. NEIL

Why would an invading army bring a bunch of whales and elephants along for the ride—unless their sip was some kind of crazy Noah's Ark?

361C. SID

Hmm, w-we have always assumed the Meteor was intended as a form of transportation. Perhaps it wasn't.

—28—

368. AKI

The meteor is a chunk of their planet that got thrown into space when they destroyed their world.

369A. NEIL

But... how could they survive the trip across outer space on a hunk of rock?

370. AKI

They didn't.

386B. NEIL

Huh! This is all beginning to make a creepy kinda sense. What do you think about all this, Captain?

388B. GRAY

I think that explains why we never had a chance. All our strategies are based on one assumption: that we were fighting alien invaders.

Close on Aki.

388D. AKI

Think of the dream Gray—how they died. Since then all they've known is suffering. They're not an invading army—they're ghosts.

76   INT. BARRIER CONTROL ROOM—NIGHT [BCR CONT'D]

General Hein leans in to look at the activity of the phantoms entering sector 31 on the floating holographic map of the city.

The soldier sits at the controls while the Major stands in the background observing the General.

372. HEIN

How many Phantoms?

The holograph reports that security has been breached as the onslaught of phantoms pour into sector 31. General Hein stands proud of his efforts.

373. HEIN

Excellent. Sound an alert. Send a squad out to eliminate them.

General Hein and the Major begin to walk away from the controls as the holograph signals phantom movement outside of sector 31. The soldier spins around in his chair alarmed.

374G. SOLDIER 1

Sir? I have numerous phantom contacts!

374H. HEIN

Well, of course you do—

374E. SOLDIER 1

Outside of sector 31, sir! And moving at incredible speed!

Major Elliott rushes over to evaluate the warning. Hein approaches the console agitated.

374F. HEIN

Major, what the hell is going on here?

The Major takes a seat and hurriedly begins operating, checking to see if this could be a computer error or not.

374A. MAJOR

They're in the pipes. They're moving with the bio-etheric energy flow.

Hein leans in to review the holograph. Large numbers of phantoms are shown dispersing at an incredible speed throughout the barrier city. The phantoms flow in large numbers through the pipes leading into other sectors.

374B. HEIN

That's impossible. No living thing could survive in those pipes.

The holograph indicated that a stray snake phantom is heading directly to the barrier control room.

374C. MAJOR

We've got a big one heading this way, sir!

The soldiers arm themselves for the impending attack. General Hein and the soldiers scan the room for the phantom. A large snake phantom becomes visible outside the Barrier window inside one of the pipes leading to the facility. General Hein looks in horror as the phantom approaches.

381. HEIN

...oh my god.

The soldiers raise their guns to shoot at the phantom. Hein raises his arm with the order.

—29—

389. HEIN

Hold your fire!

The entire group halts their effort, the snake phantom disappears. General Hein scans the room for any activity. All seems quiet. All the soldiers look down the room for a sudden attack. The soldier at the main control for the ovo tanks looks below and around him nervously. From the depths of the control room the snake phantom rises up and ills the soldier. General Hein backs up in horror as the soldier's spiritual energy is ripped from his body.

A soldier to the right of Hein begins opening fire on the snake phantom. All the soldiers follow his lead rapidly firing on the phantom. The snake phantom rears in defense, in front of the barrier control panel and the ovo tank. The soldiers' bullets pelt the casing of the controls until the system shorts and the controls begin to catch fire. The ovo tanks start to react excessively and an explosion ensues. The control room goes dark as the system shuts down. The emergency flood light system engages and the room fills with fluorescent flood lights.

The soldiers continue to fire at the snake phantom. The phantom rears and swipes its tail hitting the soldier standing next to General Hein. General Hein falls back in defense, as the phantom whips around to approach the other soldiers. The soldiers fire at the rapidly approaching phantom. The phantom exits the room and takes out the remaining two soldiers. The bullets continue to fly as the soldiers fall to their death. A stray bullet crosses the room hitting Major Elliott.

Major Elliott falls to the floor. Unaware of his fate, he reaches down and raises his hand covered in blood.

General Hein walks over in shock and looks on as Major Elliott's bloody hand drops with the last of his life.

General Hein rushes over to the Barrier control and looks on as the entire system fails and the ovo tanks begin to explode, tearing down the Barrier. Hein looks on in defeat.

389A. HEIN

What have I done?

More explosions rattle the room as the building begins to collapse. Hein rushes from the control center and ascends on the elevator as he watches the city's destruction.

81   INT. A MILITARY CELL BLOCK—NIGHT [MCB]

AKI, GRAY, SID, and the DEEP EYES are in their cells. Everyone sits listening to AKI.

389B. GRAY

Come on, Neil... we need to find a way out. Now you're our man... think.

389C. NEIL

Captain, these walls are titanium alloy, and the bars are pulse-sonic lasers. I mean it's not like I can just wave a magic wand and... woah.

Suddenly, the lights flicker and the cell doors open. They look around, no one is there. No one has entered the cellblock nor seems about to enter it. They walk out of their cells looking uneasy.

389D. GRAY

(to Neil)

Neil, I'm impressed.

389E. NEIL

(amazed)

That makes two of us.

Computer voice activates.

390. COMPUTER VOICE

Proceed to the nearest evacuation facility. Proceed to the nearest evacuation facility. Proceed to the nearest evacuation facility...

389F. NEIL

I think we should proceed to the nearest evacuation facility.

390. COMPUTER VOICE (CONT'D)

(fades out)

... Proceed to the nearest evacuation facility...

81A EXT. BARRIER CITY—NIGHT [CTY]

An overhead view of the city as the Barrier Shield shorts out and exposes the city. There is no more protection from the Phantoms.

—30—

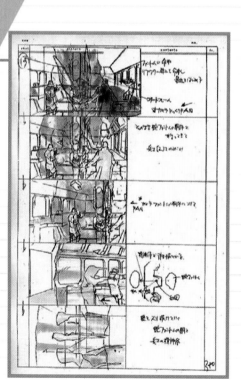

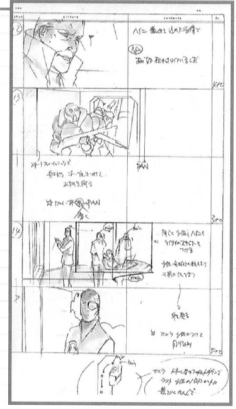

84 INT. MILITARY CELL BLOCK—NIGHT [ESC]

Gray and Aki lead everyone across a building catwalk. A large explosion outside off in the distance rattles the catwalk. Everyone stops running and looks out into what remains of the Barrier City. Escape pods rise from the fire, explosion and smoke. Phantoms rise in terror throughout the entire city.

Neil turns his head as a Human Phantom rises through the floor cutting Aki and Gray from the rest of them.

390A. GRAY

Here they come.

Like hideous ghosts, the Phantoms emerge from the walls and from the floors. Phantoms appear between GRAY and AKI and the others separating them.

GRAY takes AKI'S hand and starts to run. She looks back over her shoulder at the others but GRAY pulls her along.

391. AKI

But the others. Dr. Sid!

392. GRAY

Deep Eyes'll take care of him. Come on.

The two run down the hall toward the elevator. They press the 'down' button. They wait, then turn.

AKI and GRAY'S POV Phantoms move down the hall toward them. Coming closer and closer still.

"Ding" the elevator doors open and they hurry inside.

85 INT. THE ELEVATOR—NIGHT

AKI and GRAY wait for the doors to close.

AKI and GRAY'S POV The Phantoms float closer as the doors begin to close. One Phantom almost reaches them but the doors close just in time. Before they can relax, it passes through the door.

AKI and GRAY back up against the wall. It reaches its tentacles out at them as the elevator starts to move. The Phantoms seems to pass through the ceiling.

AKI and GRAY share a relieved look. They catch their breath.

393. AKI
(out of breath)

They look, they look different now.

394. GRAY

They must be carrying a residual charge from passing through the barrier.

86 EXT. MONORAIL—STREET LEVEL—NIGHT [BNA]

The doors open with a computer voice saying, 'Trains are not operating. We apologize for the inconvenience.' AKI and GRAY look outside.

AKI and GRAY'S POV The monorail platform is covered in corpses piled atop each other. The doors to the train open and close against the bodies.

They move along the platform on top of the corpses. But phantoms rise out of the ground and block their way. The phantoms seem to be rising right out of the bodies.

GRAY and AKI back up, but are surrounded by the encroaching Phantoms. There is no way out. The Phantoms tighten the circle. A loud crash.

An armored jeep bursts through a building façade onto the platform. NEIL is behind the wheel. Dr. SID is in the passenger seat. RYAN and JANE are firing their weapons.

402. RYAN

All aboard, Captain!

[W17 AKI & GRAY] AKI and GRAY jump inside, as multiple Phantoms approach. RYAN and JANE fire and destroy it.

NEIL hits the gas. The jeep races away down the monorail tracks.

87 EXT. BUILDING ROOFTOP—NIGHT [PNC]

Dozens of people push forward, trying to force their way into the escape pods. But the pods are full.

People are screaming, the city police are holding them back.

403A. POLICE

This is no longer a safe zone. Please proceed to your alternate evacuation facility.
(repeated 12 times)

As the pods begin to ascend, the crowd breaks through the barriers. Some jump onto the pods as they rise from the roof, dangling over the streets far below.

89 EXT. THE CITY—NIGHT

An escape pod penetrated by Phantoms veers off course crashing into another pod. Throughout the city escape pods fly wildly, crashing into each other and bursting into flames. Visible Phantoms fly through the sky. The situation is hopeless.

90 EXT. MONORAIL TRACKS—NIGHT [AIA]

Our heroes race through the tunnel in their jeep and...

405. AKI

We need to find my ship.

406. RYAN

If it was towed inside the city, it would be in the military hangar.

407. NEIL

That's a big 'if.'

91 EXT. MONORAIL TRACKS—NIGHT

Through the mouth of the tunnel, an OU-OF-CONTROL ESCAPE POD comes into view HURLING TOWARDS THEM.

At that moment, an escape pod crashes right in front of them.

They narrowly miss it, but the jeep crashes through the window onto a large passageway connecting two buildings. It is wide enough for the jeep to fit.

On both sides of the passageway are sidewalks lined with artificial trees. This is not a shopping arcade.

NEIL grins and flashes a thumbs up. They blast wildly down the passageway.

Another escape pod crashes down!

409. AKI

Look out!

NEIL moves his foot toward the brake, but GRAY'S foot SLAMS DOWN on the accelerator.

They share a look. SCREAMS and EXCLAMATIONS are nearly drowned out by the CRASH of the wreckage. They relax, but not for long.

The jeep races towards the META-PHANTOM blocking their exit.

407C. GRAY

Get us onto the platform...

He sees a piece of wreckage, and gestures.

Neil drives them up the ramp and onto the platform, and they head back the way they came.

Short pause. NO BANTER for a few moments. Just the SOUND of the ENGINE, the MUSIC and their FACES build tension. They race for the other end of the tunnel. Still clear. Everyone watches expectantly.

The JEEP accelerates...

The jeep SQUEALS around heading back the other way again. Everyone looks disillusioned. But not GRAY.

407F. NEIL

Okay, now what?

GRAY'S face is calm, hard. He decides.

407G. GRAY

We're going through the station.

In the back seat, the others look just as uncertain.

407H. SID

What? What are we doing?

-32-

407H-1. NEIL

Captain, with all due respect...

407J. JANE
(uncertain)

Excuse me, Captain...

407K. GRAY

The station, we're going through it.

407L. RYAN

It's the only way.

407L-1. SID

So I gather this will be somewhat of a rough ride?

407M. NEIL

Doc, you've got a talent for understatement.
(loud)

Hang on everybody!

Neil drives back over the ramp and release a YELL—like a frantic battle charge—as the JEEP hurls into the air and through GLASS.

Our heroes pull themselves from the wreckage.

92 EXT. AIRPORT RUNWAY—NIGHT [AIB]

The jeep crashes into the airport balancing on two wheels for a long moment before rolling over violently several times. It comes to a rest. The shock damages the jeep beyond repair. Neil lifts his head. Recovering, he looks for Sid and looks down into the passenger seat.

407N. NEIL

Doc?

Sid's head rises slowly from behind the jeep's dashboard, his eyes wide...

407P. SID

Interesting.

407P-1. GRAY

Anybody hurt?

410. JANE

Captain!

GRAY looks back—trouble! Everyone hurries to the back of the jeep. RYAN is pinned. What appears to be part of an axel protrudes from his LOWER ABDOMEN. His legs are pinned by a large piece of twisted steel.

411. NEIL

Oh, God. Talk to me Sarge.

RYAN'S breathing is measure—putting a lid on his pain.

412. RYAN
(looking at Neil)

Ouch.

411A. NEIL

Gimme a hand, Jane.

411B. JANE

Right.

411C. SID

No, wait. We're risking further injury. We need the proper tools to cut him out.

AKI hands SID a prepared hypodermic syringe.

413A. AKI

They're in my ship.

SID moves to inject RYAN.

412C. RYAN
(Grunt) No. No Doc. No drugs.

SID looks to GRAY.

-33-

412D. SID
(uncertain)
Captain...?

GRAY and RYAN look at each other in silent communication.

412A. GRAY
(to Sid)
You heard the man.
(to Ryan)
We'll find the ship and be back for you.

413B. JANE
I'll stay with you.

413C. NEIL
Me too.

413D. RYAN
Nobody's staying. Just give me a gun.

RYAN tries to move, but can't. He grimaces with pain.

Everyone looks at GRAY. He thinks a moment.

413F. GRAY
You got it.
(to Jane)
Give him a weapon.

413H. GRAY
Do it.

JANE is reluctant. GRAY sensing her misgivings gives her a nod. JANE fixes RYAN with the Jeep's cannon.

413I. GRAY
We'll be back for you, Sergeant. You <u>hear</u> me?

413J. RYAN
(to Gray)
I hear you, Captain.
(pause, to the others)
Now get outta here.

RYAN fights the pain and tries to sound as upbeat as possible. It doesn't quite work.

Short pause and then GRAY nods. He looks up at the others.

416. GRAY
Let's move out.

92A EXT. AIRPORT RUNWAY—NIGHT [AIR]

AKI, GRAY, SID, JANE and NEIL move across a dark runway. Debris from the crashed escape pods is strewn everywhere and smoke from the fires envelop them. Visibility is low. They HEAR gunfire in the distance, and SEE the glow from the beams. JANE looks back in its direction.

The smoke clears for an instant and AKI sees the Black Boa ahead of them in the distance.

For a moment the Black Boa is partially hidden by the smoke, then comes into full view.

Various equipment is connected to the underside of the Black Boa. AKI operates one of the control panels.

Panels on the underside of the Black Boa open up and an elevator with room enough for six descends. Everyone gets on.

93 INT. BLACK BOA—CARGO HOLD—NIGHT

As the lift ascends, the lights in the cargo hold come on. Seeing a Quatro among the equipment, NEIL goes over to it.

419. NEIL
A quad-axle A.T.V. This is good.

419B. SID
It can be used to retrieve Ryan and transport him safely here...

He pulls out the empty ovo packs.

419C. SID
Uh, however, we'll need to replace these spent fuel cells.

419A. JANE
There could be some live ovo-pacs in the hangar.

422. GRAY
Alright. Jane, check the hangar. Neil, get us ready for take-off. Aki and Dr. Sid, prep the Quatro. I'll go to the tower and rotate the air-tray. This city may be lost, but we are not. Let's do this thing and get the hell out of here.

NEIL runs towards the cockpit. GRAY and JANE get back on the lift. Sid moves close and hands out HEADSETS.

AKI picks up a pistol and turns toward GRAY.

426. AKI
Gray, be careful!

427. GRAY
You too.

94 EXT. AIRPORT RUNWAY—NIGHT

GRAY hurries across the runway to the Control Tower.

-34-

95 INT. MILITARY HANGAR—NIGHT

JANE climbs over the broken ovo-pacs. She spots a container. Finding a metal bar, she pries it open.

The unit is filled with rows of green glowing ovo-pacs.

428. JANE
Oh yeah.

96 INT. CONTROL TOWER—NIGHT

GRAY opens the door, and cautiously steps in. Corpses litter the floor and stairs. He climbs up the steps.

97 INT. BLACK BOA—COCKPIT—NIGHT

NEIL steps into the cockpit and begins flipping switches.

98 INT. CONTROL TOWER—NIGHT

GRAY reaches the control room. He looks around. Corpses slump in their chairs. GRAY moves to a station. Gently lowering a dead body to the floor, he takes its seat. He looks the panel over.

GRAY operates the controls, and a holographic image of the Black Boa appears. He searches the panel again, hitting a few switches that don't seem to do anything. Then the runway lights turn on. GRAY puts on a wireless headset.

429. GRAY
Neil, do you read me?

99 INT. BLACK BOA—COCKPIT—NIGHT

NEIL is also wearing a wireless headset. He flips more switches.

430. NEIL
Loud and clear, Captain... this baby'll fly itself.

100 INT. CONTROL TOWER—NIGHT

GRAY operates the controls.

431A. NEIL
Flight path is set.

The runway smolders and smokes.

GRAY is searching for something. He finds several dials to his side. Looking relieved, he reaches for them.

432. GRAY
Beginning rotation.

101 EXT. AIRPORT RUNWAY—NIGHT

Slowly, the airtray holding the shuttle begins to rotate.

102 INT. CARGO HOLD—NIGHT

AKI and SID are operating the Quatro's controls. AKI picks up her gun. A strange light rises toward them from the still lowered lift. AKI aims her pistol. Something is approaching...

JANE stands on the lift holding an ovo-pac in one hand. AKI lowers her gun, relieved.

103 INT. BLACK BOA—COCKPIT—NIGHT

423A. NEIL
Whoa. St-stop the airtray. We have a problem...

423C. NEIL
...I'm reading an impound tractor still attached to the prow of the ship.

103A INT. CONTROL TOWER

423D. GRAY
We can't take off like that.

423E. NEIL (O.S.)
Permission to go outside and detach the coupling.

Gray thinks about it. Not pleased. But:

423F. GRAY
Do it.

103C EXT. AIRTRAY

Neil and Jane rush to the impound tractor.

423I. NEIL
There's the problem.

Neil goes to the controls and opens up a panel. Starts working. Jane takes her position, and stands guard. Neil works, and the MECHANISM REACTS. Jane hears the humming from the machine and says:

-35-

423I-1. NEIL
The controls are locked, naturally. Jane, let me ask you something.

And then Jane can see the Phantoms coming.

(nervous)
423I-2. NEIL
You think we're gonna get out of here alive?

Jane starts to answer, but before she can:

423-3. NEIL (CONT'D)
I mean I wonder if anybody else has gotten OUT? You think anyone made it this far? Huh?

423I-5. JANE
Ah...

NEIL (CONT'D)
You think this "eight spirit" stuff is really gonna work against the Phantoms? I mean, what if it's all just a bunch of mumbo-jumbo?

And then the machine sparks.

423L. NEIL
Yeoww!

Neil looks irritated.

423I-1. NEIL
Jane, do you mind if we stop talking? I'm trying to concentrate here.

Jane raises her weapon and FIRES. We see a score of Phantoms emerge from obscurity.
Jane turns to Neil. Neil looks over, they don't feel good about this.
Jane cuts loose with the firepower. Neil works faster. Gray rushes to the window.

423L-3. GRAY
What's happening down there?!

423L-4. JANE
Nothing we can't handle.

423M. GRAY (O.S.)
Neil. What's your status?

423N. NEIL
Almost there.

423O. GRAY
I want you two back inside.

423P. NEIL
We're fine, sir. Jane is negotiating with extreme prejudice.

423Q. GRAY
Talk to me, Jane.

Jane is thinning out the approaching phantoms.

423R. JANE
No problem here, Captain.

Suddenly the inner mechanism reacts, Neil grins. The coupling disengages.

423S. NEIL
Yesss! Captain, we are good to go!

Neil and Jane share a relieved look. But then, Jane's face looks funny. Her expression subtly changes. Here eyes sift down.
And Neil's smile fades. He looks down, too. Down to what Jane is looking at:
There are TENTACLES sticking out of his chest. Jane sees the life depart from Neil's eyes.

444. JANE
Nooo!

In a fury, Jane fires, rushing up onto the vaporizing phantom. Jane continues to fire in a flurry of emotion. Unloading her gun, dry firing.
Jane looks up.

(ad-lib screaming)
444A. GRAY (NEW)
Jane, get out of there! Get out of there now. Go! Jane! Get the hell out of there! Jane!

We see meta phantom tentacles emerge about Jane. There's no escape. Jane is struck head on with a phantom tentacle, hitting like an oncoming truck.

111 EXT. AIRPORT RUNWAY—NIGHT
The airtray continues rotating with Black Boa on top of it. A Phantom emerges from the ground next to it.

112 INT. QUATRO—COCKPIT—NIGHT
AKI and SID are inside. AKI starts up the Quatro.

446A/448. SID
The shield is powered and ready. Where are you going?

AKI notices a display on the cockpit console controls.

449/447. AKI
To the cockpit. / The ship is set on auto-pilot. We're in countdown to lift-off.

AKI starts to get out of the Quatro.
As she jumps out, AKI hits a switch on the console generating the shield.
The Quatro is enclosed in a shield inside the cargo hold. SID yells something at AKI

450. SID
No-w-wait, it's too dangerous! Aki!

AKI heads off down the corridor after JANE.

113 INT. CONTORL TOWER—NIGHT
GRAY is operating the panel. A display reads that automated procedures in auto pilot mode are set.
GRAY watches the airtray rotate. The Boa comes into direct view through the front window. GRAY sees the Phantom next to it.
GRAY'S POV An enormous Phantom on the runway is eye level with GRAY.
GRAY picks up a chair, and shatters a window. He jumps out.

114 EXT. CONTROL TOWER—NIGHT
GRAY lands on the open terrace one story below, raises his gun toward the Phantom and fires.

453. GRAY
Over here you sonuvabitch!

Gray FIRES and the noise drowns out his curse. But the Phantom continues to slowly converge on the Black Boa.
Dozens of Phantoms emerge from out of the ground and enter the Black Boa.

115 INT. BLACK BOA—CORRIDOR—NIGHT
AKI makes it down the hall, opens the door to the lab and enters.
Phantoms are beginning to enter the room. AKI avoids them, running through the room to the cockpit.

116 EXT. CONTROL TOWER—NIGHT
GRAY fires at the Phantom. But it continues toward the Boa.
Suddenly, from GRAY'S left side a beam fires from a heavy weapon hitting the Phantom.
GRAY turns in that direction.

117 EXT. AIRPORT RUNWAY—NIGHT
The airtray has rotated. RYAN and the demolished remains of the jeep not more than 200 meters away from GRAY (close enough to recognize that this shape is RYAN). RYAN is firing.

454. RYAN
Yarghhhhhhhh!!

RYAN blasts away at the Phantom.
GRAY joins in and fires at the Phantom.
The Phantom stops, as if annoyed by the heavy weapon, turning from the Boa toward GRAY and RYAN.
In the distance, the Black Boa is preparing for launch.
Using its thrusters, the Black Boa slowly begins to ascend.
Continuing to fire, GRAY looks over at RYAN in the distance. Ryan fires, looking at Gray. Then Ryan sees something in a nearby hangar.
RYAN aims at the hangar and fires. A chain reaction begins as the ovo-pacs inside explode.
Turning its attention to this the Phantom moves swiftly over toward RYAN. Ryan keeps firing. GRAY jumps down a story shouting a warning into the wireless.
Two Phantoms appear next to GRAY. GRAY demolishes them.
Turning again toward RYAN, he sees a Phantom is about to trample him and the remains of the jeep. Ryan keeps firing.
The Phantom swallows the remains of the jeep along with RYAN.

458. GRAY
RYAN!!

118 INT. BLACK BOA—COCKPIT—NIGHT
AKI is in the cockpit, swiftly operating the controls.

445A. AKI
Gray, do you read me? What's happening?

445B. GRAY
You and Sid are getting out of here now.

445C. AKI
No. We won't leave everyone!

445D. GRAY
(emotionally)
Everyone's dead!

445E. AKI
I'm not leaving without you.

-37-

445F. GRAY
I'm sorry... but you don't have a choice. Good-bye, Aki.

The auto-pilot display disappears. AKI pulls the main pilot lever.

119 EXT. AIRPORT RUNWAY—NIGHT

The Black Boa changes direction and hovers over to the Control Tower. The hatch is open and the lift is extended out. (The same lift which will be used in the ending.)

Seeing this, the Phantom changes its direction. The Black Boa slips past it to the side continuing toward the Control Tower.

GRAY battles a mob of Phantoms that appeared out of the ground. The Boa approaches.

120 INT. BLACK BOA—COCKPIT—NIGHT

AKI shouts into the wireless.

459. AKI
Gray! Come on!!

121 EXT. AIRPORT RUNWAY—NIGHT

At the last second, GRAY jumps onto the lift.
The Black Boa is stationary as it pulls the lift back up inside and hovers over the exit.

Dozens of Phantoms enter the ship in the brief instant it was stationary in midair.

The Phantom approaches this direction preparing for another attack.

122 INT. BLACK BOA—COCKPIT—NIGHT

Phantoms enter the cockpit.

Watching out of the corner of her eye, AKI pulls the main control lever.

123 EXT. AIRPORT RUNWAY—NIGHT

The shuttle moves onto the edge of the airtray. It changes direction as it lifts off, flying diagonally toward the sky.

124 INT. BLACK BOA—CARGO HOLD—NIGHT

The lift that brought GRAY onto the ship is housed in the Cargo Bay. The Quatro shield is off and SID runs for the doorway to the hall. Dozens of Phantoms are in his way.

There are also many Phantoms around GRAY.

The ship pitches as it veers off course diagonally.

GRAY grabs a pipe.

125 EXT. MID AIR—NIGHT

The Black Boa's main nozzle begins to emit a red glow.

126 INT. BLACK BOA—COCKPIT—NIGHT

AKI hits a switch.

A Phantom appears behind her.

127 EXT. MID AIR—NIGHT

The Boa's main nozzle begins to fire, resembling a shuttle launching. The Boa starts to ascend.

128 INT. BLACK BOA—CARGO HOLD—NIGHT

The Phantoms slide down as if they have been left behind and deserted.

SID and GRAY hang on, avoiding Phantoms as they sink.

One Phantom settles directly next to SID.

140 INT. STATION AIRLOCK—DAY

The airlock opens, HEIN enters. The soldiers stand at attention and salute.

HEIN salutes, walking quickly through without stopping.

141 INT. ZEUS CONTROL ROOM—DAY

General HEIN sits at the communication panel. The hologram displays the Executive Council. They look like tiny game pieces in front of him.

490. COUNCIL MEMBER 1
What caused the barrier to fail, General Hein?

491. HEIN
(stiffly)
Ahh, I am afraid it was only a matter of time before the phantoms developed an immunity to our barriers. But I am relieved to see that you and the rest of the council were able to evacuate to Houston without incident.

HEIN waits. The tiny images of the Council Members shift a little bit.

492. COUNCIL MEMBER 1
It was a terrible loss suffered this evening...
(beat)
...the council has re-considered your proposal to fire the Zeus Cannon.

HEIN can barely sit still. He suppresses his voice not to divulge any emotion.

493. HEIN
I see.

494. COUNCIL MEMBER 1
We are transmitting the access codes to you now.

The machine beside HEIN makes a sound as the access codes are received. HEIN sits still, but his eyes follow it. He watches the code appear on the screen. There is a beep as the transmission ends. General HEIN stands up, and moves over to it quickly, but a Council Member stops him.

495 COUNCIL MEMBER 1
And General...

General HEIN waits. His face strained.

496. COUNCIL MEMBER 1 (CONT.)
...best of luck to us all.

HEIN flips a switch, and the hologram disappears.
INT. ZEUS CONTROL ROOM—DAY
HEIN enters the room. All the technicians salute.

497. HEIN
Prepare to fire the cannon.

498. TECHNICIAN 1
The target, sir?

HEIN sits in the center of the room.

499. HEIN
The Phantom crater.

138 INT. BLACK BOA—COCKPIT—NIGHT [BZS]

CLOSE UP of a hologram of a Phantom wave.

Seven other waves combine to form an opposing wave. It is almost the complete opposite, but not quite.

AKI watches the hologram. She turns as Dr. SID speaks.

465. SID
I enlarged the scanning perimeter to include an area that we had previously overlooked.

GRAY watches a hologram of the Earth. The Earth is dark.

465A. AKI
The impact crater.

The hologram displays the impact crater seen earlier. The meteorite is mostly buried.

129 INT. BLACK BOA COCKPIT—NIGHT

The Phantoms set to attack AKI are also sucked down.

130 EXT. MID AIR—NIGHT

The Black Boa accelerates into the night sky. Phantoms appear out of the inside of the ship, as if they were left behind. They descend.

131 EXT. REMAINS OF NEW YORK—NIGHT

Moving like fearsome giants, Phantoms roam between the skyscrapers. Most of the streetlights are out. Several more buildings go dark. Phantoms walk around the streets of the city, now a wasteland of death.

132 EXT. BLACK BOA—NIGHT

The Black Boa is in orbit high above the earth.

133 INT. BLACK BOA—NIGHT [LOV]

AKI floats to her favorite window and looks at the Earth. GRAY enters. AKI turns, she has been crying. Teardrops float away from her face.

GRAY'S face is a study of pain and longing as he looks at AKI. They float toward each other and into each other's arms. They drift slowly through the cabin, and quietly kiss.

460A. GRAY
I wish I could believe somehow, someway, they are in a better place.

134 EXT. ESCAPE POD—NIGHT [HAS]

Something else orbits the Earth, a military shuttle.

135 INT. MILITARY SHUTTLE—NIGHT

The CAMERA PANS the interior of the escape pod. We HEAR the sound of something breathing. Sounding tortured and pathetic, as if someone were fighting back tears, trying not to cry.

General HEIN sits weakly in the cockpit. Suddenly, he raises a gun to his temple.

He flashes back for an instant to the scene where his wife and daughter are killed.

His whole body tenses as he tries to pull the trigger.

His hand drops to the floor. He can't do it. He sits there for a moment. He is totally still. His expression is blank.

Then he hits some controls and we see that he is setting the course for the Zeus space cannon.

136 EXT. MILITARY SHUTTLE—NIGHT

The thrusters engage and the shuttle rockets out of view.

137 INT. BLACK BOA—NIGHT [LOV CONT'D]

AKI stares straight ahead. Her flowing hair and the changing background tells us she is floating. AKI turns, looking at GRAY floating next to her. It is as if they made love and have been drifting ever since. AKI touches his face. They share a smile.

139 EXT. SPACE CANNON—DAY

The Space Station orbits over the Earth looking like an enormous sword hanging over the helpless blue planet.

468. GRAY
That's a strange place to find the eighth spirit.

469. SID
Yes. Really quite astonishing.

There is a blip inside the crater. The computers hum and whir as the counter wave is completed before their eyes.

AKI stares at the hologram as if she were looking at a savior.

There is a blip inside the crater. The computers hum and whir as the counter wave is completed before their eyes.

471. GRAY
But nothing could survive in there except Phantoms.

472. SID
Precisely. Which suggests that the eighth spirit is a Phantom spirit.

AKI and GRAY look at SID. Waiting for the explanation.

473. SID
(not telling them something)
I can't explain it at the moment. But once we get down there...

473A. GRAY
Wait...

473B. SID
...you'll understand.

GRAY raises his hand stopping him.

474. GRAY
...wait, Doctor that's a one-way trip.

475. SID
Yes, yes. I expected that's how you would evaluate our chances.

476. GRAY
Well am I wrong?

477. SID
No, no, no, no, no, no... I agree, we probably won't live long enough to extract the eighth spirit from the crater.

478. GRAY
Then why should we even try it?

478A. SID
Because we don't need to extract the eighth spirit!

479. AKI
If we can't bring the final spirit here, we can go there and complete the wave inside the crater.

480. SID
Yes, exactly.

481. GRAY
And how do we do that, exactly?

482. SID
I can construct a device that would attach to Aki's chest plate to gather the eight spirits and then...

483. GRAY
And then what?

484. SID
And then, we wait and see what happens.

Trying to understand, GRAY looks at SID a moment.

485. GRAY
That's it? That's your plan? We "wait and see what happens?"

486. SID
Yes.

GRAY stops. He looks at the hologram, then at AKI.

—41—

153 **EXT. IMPAT CRATER—DAY**
The Quatro descends toward the crater. The shield sparks as it contacts the Phantoms. The crater begins to appear larger as they approach.

154 **INT. ZEUS CONTROL ROOM—DAY [ESS]**

509. TECHNICIAN 1
Ready to fire in three minutes.

510. TECHNICIAN 2
Ovo-pacs at maximum. Transferring plasma flow to auto.

HEIN sits in the center of the room, and waits.

511. TECHNICIAN 3
Counter-thrusters are engaged.

512. TECHNICIAN 2
Lox flow decoupled... status is green.

All of this is music to HEIN'S ears. Then an alarm sounds. The Technicians look.

513. TECHNICIAN 4
We have something on radar over the impact site, sir.

HEIN leaps from his chair, and looks into the scanner. His expression turns to anger and hate. It's the Quatro.

514. HEIN
It's her.

515. TECHNICIAN 1
Sir?

516. HEIN
Just a traitor under the influence of the enemy. Continue the countdown.

HEIN takes his seat again.

517. HEIN
We'll take them all out at the same time.

156 **INT. QUATRO—DAY [CRA]**
AKI and GRAY look tense as they approach the blip. They begin to be able to make out the shape of the phantom.

518. AKI
We're closing on the phantom. Contact in thirty seconds.

157 **INT. ZEUS CONTROL ROOM—DAY [ESS/SSF]**
HEIN sits there until he hears the technician speak.

519. TECHNICIAN 1
Target locked! Ready to fire on your command.

158 **EXT. ZEUS SPACE CANNON—DAY**
The lights of the Space Station begin to dim in order to channel Zeus' full power into the cannon.

Ovo-pacs. Their inner cells are reacting eerily. The thrusters open and the safety valves are disengaged.

One after the other, the mechanisms on the Station come to life and the cannon barrel begins to spin as it finally opens up...

161 **INT. BLACK BOA—DAY [CRA]**
Dr. SID operates the holograph. The eighth spirit merges above the crater and the holograph of the wave forms an exact opposite of that of the Phantom.

INSERT—HOLOGRAPHIC DISPLAY which reads "PERFECT MATCH."

BACK TO SCENE

—43—

487. GRAY
Oh good. Well, I got my own plan. We keep scanning the surface from orbit, and maybe we'll find a compatible spirit somewhere else.

AKI places her hand inside the hologram. As if touching the impact crater.

489. AKI
I say we go in.

143 **EXT. IMPACT CRATER—DAY [CRA]**
The Black Boa descends over the crater. It is located roughly one mile from Earth.

145 **EXT. IMPACT CRATER—DAY**
The cargo bay opens and the Quatro descends by cable. It dangles over the crater below.

146 **INT. QUATRO—DAY**
Inside the Quatro AKI and GRAY are surrounded by control panels. Holograms appear all around them.

502. AKI
Powering the shield.

147 **EXT. IMPACT CRATER—DAY**
A phantom shield appears around the Quatro as it descends.

148 **INT. QUATRO—DAY**
AKI and GRAY operate the controls producing an image of the crater. The landscape looks barren. The twisted tip of the meteor protrudes from the center.

503. GRAY
Okay. We're over the meteor.

GRAY pushes a button, and images of Phantoms pouring out of the meteor appear. Grotesque and horrifying, it resembles a giant anthill. They infest the meteor site.

Aki and Gray share a heinous look. What lies below them seems like certain death. After a moment, they both look away, forcing themselves back to business.

504. GRAY
Do you have it in sight, Doctor?

149 **INT. BLACK BOA—DAY**
Dr. SID IS INSIDE THE Boa monitoring his holograms. He operates them and for an instant a blip moves across the crater.

504A. SID
There are so many of them...

Suddenly, a blip moves across the screen.

505. SID
Wait! Yes. I'm tracking the eighth spirit moving along the crater's surface!

150 **INT. QUATRO—DAY**
Something else catches GRAY'S attention. He frowns.

503. GRAY
Alright. Now let's take a closer look...

151 **EXT. IMPACT CRATER—DAY**
The Quatro dangles above the crater. Phantoms attempt to enter it becoming visible when the shield repels them.

152 **INT. INSIDE THE QUATRO—DAY**
AKI and GRAY look at each other as the interior lights fade.

—42—

521. SID

It's a match. It's a perfect match!

159 INT. ZEUS CONTROL ROOM—DAY

HEIN gestures.

520. HEIN

FIRE!

161A INT. BLACK BOA—DAY [CRA]

An alarm sounds. The displays show an enormous energy reaction approaching.

As he looks up, SID'S expression hardens into one of fear.

The beam from the Zeus Cannon passes outside the window bathing the inside of the ship in blinding light. The crater is no longer visible. It is as if everything has been turned completely white.

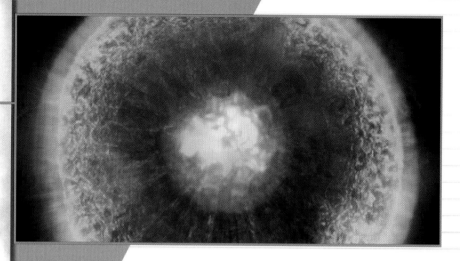

162 EXT. CRATER—DAY

The beam directly hits the meteor in the crater.

Hundreds of Phantoms become visible the instant it explodes, reacting to the discharge.

Hundreds of Phantoms overflow in this eerie scene.

164 INT. QUATRO—DAY

AKI and GRAY try to hold on as the rover swings on the cable.

164A EXT. CRATER—DAY

Wide shot. The entire crater and small Quatro hanging above it.

164B INT. INSIDE THE QUATRO—DAY

523. AKI

What was that?

524. GRAY

It's the Zeus. They're firing on the crater.

522. SID (VO)

Aki? Captain? Are you all right?

522A. GRAY

A little shaken. Stand by.

AKI realizes the blip has vanished.

525. AKI

Sid, the eighth spirit is not on our scanner. Do you have it?

165 INT. BLACK BOA—DAY

Dr. SID reads hologram and data.

526. SID

(with deep realization)

The eighth spirit... has been destroyed.

166 INT. QUATRO—DAY

AKI and GRAY look at each other.

527. AKI

What are we going to do now?

528. GRAY

Nothing. This mission is over. We have to get outta here.

166A INT. BLACK BOA—DAY

Sid turns as an alarm sounds on the ship. His face reacts.

526A. SID

Incoming!

169 EXT. IMPACT CRATER—DAY

The energy beam strikes the crater, revealing something new. Something huge emerges out of the meteor. It is the Phantom's Gaia with its thousands of writhing tentacles.

170 INT. QUATRO—DAY

AKI and GRAY hold on as the Quatro rocks violently. AKI looks out the window. She gasps.

529A. AKI

(gasps)

530. GRAY

What is that?

-44-

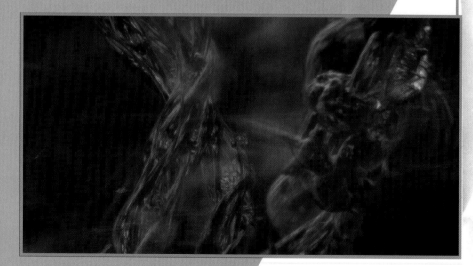

171 EXT. IMPACT CRATER—DAY

An enormous writhing behemoth, the Phantom's Gaia rises up at the small Quatro dangling by a cable.

172 INT. QUATRO—DAY

AKI looks at GRAY.

530A. AKI

If you're gonna get us out of here, you better do it now.

GRAY sees her and immediately begins working. He hears a wrenching and looks up.

531A. GRAY

Hold on!

173 EXT. IMPACT CRATER—DAY

The cable holding the Quatro is twisted and bent out of shape. Finally it snaps and the Quatro drops. It falls directly toward the enormous Phantom's Gaia, which looks like the bottom of the Red Sea through the wriggling tentacles.

175 INT. QUATRO—DAY

The Quatro is capsized.

GRAY somehow manages to release the gel pac from the Quatro.

176 EXT. PHANTOM GAIA—DAY

Gel pacs are automatically ejected and the Quatro lands safely on the crater surface.

Aki, recovering from the shock of the impact.

Phantoms bubble out of the Phantom's Gaia as if being spawned from the Red Sea surrounding them. Phantoms draw near, cling to the Quatro, but are stopped by the ship's shield.

177 INT. QUATRO—DAY

AKI and GRAY look out the window at a Phantom trying to get in.

532. SID'S VOICE

... [static interference] ... come in... come in, please... [more static] Aki, Gray, can you hear me?

533. AKI

Sid, I need to talk to the station. Can you patch us through?

178 INT. ZEUS CONTROL ROOM—DAY [ESS]

HEIN looks at the holograph over the shoulder of a technician.

534. HEIN

What is that thing?

535. TECHNICIAN 1

I don't know sir.

Suddenly, another technician swings around in his chair.

536. TECHNICIAN 4

Incoming message, sir...

Surprised, HEIN looks at a hologram of AKI in the room. It is a poor connection.

537. AKI

(fast, with immediacy)

General Hein, you must cease fire immediately. What you are looking at in the crater is the living spirit of an alien's home world. Their planet was destroyed and part of it landed here. This is not an invasion. It never was.

538. HEIN

(sarcastically)

Oh, I see. And what have we been fighting all this time, Doctor? Ghosts?

539. AKI

Yes.

(Hein, "mmmmm")

Spirits that are confused, lost and angry.

539A. HEIN

Ahh, right. And these spirits are coming out of this 'Gaia' thing.

539B. AKI

General Hein, you have to listen—

540. HEIN

"Alien Gaia, Earth Gaia"... Doctor, even if I believed in such nonsense the fact remains, the Earth is under attack from an aggressor who must be destroyed at all costs.

541. AKI

The cost may be the entire planet, sir. Firing on the alien Gaia will only make it stronger.

-45-

542. HEIN
Well since you are under the alien's influence, Doctor, I will take your protest to mean that we are in fact pursuing the correct course of action. So, I suggest you take your last few moments and prepare to meet your "Gaia."
(Pause, to his men)
Continue to fire until the invader has been destroyed!

180 EXT. IMPACT CRATER—DAY
The Beam continues to fire, raining down on the crater, cracking the earth's surface.

181 INT. QUATRO—DAY
AKI and GRAY are rocked violently by the new blasts.

182 EXT. IMPACT CRATER—DAY
The Phantom's Gaia absorbs the energy blast and grows.
The enlarged phantom Gaia begins to engulf the Quatro.
The edge of a cliff. The Quatro's wheels are embedded so deeply that it cannot move.
One large tentacle nears the Quatro.

185 INT. QUATRO—DAY
GRAY watches the tentacle from the phantom Gaia approach through the window.

186 EXT. PHANTOM GAIA—DAY
The Quatro is engulfed by the tentacle. Then...
The Quatro is engulfed in the Phantom Gaia, which is flowing down the cliff and it falls. A violent burst of electricity is discharged from the shield, after having come in contact with the Phantom Gaia. The Quatro plummets into the fissure.

187 INT. BLACK BOA—DAY
Dr. SID is in the cockpit. He grabs the lever and jerks it hard.

188 EXT. IMPACT CRATER—DAY
The Black Boa tries to evade the rapid fire of the beam. To no avail, one of its wings is hit.
The Black Boa disappears in the light of the beam.

190 EXT. CRATER—DAY
Black Boa manages to land safely on the surface.

191 INT. ZEUS CONTROL ROOM—DAY [ESS]
General HEIN watches the screen, frowning.

545. TECHNICIAN 1
General. The system is overheating, sir.
546. HEIN
We're going to hit it again and again, and keep on hitting until it's dead!
547. TECHNICIAN 1
But sir, we're not even sure if it's having any effect on the creature.
548. HEIN
No effect? We've got them on the run, soldier. This is our moment of victory. I order you to fire.
549. TECHNICIAN 1
The system won't allow us to fire again...
550. HEIN
(interrupting)
We'll see about that.

HEIN walks out the door.

192 INT. QUATRO—DAY [CRA]
GRAY and AKI inside the Quatro. They both look worse for wear. Gray turns and raises his chin a little, in an unspoken question. Aki nods that she's all right. Then he starts working the controls. Their energy shield is gone.
551A. GRAY
Our shield is out. We're sitting ducks in here. Come on.

193 EXT. DEEP IN A FISSURE
AKI and GRAY step out. They look around and then up at the Phantom Gaia's red plasma over them.
552. GRAY
This is not a good place to be.

They look below them from the ridge.
Their POV. Something else is visible. A shimmering blue plasm.
553. GRAY
What the hell is that? That's not what I think it is, is it?
554. AKI
Yes. It's Gaia.

Gray looks up at the red Gaia... and then down at the blue Gaia.
555. GRAY
This is definitely not a good place to be.

AKI looks as if she is in pain. Gray turns.
555B. GRAY
Hey. Are you alright?
555C. AKI
I'm fine. I have to talk to Dr. Sid.

194 INT. BLACK BOA—DAY
Inside the crash-landed Boa. The cockpit tilts sideways.
In the front of the cockpit, Dr. SID places his left hand on his right shoulder in pain. It might be dislocated. He slouches back in his chair.
556. AKI'S VOICE (HOLOGRAPH)
(urgently)
Sid? Do you read me?
557. SID
Go ahead. I'm still here.
558. AKI'S VOICE (HOLOGRAPH)
We're looking at Gaia. Do you hear me, Sid? Gaia. I think this explains why the eighth spirit appeared here.

Sid thinks. Stretches out his left and operates the holograph.
On the holograph. New particles of life are shown being born of Gaia located below the Phantom's Gaia. A text explanation on the holograph is also displayed (the phenomenon of reincarnation).
By putting a larger particle returning to the Gaia in contact with a smaller particle just born, the smaller particle will carry part of the larger one.
The display reads: 45% of memory transferred.
He notices a certain percentage of the Gaia-born particles merge with some of the Phantom's Gaia particles.
SID finally regains his sense.
559. SID
Yes, yes! That's it!

195 EXT. DEEP IN A FISSURE
AKI is looking at the same holograph image as Sid.

-47-

560. SID'S VOICE (HOLOGRAPH)
A single phantom must have come into contact with a new spirit born from our own Gaia. If so, it would have been given a different energy signature that set it apart from the other Phantoms.

196 INT. BLACK BOA—DAY
561. SID
Oh, you two could not have hoped for a better location to find a new compatible spirit.

200 EXT. DEEP IN A FISSURE
562. SID (OS)
Whatever you do, don't move! Stay right where you are!
GRAY notices a phantom approaching from above him.
563. GRAY
Staying right where we are may not be as easy as it sounds.
GRAY lifts his weapon and fires.
GRAY fires. The energy beam strikes the closest phantom point blank. The phantom vaporizes.
567. SID
Don't shoot any of them! You could very well destroy out last hope.

201 INT. BLACK BOA—DAY
Dr. SID is working and watching his read-outs.
567A. GRAY (OS)
Then what do you suggest I do, Doctor? Ask them to play nice?
567B. SID
(ignoring his tone)
Combat strategy is your area of expertise, Captain, not mine.
There is a familiar blip on the hologram, and Sid reacts.
569. AKI
I have a reading here in the fissure. Do you see it?

201A INT. QUATRO—DAY
571. SID
Yes. A compatible spirit. It must be very near you.

202 EXT. DEEP IN A FISSURE
A dozen phantoms float toward GRAY.
570. GRAY
Well... which one is it? Which one?
He aims his gun to fire... but hesitates. GRAY backtracks, trying to get away from the tentacles extending toward him. Without the ability to fire, this fissure is a deadly ever-tightening maze of phantoms moving closer and closer.
570A. SID (VO)
I'm-I'm having difficulty narrowing it down. Just a moment, please.
GRAY makes a face, like he can't believe this. He hesitates a moment to find an open path and then keeps moving, dodging.
568. GRAY
Doctor, it's getting crowded in here!
More phantoms move toward him. Gray runs toward the Quatro.
568C. GRAY
Aki, we don't have much time. Aki!
GRAY sees that Aki is slumped down on a chair in the Quatro cockpit.
568D. GRAY
Aki!
A phantom is just about to consume Gray. He turns and FIRES!
White out.

-48-

205 EXT. ALIEN LANDSCAPE—DREAM [DRF]
AKI sees countless corpses of Phantom soldiers scattered about. Suddenly the alien particles inside her emerge from her body and burrow into the clear ground. The Phantom soldiers' armor falls off and is absorbed into the sand as blue spirits emerge from the armor. A new phantom rises from the ground.
The Phantom gestures at the barren landscape.
The spirits of the Phantoms begin to sink into the ground feet first. Vegetation begins to return around AKI'S feet.
AKI turns, and looks down on the land from the top of the ridge. Life is regenerating at an accelerated rate.

206 EXT. DEEP IN A FISSURE [CRA]
Aki wakes with a start, and sees:
AKI'S POV: GRAY fires on the attacking phantoms. This is the last stand. The phantoms vaporize.
AKI activates the holograph on her chest plate. The membrane is still there, but the Phantom particles have disappeared.
She looks at the complete spirit wave displayed on it.
587. AKI
I have it!
Outside the ship, Gray turns at the sound of her voice, and looks relieved to see her conscious. Then he turns, FIRES.
587A. AKI
Gray—get in here. I need you!

205A INT. BLACK BOA—DAY
SID listens to the transmissions from AKI. He looks excited.
587B. AKI'S VOICE
Have you been listening, Doctor? The wave pattern is complete!
587C. SID
Yes, I read you! Th-this is wonderful! Bu-I-I-I don't see how you could have found the final spirit—

207 INT. QUATRO—DAY
AKI uses a wire extending from her chest plate to connect herself to the Quatro equipment.
589. AKI
It found me, Doctor!

208A INT. BLACK BOA—DAY
SID looks at the holograms showing Aki's physical read-outs. He looks very excited, all of his theories proven true, all his hopes for Aki fulfilled—then he sees something. Something that makes him frown. But slowly his face shows realization.
587E. SID
(as if delighted)
Oh my word. I see now. I understand.

209 INT. QUATRO—DAY
GRAY fights off the wave of phantoms converging on him, and steps into the Quatro with:
588. GRAY
Well, I don't understand! What the hell is going on?
AKI is furiously jury-rigging the equipment.
588A. AKI
Give me your ovo pac! I need to power up the shield!
588B. GRAY
But we'll be defenseless—
588C. AKI
Just do it!
Gray disengages the ovo-pac from his rifle. He gives it to her.

-49-

Aki works hurriedly. Gray takes his seat inside the cockpit. The phantoms draw closer to the Quatro.

588D. GRAY

I hope you know what you're doing, Aki.

Aki inserts the ovo-pac into the instrumentation. She works. Gray sits there looking nervous.

588E. AKI

We have to project the completed wave.

588F. GRAY

What?

588G. AKI

Dr. Sid's theory was right. I have it. The eighth spirit. I'm cured, Gray.

590A. GRAY

Are you sure you have the final spirit?

Aki keeps rigging the wires and hitting switches.

590B. AKI

Yes, yes, I'm sure.

590C. GRAY

But how? H-how can you know that?

Finally, Aki looks at him, and smiles:

590D. AKI

Don't worry. A phantom told me.

This does not make Gray feel any better.

590E. GRAY

Oh... great.

Gray turns around. Phantom tentacles are penetrating through the Quatro's hatch. Aki hits her last switch as she yells:

590F. AKI

That's it. Shield on!

... but nothing happens. Aki and Gray share a look. They sit next to each other in cockpit seats divided by an aisle. They hold their breath as phantom tentacles gradually approach.

590G. GRAY

It's not working. We have to do something before it's too late—

But Aki places her hand over his. His eyes lock onto hers. It stops him.

590H. AKI

(almost softly)

If this doesn't work, then it's already too late.

He doesn't take the pack. Gray looks back out to see the phantoms drawing closer. Aki and Gray look into each other's eyes.

590F. AKI

Gray, trust me.

Gray releases the pack.

Just as the Phantom tentacles are about to wrap around AKI and GRAY, the instrumentation kicks in and the shield forms around the Quatro. The phantoms' tentacles are diffused.

An electrical discharge is given off as the Phantoms come in contact with the barrier. The spirit wave changes the color of the shield to an even deeper blue.

Aki turns. Looks at Gray. She pulls him closer for a kiss.

209A INT. BLACK BOA—DAY

SID frowns as he hears the sounds of a kiss over this headset. Then he looks relieved, and grins.

---

215 EXT. ZEUS SPACE CANNON—DAY

Because the cannon was force fired, the ovo-pacs cause electrical reactions and begin to explode. Fire and discharge are visible throughout the Space Station. The firing pushed it too far.

The Space Station explodes.

The explosions cause the Habitat Area to break off from the Space Station causing a second explosion. It speeds up and falls directly down towards the Manual Control Room where HEIN is.

216 INT. ZEUS SPACE CANNON—DAY

595A. HEIN
(ad-lib)

Fire. Fire damn you! Come on do it for me... Fire!!! ...Argh, system...

And then HEIN turns around. Sees it.

596. HEIN
(softly)

Oh.

HEIN'S POV The Habitat Area closes in on him.

217 EXT. ZEUS SPACE CANNON—DAY

The Habitat Area crushes the area containing HEIN.

And then, another explosion begins to spread out and the Space Station splits exactly in two.

The upper part is engulfed in explosions and the lower area falls toward the atmosphere. It bursts into flames piercing the clouds.

213 EXT. DEEP IN A FISSURE [CRA]

The beam pierces through the Phantom's Gaia, bearing down on the Quatro.

The Quatro is not visible in the light beam. The beam pierces into the Gaia.

218 EXT. IMPACT CRATER—DAY

The Phantom's Gaia grows larger, its tentacles writhing.

219 INT. BLACK BOA—DAY

Sid watches the phenomena unfold before his eyes. Phantoms erupt out of the central crevasse of the crater as if it were a volcano. They spread out along the surface of the earth.

222 EXT. DEEP IN A FISSURE

The Quatro is a wreck, nothing but rocks, boulders, and twisted metal. AKI tries to communicate with the Black Boa.

There is no response. Aki turns and sees Gray trying to rise up into a sitting position. He looks to be in serious pain. She hurries over and helps him lean up against a rock.

597F. AKI

Gray, Gray.
(big pause)
Don't leave me, Gray.

605. GRAY
(sounding weak)

Told Sid this was a one-way trip. Looks like I was right.

Aki holds him and tries to keep him conscious.

605A. AKI

No Gray. Hang on please. I need you! We need you!

605B. GRAY

Aki.

She interrupts.

608C. GRAY

We're not gonna make it.

608C-1. AKI

-82-

209BINT. INSIDE THE QUATRO—DAY

AKI and GRAY pull away from each other, just a little. Aki and Gray both start working the controls. Aki hits the switch and...

209CEXT. DEEP IN A FISSURE

The energy wave released from the Quatro slowly begins to purify the phantom Gaia.

290DINT. INSIDE THE QUATRO

Aki glances at Gray and smiles.

210 INT. ZEUS SPACE CANNON—DAY [ESS]

The readout indicates that preparations are compete.

592. HEIN

I'll blast you all to hell.

Then HEIN pushes the firing button.

211 EXT. ZEUS SPACE CANNON—DAY

The Zeus Cannon fires again.

212 INT. QUATRO—DAY [CRA]

AKI works the controls... but then sees something approaching. It is the laser beam. Slowly her face shows realization, and GRAY turns. Sees her face. He looks up as the energy slowly descends through the Phantom Gaia.

593. AKI

Oh no... No!

Gray throws Aki to the floor, covering her with his own body.

GRAY looks up. The beam's energy slowly descends through the Phantom's Gaia.

199 INT. ZEUS CONTROL ROOM—DAY [ESS/SSE]

565. COMPUTER VOICE

Warning! System Overload!

564A. HEIN

I know.

565. COMPUTER VOICE

Warning! System Overload!

564A. HEIN

I knowwww!

565. COMPUTER VOICE

Warning! System Overload!

564A. HEIN

I KNOWWWW!!

565. COMPUTER VOICE

Warning! System Overload!

566. HEIN

But it must be done.

565. COMPUTER VOICE

Warning!

We're going to make it.

608C-2. GRAY

We both know that isn't true.

A moment—they both know. Aki is frozen, unable to admit the truth. Gray begins to stand then stumbles.

608H. AKI

Gray!

Gray gets his legs under him, trying again.

608I. GRAY

Help me.

608J. AKI

Gray!

608D. GRAY

Listen to me. You saved my life once. Now I want you to save yourself.

Gray holds Aki by the shoulders, moving her towards a ledge just beneath the platform. She steps onto it as...

608K. AKI

Gray, no! Please!

608L. GRAY

Let me do this, Aki. Trust me.

608G. AKI

Don't leave me, Gray

610. GRAY

You've been trying to tell me that death isn't the end. Don't back out on me...
(short pause)
... now that I finally believe...

Gray stands upright.

610A. GRAY

I love you.

Aki weeps. Gray stands with new found strength. The arm of the Alien Gaia swings towards Gray with deliberate force. He looks into Aki's eyes—love, strength, and resolve. The arm passes through him and his body falls limp. A moment—death. Hopeless, then...

GRAY'S SPIRIT RISES UP OUT OF HIS BODY. Aki moves back, just a bit, her expression filling with surprise and wonder. HIS SPIRIT PASSES THROUGH AKI—taking on Gray's profile—and she reaches out, as if to touch him. Gray's spirit continues out into the phantom Gaia, taking along with it the completed spirit wave.

Gray's spirit intersects with the tip of the phantom Gaia and the light particles take the form of a ribbon flowing upward.

The Gaia's color becomes cloudy.

229 EXT. CRATER—DAY

Dr. SID watches the spirit wave rise up inside the Phantom Gaia... and the Phantom Gaia turns blue—becoming beautiful. Sid watches as the blue light particles rise toward the sky.

The alien Gaia becomes a glittering river of light streaking toward the heavens.

234A EXT. CRATER—DAY [CRA]

The particles of light surround the smiling Dr. Sid.

603. SID

Oh, it's warm.

The blue light pierces through the clouds, PASSES THE CAMERA and ascends into space.

231 EXT. DEEP IN A FISSURE

GRAY'S SPIRIT descends and AKI watches as it RETURNS TO GAIA.

231A EXT. CRATER—DAY

"The Bird Flying" section
FADE OUT.
THE END

-83-

EXTRAS

CHOCOBOS

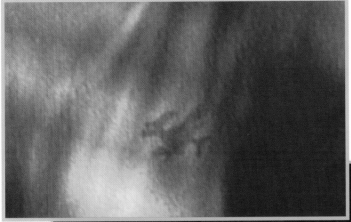

Those people familiar with the Final Fantasy universe are undoubtedly well aware of the little feathered creature called a chocobo. The chocobo has been a staple in the Final Fantasy series of games. They have now made the transition to the big screen in *Final Fantasy: The Spirits Within*.

The chocobo makes an appearance!

HIRONOBU SAKAGUCHI

Even the Director makes an appearance in the film. Pay close attention during the scene in which Dr. Sid addresses the council in the conference room. None other than Hironobu Sakaguchi is one of the council members!

FINAL FANTASY TEASER

In their spare time, some of the talented folks at Square USA created an outtake starring the cast of *Final Fantasy: The Spirits Within*. In the video Aki, Dr. Sid, and the Deep Eyes perform their rendition of a famous music video.

FINAL FANTASY
THE SPIRITS WITHIN

FILM CREDITS
Produced and Directed by: HIRONOBU SAKAGUCHI; Produced by: JUN AIDA; Co-Director: MOTO SAKAKIBARA; Produced by: CHRIS LEE; Original Story by: HIRONOBU SAKAGUCHI; Written by: AL REINERT, JEFF VINTAR; Music Composed by: ELLIOT GOLDENTHAL; Music Supervisor: RICHARD RUDOLPH; Associate Producer: KATSUHIKO TOYOTA; Casting and Voice Director: JACK FLETCHER

CAST
Doctor Aki Ross: MING-NA; Captain Gray Edwards: ALEC BALDWIN; Ryan: VING RHAMES; Neil: STEVE BUSCEMI; Jane: PERI GILPIN; Doctor Sid: DONALD SUTHERLAND; General Hein: JAMES WOODS; Council Member #1: KEITH DAVID; Council Member #2: JEAN SIMMONS; Major Elliot: MATT MCKENZIE

Animation Director: ANDY JONES; Line Producer: DEIRDRE MORRISON; Editor: CHRISTOPER S. CAPP; Staging Director: TANI KUNITAKE; Computer Graphics Supervisor: GARY MUNDELL; Sequence Supervisors: EIJI FUJII, HIROYUKI HAYASHIDA, KENICHI ISAKA, TAKUMI KIMURA, CLAUDE PRECOURT, STEVE PREEG, TERU "YOSH" YOSHIDA; Layout Supervisor: TAKASHI KUBOTA; Character Supervisor: TAIJI OKUSAWA; Creature Supervisor: TAKAO NOGUCHI; Sets & Props Supervisor: TADAO ODAKA; Lighting Supervisor: DAVID SEAGER; Visual Effects Art Director: TAKAHIKO AKIYAMA; Visual Effects Supervisor: REMO BALCELLS; Compositing Supervisor: JAMES ROGERS; R & D Supervisor: KAZUYUKI HASHIMOTO; Motion Capture Directors: JACK FLETCHER, REMINGTON SCOTT; Motion Capture Supervisor: YOSHINOBU SHIMA; Production Systems Supervisor: TROY BROOKS; Production Software Supervisor: SHINICHI SOEDA; System Director: KOICHI ISE; System Administration Supervisor: MASAYUKI KASUYA; Rendering & Shading Supervisor: KEVIN BJORKE; Image Supervisor: MICHAEL GIBSON; Computer Graphics Producer: CAMERON STEVNING

ART
Conceptual Design Artist: KAZUNORI NAKAZAWA

CONCEPT ARTISTS
ERIC BROWN, PATRICK JANICKE, THOMAS ROLAND JOHNSON, TONY KIM, JOSEPH MORO, SHUKO MURASE, NOBORITO SUE; Mechanical Designer: YOSHINORI SAYAMA

STORYBOARD ARTISTS
JOHN FOX, TREVOR GORING, RAYMOND HARVIE, TIM HOLTROP, ED KLAUTKY, SHINSAKU KOZUMA, MARK MORETTI, AKIRA OGURO, MASAO OKUBO, MARC VENA, MASAHITO YAMASHITA

LAYOUT
YOSHINORI KANADA, SHINICHI KIMURA, YOSHIHIRO KITANO, MAMORU KUROSAWA, ANDREA MAIOLO, YUICHI NAKAMURA, HIDEKI SUDO; Layout Assistant: YASUSHI MATSUMURA

ANIMATION
Lead Character Animators
Doctor Aki Ross: ROY SATO; Captain Gray Edwards: TOBY M. HARUNO, BEN RUSH; Ryan: CHRISTOPHER ERIN WALSH; Neil: JAY RANDALL; Jane: ALICE KAISERIAN; Doctor Sid: LOUIS LEFEBVRE; General Hein: MATTHEW T. HACKETT; Major Elliot: TIMOTHY HEATH; Lead Animator: JONGBO KIM
Character Animators
ROBIN AKIN, WALTON BURGWYN, KELLY HARTIGAN GOLDSTEIN, YOSHINOBU INANO, YUNG SHENG JONG, MICHAEL KITCHEN, KANJI NISHIDA, KUNIHIKO NOGUCHI, JEFF SCHU, ERIC WEISS, KAZUYOSHI YAGINUMA, CINDY YAMAUCHI

CHARACTER
Original Character Design by: SHUKO MURASE; Lead Character Artist: STEVEN ERIC GIESLER; Character Artists: FRANCISCO A. CORTINA, VERONIQUE GARCIA, KOICHI IWATSUKA, TATSUYA KOSAKA, RENE MOREL, JEREMY RAY; Cloth Simulation Artists: PATRICIA PAWLAK, CHERYL RYE; Character Technical Directors: BENJAMIN CHEUNG, NAOTAKA HORIGUCHI, AYUMU IMAIZUMI, KEVIN M. OCHS

CREATURE
Creature Design by: YASUSHI NIRASAWA; Creature Technical Director: YOSHINORI MORUZUMI; Creature Effects Artists: KOJI KAWAMURA, KENGO TAKEUCHI, KOJI TANAKA, TAKUJI TOMOOKA, MASAHITO YOSHIOKA

SETS & PROPS
Lead Sets & Props Artists: DANIEL CASEY, ANDREW HARBECK, HIROSHI "DUCK" KAMOHARA, KOJI KOBAYASHI, TATSURO MARUYAMA, BO MOSLEY; Sets & Props Artists: SERGIO GARCIA ABAD, ERIKO ARATA, ROBERT BOURGEAULT, KARL COYNER, JAMES DARGIE, ALEJANDRO GIL, TAKUYA HADA, TAKEHIKO HOASHI, MASAHISA KANEKO, JAE KIM, LISA KIM, EDMUND LEO, TAKAHIRO MATSUHIRA, CLEAR MENSER, ANDREA MERLO, MOTOHITO NASU, BEHROOZ ROOZBEH, JAKE ROWELL, NAOYA SHIGEMATSU, ERIC STERNER, SUAN CHING TAN, MICHAEL WITHEM; Texture Artists: CLAUDIA CANDIA, ROBIN FOLEY, TAKAYUKI HAYASHI, HIROSHI MORI
Graphic Designers: KANWA NAGAFUJI, OSAMU YAMAZAKI

LIGHTING
Lead Lighting Artists: ANGELA M. ELIASZ, GREG LEV, JOHN MONOS, JEFF STERN; Lighting Artists: BELA BROZSEK, HERMAN CHENG, MARK DE LA GARZA, MICHAEL FOLEY, HASKELL FRIEDMAN, RIKA FUJIMOTO, HSUN HO, YOSHIHITO IKUTA, RYAN LEASHER, STANLEY MISKIEWICZ, FRANK RITLOP, SABA ROUFCHAIE, HIROYUKI SESHITA, MICHIKO SESHITA, DON TAYLOR, CARLOS A. VIDAL

VISUAL EFFECTS
Lead Visual Effects Artists: YASUKO ASAKURA, SPENCER KNAPP, GUSTAV MELICH, DAVID TANNER, JOANNE THIEL; Visual Effects Artists: JEFFREY BENDIT, ANDY CHEN, MATTHEW DAVIES, PETRONELLA EVERS, MICHAEL FADOLLONE, STEVEN GALLE, DAVID HOWE, KENNETH IBRAHIM, MUQEEM KHAN, MACH TONY KOBAYASHI, HAE-JEON LEE, ROSA LIN, JEFFREY MARTIN, SANDOR RABB, MICHAEL RIVERO, ROBERT SHRIDER, NEVILLE SPITERI, PAUL VAN CAMP

MATTE PAINTING
Digital Matte Painters: RONALD BUSHAW, ROGER GIBBON, ROGER KUPELIAN, RICHARD MAHON, CRAIG MULLINS, CHRISTIAN LORENZ SCHEURER, MASAHIKO TANI, KAZUMASA UCHIO

COMPOSITING

Senior Compositor: TIM CROSBIE; Lead Compositors: MIKU KAYAMA, STEPHEN R. LUNN, RON ROBERTS, YASUHARU YOSHIZAWA; Compositors: JONATHAN BOWEN, SONIA CALVERT, FERIC YI FENG, JERRY HALL, LILY VASCONCELLOS IBBOTSON, KORY JUUL, DON KLINGLER, TETSUO MAEDA, WILLIAM MCCOY, HEIJI MORISHITA, ADAM K. MOURA, HIDETO OZAKI, GEOFFREY RICHARDSON, JOSHUA SAETA, ANDREW SCHWARTZ, TOMOKO SHIN, SHARMISHTHA SOHONI, KAT SZUMINSKA, LINDA TREMBLAY

EDITORIAL

Associate Editor: KEIICHI KOJIMA; First Assistant Editor: WILLIAM STEINBERG; Assistant Editor: PATRICK DAY KENNEDY

RESEARCH & DEVELOPMENT

Manager: KAVEH KARDAN; Senior Programmers: GERARD BANEL, PER CHRISTENSEN, LI-HAN CHEN, TOSHI KATO, SHIRO KAWAI, JACK LIAO, HITOSHI NISHIMURA; Programmers: PAOLO COSTABEL, TADASHI ENDO, PETER JU, JUNICHI KIMURA, CYRIAQUE KOUADIO, YONG HWAN LEE, TAMOTSU MARUYAMA, BERND RAABE, JONATHAN RICE, JUN SAITO, ANDREI SHERSTYUK, SHAWN TARAS; Coordinators, AYUMI BABA, MASAHIRO YOSHIBA

MOTION CAPTURE

Motion Capture Engineers: UDAI HARAGUCHI, MATTHEW KARNES; Set Designer: RON PERRY; Motion Capture Staff: JAMES BRENNAN, GEMINI BURKE, JAMIE DIXON, TORI MEI-LIN ELDRIDGE, ROD GNAPP, WESLEY MANN, MATT MCKENZIE, MICHAEL SCOTT RYAN, ERIK SEBUSCH; Motion Capture Director: BRADLEY G. BATE

SOFTWARE & SYSTEMS

Production Software Programmers: MOTOHISA ADACHI, SCOT BREW, ATSUSUHI EBISAWA, JUNKO IGARASHI, SAED MIRSEPASSI, KOJI NAGASHIMA, SEYMOUR, SHINYA YARIMIZO; System Administration: TAKAAKI CHO, TOMOHIRO HAYASAKA, YUJI SATO, BRYCE WATANABE, YUKIKO YAMANAKA; System Administration Assistants: MAKIKO NAGAKURA CRONIN, ETSUKO ONO, CHIKAKO TERASHITA

RENDERING & TECHNICAL SUPPORT

Rendering Technical Directors: KELLY COWLES, MICHAEL FU, BRET HUGHES, SATOMI UCHIDA; Sequence Technical Directors, JAY CARINA, TETSUCHIRO KITAGAWA, KEN SAITO, ERIC SALITURO, KIYOSHI SHIGENAGA; Rendering Technical Assistants: ANTHONY HIGA, JUDITH KAZEL, CATHERINE MITSUNAGA, CHIH-CHIEH (MICHAEL) YANG; Data Wranglers: JASON J.K. ANTONIO, MICHAEL BUSH, WAI CHI CHAN, CINDY P.Y. CHU, DUANE JOSEPH DUBUQUE, SEAN EYESTONE, CHRISTINE L. GALIZA, RUSSELL JARALBA, KEN KYUNG NAM KANG, MICHAEL K. KOGA, SAMSON LEE, RONNIE LIVINGSTON, STEVE LUH, CUONG NGUYEN, REID OISHI, CHRISTOPHER RICHMOND, JOSEPH TUMPAP, HOLLY S. YOKOMICHI

PRODUCTION

Production Managers: HIROYOSHI HAMADA, KAORU HIYAMA ROGERS, TERRI SASAKI, KENJI TAKEMOTO; Computer Graphics Managers: IVY AGREGAN, REI MATSUOKA, NAOKO MULDOWNEY, KEN NIIYAMA, MEGHAN NISHIMIZU, KAY SASATOMI, HIROSHI TANAKA; Post Production Manager: KERRY SHEA; Editorial Manager: HEATHER ELISA HILL; Editorial Coordinator: KEIKO SHINOZUKA; VFX Manager: CHRISTOPHER PAIZIS; Production Coordinators: MAYUMI ARAKAKI, ARTEMIO DE PALA, CHRISTINA DE SILVA, THOMAS HENDRICKSON, KEIKO JAFFUEL, NORIKO WADA, CAROLINE WINKLER; Production Assistants: MINORI HASHIMOTO HUNG, KATHY KEEGAN, YOSHIKO MAYEAUX, SHERRY SASUGA, MAYA ZIBUNG; Associate Producer: DAN KLETZKY

DIGITAL FRONTIER INC.

Compositor: YASUHIRO OHTSUKA

ITOCHU TEHCNO-SCIENCE CORPORATION

KUSANAGI CO., LTD.

Director: YOJI NAKAZA; Designers: HIDEYASU HARITA, TADASHI IWASA, KAZUO OGURA, KEN ARAI, KAZUYUKU HASHIMOTO, SADAHIKO TANAKA

PHOTOGENIC CO., LTD.

Director: KAZUKI AKANE

POLYGON PICTURES INC.

Director: TOSHIFUMI KAWAHARA

OVERLOAD CO., LTD.

SHUJI ASANO

OZ COMPANY CO., LTD.

KO YOKOYAMA

SHIROGUMI INC.

Producer: TOSHIO YAMAMOTO; CG Designers: SHOICHI MATSUBARA, TAKAYUKI TAKETA, SEMIN THO, YOSHIHIRO KOMORI; Conceptual Designer: HITOSHI YONEDA; Mechanical Designers: SHINJI ARAMAKI, REI NAKAHARA; Pro Production Writers: GITI OHTSUKA, SHIGERU KIMIYA; Makeup Artist: DAISUKE DOBASHI; Lighting Artist: SHIGEKI HAYASHI

POST PRODUCTION

Post Production Sound Services provided by: SKYWALKER SOUND, a division of LUCAS DIGITAL LTD., LLC, Marin County, California
Sound Design: RANDY THOM; Re-recording Mixers: RANDY THOM, GARY RIZZO; Supervising Sound Editor: DENNIS LEONARD; ADR Editor: SUE FOX; Sound Effects Editor: DAVID C. HUGHES; Foley Editor: ANDREA STELTER GARD; Supervising Assistant: ERICH STRATMAN; Sound Designer Assistant: STUART MCCOWAN; Effects Assistant: COLIN O'NEIL; ADR Assistant: SAM HINKLEY; Sound Design Apprentice: MAC SMITH; Foley Artists: DENNIE THORPE, JANA VANCE; Foley Mixer: TONY ECKERT; Foley Recordist: FRANK "PEPE" MEREL; Additional Sound Effects Editing: BOB SHOUP, DAVID FARMER, JIM MCKEE, CHRIS SCARABSOSIO, ANDREA STELETER GARD; Additional Sound Effects Assistants: DOUG WINNINGHAM, DEE SELBY; Mix Technician, GABRIEL GUY; Re-Recordist: RON ROUMAS; Machine Room Operators: STEVE ROMANKO, SEAN ENGLAND; Digital Transfer: JOHNATHAN GREBER, CHRISTOPHER BARRON, TIM BURBY, JOHN COUNTRYMAN; Video Services: ED DUNKLEY, JOHN "J.T." TORRIJOS; Engineering Services: JOHN TAYLOR, CHRIS BARNETT; Digital Editorial Services: DAVID HUNTER, BRIAN CHUMNEY, NOAH KATZ; Client Services: MIKE LANE, EVA NAPOLEAN, MEGA FOUTS, GORDON NG

ADDITIONAL DIALOG BY:

JACK FLETCHER; Actions Sequence Director: COLIN FONG; Casting Agent: ANNA FISHBURN; ADR Voice Casting: BARBARA HARRIS

ADDITIONAL CAST

BCR Soldier #1, Space Station Technician #2: JOHN DEMITA; BFW Soldier #1: JOHN DIMAGGIO; Space Station Technician #3: ALEX FERNANDEZ; Space Station Technician #1 & 4: DAVID RASNER; Scan Technician: DWIGHT SCHULTZ; Additional Voices: MATT ADLER, STEVE ALTERMAN, DAVID ARNOTT, CATHERINE CAVADINI, LANEI CHAPMAN, VICKI DAVIS, JOHN DEMITA, JUDI DURAND, GREN FINLEY, JACK FLETCHER, JULIA FLETCHER, BARBARA ILEY, DAVID MCCHAREN, TRACY METRO, DAVID MICHIE, RICHARD PENN, DAVID RANDOLPH, ANDREA TAYLOR

THE MAKING OF
FINAL FANTASY
THE SPIRITS WITHIN

Brady Publishing

An Imprint of Pearson Education
201 West 103rd Street
Indianapolis, Indiana 46290

ISBN: 0-7440-0071-8
Library of Congress Catalog No.: 2001-135054
Printing Code: The rightmost double-digit number is the year of the book's printing; the rightmost single-digit number is the number of the book's printing. For example, 01-1 shows that the first printing of the book occurred in 2001.

04 03 02 01   4 3 2 1

Manufactured in the United States of America.

240

BRADYGAMES STAFF

DIRECTOR OF PUBLISHING
David Waybright

CREATIVE DIRECTOR
Robin Lasek

ASSISTANT LICENSING MANAGER
Mike Degler

EDITOR-IN-CHIEF
H. Leigh Davis

ASSISTANT MARKETING MANAGER
Susie Nieman

MARKETING MANAGER
Janet Eshenour

///II BRADYGAMES®

BradyGAMES would like to sincerely thank everyone at Square USA for supporting us during this project. In particular, we would like to thank Yumi Ozaki, Cameron Stevning, Lani Mathews, and Naoko Muldowney. This book would not have been possible without your tremendous effort and cooperation.

CREDITS

TITLE MANAGER
Tim Cox

LEAD DESIGNER
Ann-Marie Deets

DESIGN TEAM
Carol Stamile
Doug Wilkins

PRODUCTION DESIGNERS
Jane Washburne
Tracy Wehmeyer

GRAPHICS EDITOR
Michael Owen